Hands-on Cryptography with Python

Master Cryptographic Foundations with Real-World Implementation for Secure System Development Using Python

Md Rasid Ali

www.orangeava.com

First Published: January 2025

Published By: Orange Education Pvt Ltd, AVA®

Address: 9, Daryaganj, Delhi, 110002, India

275 New North Road Islington Suite 1314 London,
N1 7AA, United Kingdom

ISBN (PBK): 978-93-48107-51-0
ISBN (E-BOOK): 978-93-48107-73-2

Scan the QR code to explore our entire catalogue

www.orangeava.com

Dedicated To

Abba, Maa

and

My beloved Nephews and Niece,

Ayan, Ayat, Mahir

About the Author

Md Rasid Ali is a seasoned cryptography and security expert specializing in firmware development for resource-constrained devices. Currently a Senior Engineer at Qualcomm Inc., Rasid focuses on Root-of-Trust (RoT) firmware and cryptographic protocol development. Beyond his professional work, he actively collaborates with research institutions on advanced topics such as Lightweight Cryptography and Post-Quantum Cryptography, bridging the gap between industry and academia. His work fosters innovation and contributes to the ongoing evolution of cryptographic technologies.

Rasid holds a Master of Science (by Research) in Computer Science and Engineering from IIT Kharagpur, where his thesis on Cryptography was published in several prestigious journals. His professional career also includes significant contributions as a Junior Project Officer, where he worked for three years on a cryptanalysis-focused project funded by the Ministry of Electronics and Information Technology, Government of India.

Rasid has authored multiple conference and journal articles, with two of his recent papers published in high-impact journals: the *Journal of Supercomputing* and IEEE *Transactions on Emerging Topics in Computing* (TETC), which ranks among the top 4% of computer science journals. His research continues to contribute to the advancement of cryptographic methods in securing digital systems.

Outside of his professional and academic achievements, Rasid enjoys listening to folk songs, a hobby that offers him relaxation and creative inspiration. With a passion for both cryptographic research and music, he embodies the blend of technical expertise and personal interest that makes his work both impactful and well-rounded.

About the Technical Reviewer

Kumar Kanishk is a skilled developer specializing in crafting innovative software solutions. Proficient in Django, Artificial Intelligence, and Machine Learning, he has spearheaded over twenty-five projects in AI and AIoT, and made significant contributions to cybersecurity and blockchain. As an active bug bounty hunter, Kanishk has a proven track record of identifying and addressing critical vulnerabilities, earning recognition such as a Hall of Fame distinction from Akeyless. He also has experience building smart contracts in blockchain, showcasing his expertise in decentralized technologies. Since 2024, Kanishk has been a Technical Project Engineer at Thinknyx Technologies, where he has developed robust certification and skill academy portals, enhanced website security, and led initiatives to optimize system performance and scalability. His standout projects include a face-recognition-based attendance system, a vulnerability scanner, and an AI chatbot, demonstrating his ability to solve real-world problems through technology.

Beyond his professional roles, Kanishk is a passionate educator. He has conducted workshops at institutions such as Amity University and Graphic Era Hill University, sharing his expertise in emerging technologies. These efforts have earned him accolades, including the Outstanding Co-Instructor Award. His contributions extend to developing over five blockchain projects and co-authoring more than four Udemy courses, further cementing his impact in the tech community. His achievements, coupled with a strong foundation in software development, AI, blockchain, and cybersecurity, position him as a dynamic professional capable of driving innovation across multiple domains.

Acknowledgements

I am profoundly grateful to the many individuals whose unwavering support and encouragement have been instrumental in the completion of this book. Foremost, I extend my heartfelt thanks to my MS supervisor, Prof. Dipanwita Roy Chowdhury, for her trust in my abilities and for kindling the spark of writing within me. I am equally indebted to my sisters, Jumatan and Sunifa, whose constant motivation has been a source of strength. My deepest gratitude also goes to my parents and brother, whose steadfast support has been a cornerstone of my journey. Finally, I am sincerely thankful to my friends, Imam and Pratyusha, for their invaluable assistance and encouragement along the way.

I would also like to acknowledge the incredible team at AVA Publication for their continuous support throughout the writing and review process. Their patience and encouragement allowed me the time needed to complete this book. A special note of appreciation goes to Kanishk Kumar, the technical reviewer, for his insightful feedback and valuable contributions.

Preface

Cryptography has become an indispensable cornerstone of our digital age, safeguarding data, securing communications, and enabling trust in a rapidly evolving technological landscape. This book aims to bridge the gap between theoretical cryptography and its real-world applications by providing a holistic journey through the fundamentals, modern developments, and implementation of cryptographic techniques. Using Python as a reference programming language, we demonstrate the practical aspects of cryptographic protocols and algorithms, empowering readers to apply these concepts in real-world scenarios.

The book is structured into ten chapters, each designed to build a comprehensive understanding of cryptography, ranging from historical roots to cutting-edge advancements.

Chapter 1. Platform Setup and Installation: This chapter provides a brief introduction to Python for newcomers and covers key libraries such as ECPy, cryptography, and pyCryptodomex, which are used throughout the book.

Chapter 2. Introduction to Cryptography: This chapter explores the evolution of cryptography, from ancient ciphers to modern encryption. It highlights the ingenuity of early civilizations, the impact of cryptographic machines like the Enigma, and the emergence of techniques that secure today's digital world. This serves as a foundation for deeper exploration of cryptographic algorithms, mathematical principles, and ethical considerations in later chapters.

Chapter 3. Symmetric Key Cryptography: In this chapter, we delve into symmetric key cryptography, which uses a shared secret key for encryption and decryption. This chapter explores key management, symmetric encryption algorithms, modes of operation, and real-world applications. It serves as a stepping stone to understanding the broader cryptographic landscape, preparing us for public key cryptography in subsequent chapters.

Chapter 4. Asymmetric Key Cryptography: In this chapter, we transition from symmetric key cryptography to the innovative world of asymmetric key cryptography, where public and private key pairs revolutionize encryption. The chapter explores the intricate mechanisms of asymmetric encryption, key generation processes, and the role of randomness in ensuring secure, unique keys. We delve into Public-Key Infrastructure (PKI), examining the trust model, Certification Authorities (CAs), and digital certificates that uphold cryptographic integrity. Key algorithms like RSA, ElGamal, and Elliptic Curve Cryptography (ECC) are highlighted, showcasing their unique strengths and applications in enhancing security and advancing cryptographic sophistication.

Chapter 5. Hashing: This chapter explores hashing, a foundational concept in cryptography that transforms variable-length data into fixed-size hash values. We delve into key properties including collision resistance, preimage resistance, and the avalanche effect, which ensure security and reliability. Practical applications include password security, digital signatures, and data integrity checks, demonstrating the versatility of hash functions in modern cryptographic systems. By bridging theory and real-world use, this chapter highlights hashing's critical role in securing digital interactions.

Chapter 6. Message Integrity: In the previous chapter, we explored the world of hashing, examining the properties and applications of various hash algorithms. Now, we turn our attention to Message Integrity, a critical element in secure communication. Unlike encryption, which focuses on confidentiality, integrity mechanisms ensure that transmitted data remains unaltered and trustworthy. In this chapter, we focus on Message Authentication Code (MAC), its construction, and its role in cryptographic schemes, with a particular emphasis on HMAC (Hash-Based MAC). We also explore the limitations and challenges of MAC, while introducing Authenticated Encryption, a method that combines confidentiality and integrity for enhanced security.

Chapter 7. Miscellaneous Crypto Schemes: This chapter covers advanced cryptographic techniques, building on previous concepts to explore digital signatures for authenticity, key exchange protocols like Diffie-Hellman for secure communication, and key derivation functions (KDFs) for enhanced security. We also examine homomorphic encryption for computations on encrypted data, zero-knowledge proofs for authentication without revealing sensitive information, and multiparty computation (MPC) for secure collaborative calculations. These techniques play a crucial role in securing digital communications and offer practical solutions to modern security challenges.

Chapter 8. Security is Only as Strong as the Weakest Link: In cybersecurity, the strength of a system is determined by its weakest link. Even the most advanced technologies can be compromised by a single vulnerability, whether it is a misconfigured firewall, outdated software, or human error. This chapter highlights the importance of a holistic security approach, addressing every potential weak spot in the system. Through real-world examples, we will explore how organizations can better manage risks, identify vulnerabilities, and strengthen their defenses to build more resilient security systems.

Chapter 9. TLS Communication: In the previous chapter, we explored the principle that security is only as strong as its weakest link. Now, we shift our focus to Transport Layer Security (TLS), the protocol that ensures secure communication over the internet. This chapter covers TLS's inner workings, including its handshake process, cryptographic algorithms, and key differences between TLS 1.2 and 1.3. We also explore the role of TLS certificates and Certificate Authorities (CAs), best practices for secure implementation, and emerging trends in TLS, all emphasizing its critical role in safeguarding digital communications.

Chapter 10. Latest Trends in Cryptography: Cryptography is a dynamic field, evolving to meet new technological advancements and emerging threats. This chapter explores the latest trends, including post-quantum cryptography to combat the threat of quantum computing, and homomorphic encryption for secure data processing without decryption. We also examine zero-knowledge proofs, now used in blockchain and privacy applications, and lightweight cryptography for resource-constrained environments like IoT. Additionally, privacy-enhancing technologies and cryptographic agility are discussed, highlighting the future of secure communication and data protection.

Get a Free eBook

We hope you are enjoying your recently purchased book! Your feedback is incredibly valuable to us, and to all other readers looking for great books.

If you found this book helpful or enjoyable, we would truly appreciate it, if you could take a moment to leave a short review with a 5 star rating on Amazon. It helps us grow, and lets other readers discover our books.

As a thank you, we would love to send you a free digital copy of this book, and a **30%** discount code on your next cart value on our official websites:

www.orangeava.com

www.orangeava.in (For Indian Subcontinent)

☑ **Here's how:**

Leave a review for the book on Amazon.

Take a screenshot of your review, and send an email to **info@orangeava.com** (it can be just the confirmation screen).

Once, we receive your screenshot, we will send you the digital file, within 24 hours.

Thank you so much for your support – it means a lot to us!

Downloading the code bundles and colored images

Please follow the links or scan the QR codes to download the ***Code Bundles and Images*** of the book:

https://github.com/ava-orange-education/Hands-on-Cryptography-with-Python

The code bundles and images of the book are also hosted on ***https://rebrand.ly/a72cec***

In case there's an update to the code, it will be updated on the existing GitHub repository.

Errata

We take immense pride in our work at **Orange Education Pvt Ltd,** and follow best practices to ensure the accuracy of our content to provide an indulging reading experience to our subscribers. Our readers are our mirrors, and we use their inputs to reflect and improve upon human errors, if any, that may have occurred during the publishing processes involved. To let us maintain the quality and help us reach out to any readers who might be having difficulties due to any unforeseen errors, please write to us at :

errata@orangeava.com

Your support, suggestions, and feedback are highly appreciated.

DID YOU KNOW

Did you know that Orange Education Pvt Ltd offers eBook versions of every book published, with PDF and ePub files available? You can upgrade to the eBook version at **www.orangeava.com** and as a print book customer, you are entitled to a discount on the eBook copy. Get in touch with us at: **info@orangeava.com** for more details.

At **www.orangeava.com**, you can also read a collection of free technical articles, sign up for a range of free newsletters, and receive exclusive discounts and offers on AVA® Books and eBooks.

PIRACY

If you come across any illegal copies of our works in any form on the internet, we would be grateful if you would provide us with the location address or website name. Please contact us at **info@orangeava.com** with a link to the material.

ARE YOU INTERESTED IN AUTHORING WITH US?

If there is a topic that you have expertise in, and you are interested in either writing or contributing to a book, please write to us at **business@orangeava.com**. We are on a journey to help developers and tech professionals to gain insights on the present technological advancements and innovations happening across the globe and build a community that believes Knowledge is best acquired by sharing and learning with others. Please reach out to us to learn what our audience demands and how you can be part of this educational reform. We also welcome ideas from tech experts and help them build learning and development content for their domains.

REVIEWS

Please leave a review. Once you have read and used this book, why not leave a review on the site that you purchased it from? Potential readers can then see and use your unbiased opinion to make purchase decisions. We at Orange Education would love to know what you think about our products, and our authors can learn from your feedback. Thank you!

For more information about Orange Education, please visit **www.orangeava.com**.

Table of Contents

CHAPTER 1
Platform Setup and Installation

Introduction

Before starting to dive in we need a place to swim. In this chapter, we discuss a little about the introduction to the Python programming language, only for those who are unfamiliar with the language. Then we discuss the libraries that we will use throughout the chapter, such as pyOpenSSL and cryptography..

Structure

In this chapter, the following topics will be covered:

- Software Installation and Platform Setup
- The `pyOpenSSL` Module
- The Cryptography Module

Introduction to Python

Python is a powerful and versatile programming language known for its simplicity, readability, and efficiency. Created by Guido van Rossum in the late 1980s, Python has rapidly grown in popularity and has become a favorite among beginners and seasoned developers alike. Its clear and expressive syntax allows programmers to focus on solving problems rather than wrestling with complicated code structures.

Before diving into the exciting world of cryptography using Python, it's essential to choose a suitable platform for your development. Python is compatible with various operating systems, including Windows, macOS, and Linux. It's essential to understand the different Python versions available. As of the time of writing, the two main versions are Python 2 and Python 3. However, Python 2 has reached its end of life, and it is strongly recommended to use Python 3 for all new projects.

Windows Installation:

To install Python on Windows, follow these steps:

1. Visit the official Python website at https://www.python.org/downloads/.
2. Download the latest stable version of Python 3.x for Windows.
3. Run the installer and select the option to add Python to the system PATH.
4. Complete the installation by following the on-screen instructions.

macOS Installation:

Python comes pre-installed on most macOS systems. However, you can install a newer version if needed,

1. Visit the official Python website at https://www.python.org/downloads/.
2. Download the latest stable version of Python 3.x for macOS.
3. Run the installer and follow the on-screen instructions.

Linux Installation:

Python is typically included in most Linux distributions. To install Python on Linux, open a terminal and use the package manager specific to your distribution:

- **For Debian/Ubuntu**: `sudo apt-get install python3`
- **For Fedora**: `sudo dnf install python3`
- **For CentOS/RHEL**: `sudo yum install python3`

Tutorials on Introduction to Python:

If you're a complete beginner stepping into the world of programming or someone very new to Python, then this introduction will take you through the fundamental concepts of Python programming with illustrative examples to demonstrate its ease and practicality.

Hello, World! - Your First Python Program: Let's start with the classic "Hello, World!" program, which prints a simple message to the screen.

Types: Python is dynamically typed, meaning you don't need to declare variable types explicitly. Here are some common data types.

```
# Integer
age = 25
# Floating-point number
pi = 3.14
# String
name = "Alice"
# Boolean
is_student = True
```

Arithmetic Operations:

Python supports all standard arithmetic operations: addition, subtraction, multiplication, division, and modulus.

Conditionals statements:

Conditionals allow you to execute code based on certain conditions.

```
x = 10
if x > 0:
    print("x is positive")
elif x == 0:
    print("x is zero")
else:
    print("x is negative")
```

Output:

```
>>x is positive
```

Loops (for and while):

Loops are used to repeat blocks of code.

```
# For loop
for i in range(5):
    print(i)
```

Output:

```
>>0
>>1
>>2
>>3
>>4
```

```
# While loop
count = 0
while count < 5:
    print("Count:", count)
    count += 1
```

Output:

```
>>Count:0
>>Count:1
>>Count:2
>>Count:3
>>Count:4
```

Lists and List Comprehension:

Lists are collections of items, and list comprehension provides a concise way to create lists.

```
# Creating a list
fruits = ["apple", "banana", "orange", "grape"]

# List comprehension
squares = [x ** 2 for x in range(1, 6)]
```

Functions:

Functions in Python are blocks of reusable code that perform specific tasks. They help organize code and make it more maintainable.

```
def greet(name):
    return "Hello, " + name + "!"

message = greet("Alice")
print(message)
```

Output:

```
>>Hello, Alice!
```

Dictionaries:

Dictionaries store data in key-value pairs.

```
# Creating a dictionary
person = {
    "name": "Alice",
    "age": 30,
    "occupation": "Engineer"
}

# Accessing values
print(person["name"])
```

Output:

```
>>Alice
```

File Handling:

Python makes it easy to read from and write to files.

```
# Writing to a file
with open("example.txt", "w") as file:
    file.write("Hello, Python!")

# Reading from a file
```

```
with open("example.txt", "r") as file:
    content = file.read()
    print(content)
```

Output:

```
>> Hello, Python!
```

Classes and Objects:

Python supports object-oriented programming.

```
class Dog:
    def __init__(self, name, age):
        self.name = name
        self.age = age

    def bark(self):
        return "Woof!"

# Creating an object
dog1 = Dog("Buddy", 3)
print(dog1.name)
>> Buddy
print(dog1.bark())
>> Woof!
```

Python offers many more concepts and features, allowing you to build complex applications with concise and readable code. This introduction provides a glimpse into the language's capabilities, and as you continue your journey in Python, you will discover its vast ecosystem and applications in various domains. Now we will discuss two Python modules that we will use extensively throughout the book.

The pyOpenSSL Module

The '**pyOpenSSL**' module is a Python wrapper around the OpenSSL library, which provides tools for working with Secure Sockets Layer (SSL) and Transport Layer Security (TLS) protocols, as well as various cryptographic operations. It allows Python developers to implement secure communication, work with certificates, and perform various cryptographic tasks using the OpenSSL library's capabilities.

Key features of the cryptography Module:

- **SSL/TLS Communication**: The module enables the implementation of SSL and TLS protocols, which are essential for securing data transmission over networks. It allows you to create both SSL clients and servers.
- **Certificate Management**: With '**pyOpenSSL**', you can manage X.509 digital certificates and private keys. This includes generating certificates, creating certificate signing requests (CSRs), and handling certificate chains.

- **Cryptographic Operations**: The module provides interfaces for various cryptographic operations, including encryption, decryption, hashing, digital signatures, and more.
- **Validation and Verification:** '**pyOpenSSL**' allows you to validate certificates and verify digital signatures, ensuring the authenticity and integrity of data.

To use the `` `pyOpenSSL` `` module in your Python projects, follow these installation steps:

Install OpenSSL Libraries: Before installing the `` `pyOpenSSL` `` module, you need to have the OpenSSL libraries installed on your system. Depending on your operating system, you may need to install them separately.

- **On Linux**: Use the package manager for your distribution to install OpenSSL. For example, on Debian-based systems, you can use the following command:
  `pip install openssl`
- **On macOS**: OpenSSL is usually pre-installed on macOS. If not, you can use package managers such as Homebrew to install it
- **On Windows**: You can download the OpenSSL binaries for Windows from the official website (https://slproweb.com/products/Win32OpenSSL.html) or use package managers such as Chocolatey.

Install pyOpenSSL: After setting up the OpenSSL libraries, open a terminal or command prompt, and run the following command to install the `` `pyOpenSSL` `` module.

Verify Installation: To verify that the installation was successful, open a Python interpreter or create a Python script and import the `` `OpenSSL` `` module.

If the installation is successful, it will display the version number of the '**pyOpenSSL**' module.

The Cryptography Module

The 'cryptography' module in Python is a powerful library that provides various cryptographic functionalities to secure data, ensure data integrity, and implement secure communication. It is built on top of the 'cryptography.io' library, which is a set of low-level cryptographic primitives. The 'cryptography' module simplifies the usage of these primitives and makes it easier for developers to implement secure cryptographic operations.

Key features of the cryptography Module:

- **Symmetric and Asymmetric Encryption**: The library supports both symmetric and asymmetric encryption schemes. It provides implementations of popular symmetric ciphers such as AES and DES, as well as RSA and ECC for asymmetric encryption.

- **Hash Functions**: Cryptography supports various cryptographic hash functions, such as SHA-256, SHA-384, and SHA-512, which are used to generate hash codes for ensuring data integrity.
- **Digital Signatures**: It enables the creation and verification of digital signatures using algorithms such as RSA and ECDSA. Digital signatures are crucial for verifying the authenticity and integrity of data.
- **Key Derivation Functions**: The module supports key derivation functions such as PBKDF2 and HKDF, which are essential for securely deriving cryptographic keys from passwords or passphrases.
- **Random Number Generation**: It provides facilities for generating secure random numbers, which are crucial for cryptographic operations that require randomness, such as key generation.
- **Serialization and Key Management**: Cryptography allows for serialization of cryptographic objects, enabling secure storage, and retrieval of keys and other cryptographic data.

Install '`cryptography`': After setting up Python, open a terminal or command prompt and run the following command to install the cryptography module:

```
pip install cryptography
```

Verify Installation: To verify that the installation was successful, open a Python interpreter or create a Python script and import the '**`cryptography`**' module:

```
import cryptography
print(cryptography.__version__)
```

If the installation is successful, it will display the version number of the cryptography module.

With the '**`cryptography`**' module installed, you can now utilize its cryptographic functionalities to implement secure communication, data integrity verification, digital signatures, and more in your Python projects. Now we are ready to dive into the world of cryptography concepts.

Conclusion

This chapter provided a foundational understanding of the Python programming language and its significant role in cryptographic applications. We began with installing Python and configuring a development environment tailored for cryptography-focused projects. This setup ensures a smooth and efficient workflow as we delve deeper into the complexities of secure programming.

Additionally, we introduced essential cryptographic libraries, such as **`pyOpenSSL`**, and cryptography. These libraries serve as the building blocks for implementing secure communication protocols, managing digital certificates, creating digital signatures, and other cryptographic functionalities. Through clear installation steps and basic examples, we equipped you with the practical tools necessary to begin exploring these powerful modules.

Looking ahead, the next chapter will delve into the Introduction to Cryptography, providing a comprehensive overview of the field's fundamental principles and objectives. We will explore core concepts, such as encryption, decryption, hashing, and digital signatures, setting the stage for the detailed implementation of these concepts in subsequent chapters. This transition from platform setup to cryptographic theory will form the basis of your journey into mastering cryptographic systems using Python.

Chapter 2
Introduction to Cryptography

Introduction

This chapter embarks on a journey through time, tracing the evolution of cryptography from its ancient origins to its modern-day prominence. As we delve into the pages of history, we will explore the art of encoding secrets, decipher the tales of ancient ciphers, and witness the transformative power of cryptographic machines.

From the enigmatic Enigma machine that played a pivotal role in World War II to the dawn of the digital age and the birth of modern cryptographic methods, our odyssey will illuminate the fascinating interplay between cryptography and human history. We will uncover the ingenious techniques employed by ancient civilizations to protect their most sensitive information, and we will chart the emergence of cryptographic technologies that secure the digital foundations of our interconnected world.

Yet, this chapter is just the beginning of our exploration. In the chapters that follow, we will venture deeper into the realms of cryptographic algorithms, unravel the mathematical mysteries that underpin encryption, and navigate the complex ethical and legal considerations that surround this essential field. Together, we will embark on a thrilling journey through the heart of cryptography, unlocking its secrets and discovering the pivotal role it plays in shaping our digital future.

Structure

In this chapter, the following topics will be covered,

- Ciphers of Antiquity
- From Paper to Machine
- The Enigma of World War II
- Digital Dawn and Modern Cryptography
- Modern Cryptographic Algorithms

- The Role of Cryptography Today
- Ethical and Legal Considerations
- Ongoing Evolution
- Conclusion – A Journey Through Time

Ciphers of Antiquity

In the annals of history, the art of concealing information has always been a necessity, leading to the birth of cryptography. Ancient civilizations employed ingenious methods to safeguard their secrets, giving rise to a variety of ciphers that were far ahead of their time. These cryptographic techniques were driven by the fundamental desire for secrecy and the need to protect sensitive information from prying eyes.

The two earliest cryptographic endeavors are:

- Substitution cipher
- Transposition cipher

Substitution Cipher

The substitution cipher stands as a testament to the ancient art of secret communication. This ingenious technique involves the systematic replacement of individual letters or symbols in plaintext with other symbols, creating an intricate web of transformations that renders the original message inscrutable to anyone without knowledge of the key. The concept behind the substitution cipher is deceptively simple: By substituting each letter with another, a coded message emerges that is remarkably different from the original yet retains its underlying structure.

One of the most iconic examples of the substitution cipher is the Caesar cipher, named after Julius Caesar, who is said to have used it during his campaigns. In the Caesar cipher, each letter in the plaintext is shifted by a fixed number of positions down or up the alphabet. For instance, with a shift of 3, **A** becomes **D**, **B** becomes **E**, and so on. This transformation creates a new alphabet, reshaping the message into an unreadable series of characters. In Table 2.1, the message MAYDAY is encrypted as PDBGDB, which clearly does not make any sense. The recipient of the coded message, armed with the knowledge of the shift value, can decipher the message by simply reversing the process.

Throughout history, cryptographers in various cultures employed these early ciphers to safeguard military strategies, diplomatic correspondence, and other sensitive information. From the Spartan scytale to the Atbash cipher of ancient Hebrews, these techniques showcased the ingenuity of ancient civilizations in devising methods to ensure the confidentiality of their communications.

Plain	M	A	Y	D	A	Y
Cipher	P	D	B	G	D	B

Table 2.1: *An example of Caesar Cipher Encryption*

While seemingly straightforward, the substitution cipher represented a significant advancement in confidentiality during ancient times. It allowed individuals and organizations to exchange sensitive information without fear of interception or comprehension by unintended recipients. Despite its relative simplicity, the substitution cipher was a formidable barrier for those attempting to decipher the coded messages without the key. It laid the groundwork for subsequent cryptographic developments and paved the way for more complex encryption methods. The substitution cipher, with its ability to transform ordinary language into cryptic puzzles, captured the imagination of cryptographers throughout history.

Transposition Cipher:

The ciphers of antiquity laid the groundwork for modern cryptographic principles, serving as a testament to humanity's enduring pursuit of secrecy and the protection of knowledge. These early encryption methods, while simplistic by today's standards, played a vital role in shaping the evolution of cryptography, leading to the sophisticated techniques that secure our digital world today.

The limitations of manual encryption were evident. These methods were inherently slow, prone to errors, and required a considerable amount of training and expertise to execute effectively. Additionally, maintaining the secrecy of the key was challenging, as physical copies of keys could be stolen or lost, compromising the security of the system.

Nonetheless, manual encryption was a critical stepping stone in the evolution of cryptography. It reflected humanity's early efforts to grapple with the fundamental challenges of secrecy and secure communication. As we delve further into the annals of cryptographic history, we witness the remarkable transformation from these manual methods to the mechanized precision of cipher machines, a pivotal transition that would revolutionize the field of cryptography.

From Paper to Machine: Mechanization of Encryption

When discussing mechanical forms of encryption, there are several key points and aspects you can explore to provide a comprehensive view of this fascinating period in the history of cryptography. Here are some points to consider.

Emergence of Mechanical Cipher Machines

In the historical context of cryptography, the emergence of mechanical cipher machines marked a transformative period. These ingenious devices appeared during an era when societal and technological advancements intersected, creating fertile ground for cryptographic innovation. This pivotal juncture in history witnessed the rise of machines designed to automate and streamline the encryption and decryption processes, setting the stage for revolutionary changes in the field of cryptography.

Early Mechanical Devices

Among the early mechanical cipher machines, standouts such as the Jefferson disk and the Alberti cipher disk captured the imaginations of cryptographers and security enthusiasts alike. These mechanical marvels were designed to simplify the encryption process while enhancing security. Typically composed of rotating wheels or disks, they allowed users to encode and decode messages by manipulating the machine's settings. The ingenuity of these devices lies in their ability to automate the complex task of substitution ciphers, offering both speed and precision in cryptographic operations.

Advantages Over Manual Methods

The advantages of mechanical cipher machines over their manual counterparts were multifaceted. These machines eliminated the labor-intensive nature of manual encryption methods, reducing the possibility of errors introduced by human calculation. Moreover, they accelerated the encryption and decryption processes, allowing for the rapid exchange of secure messages. This combination of improved accuracy and efficiency made mechanical machines a quantum leap in the evolution of cryptography, enhancing the confidentiality of sensitive information.

The Jefferson Disk

The Jefferson disk, a notable example of early mechanical encryption devices, featured a set of concentric disks, each inscribed with the letters of the alphabet. By aligning the disks in a specific configuration, users could encode and decode messages. Thomas Jefferson, one of its creators, utilized this disk to protect sensitive correspondence during his time. Its elegant design and effectiveness made it a prime example of the potential of mechanical cipher machines, revolutionizing the way information was secured and transmitted.

Influential Figures

The development and use of mechanical cipher machines were often intertwined with the contributions of influential figures in the world of cryptography. Individuals such as Thomas Jefferson, Leon Battista Alberti, and others played pivotal roles in advancing the field through their design and deployment of these machines. Their work not only enhanced the security of communication but also laid the groundwork for future cryptographic innovations.

Cryptanalysis of Mechanical Machines

The advent of mechanical cipher machines also sparked the interest of cryptanalysts who sought to break their security. These early attempts at cryptanalysis formed the basis for later, more sophisticated techniques. While some mechanical machines posed formidable challenges, others succumbed to determined codebreakers, illustrating the ongoing cat-and-mouse game between cryptographic innovators and those seeking to decipher their messages.

Legacy of Mechanical Encryption

The legacy of mechanical cipher machines endures in the world of cryptography. These early innovations in automation and encryption set the stage for the development of more sophisticated cryptographic devices and algorithms in the digital age. The principles and concepts behind these machines continue to influence modern cryptographic systems, reminding us of the enduring impact of mechanical encryption on the security of information.

Transition to Modern Cryptography

The transition from mechanical cipher machines to modern cryptography represents a critical chapter in the field's evolution. As technology continued to advance, the fusion of human innovation with mechanical precision foreshadowed the increasing importance of technology in cryptography. This transition paved the way for the digital encryption methods that safeguard our digital world today, marking a pivotal moment in the history of securing information.

Aspects	Mechanical Cipher	Modern Cipher
Era of Use	Primarily used during the early 20th century, especially in military and diplomatic communications	Used extensively in the digital age to secure data across industries and applications worldwide
Key Type	Typically used fixed, manually set keys (for example, rotor settings)	Utilizes mathematically complex keys, often generated by software or hardware, ranging from 128 to 4096 bits or more

Encryption Process	Mechanical and manual, involving physical components, such as rotors, wheels, and plugboards	Completely digital, involving algorithms and high-speed computation
Strength	Mechanical and manual, involving physical components, such as rotors, wheels, and plugboards	High strength due to computational complexity; resistant to brute-force attacks when using appropriate key sizes
Speed	Slow and labor-intensive, requiring human intervention for setting and operation	Extremely fast and automated, capable of securing large volumes of data in milliseconds
Adaptability	Limited to specific use cases (for example, military, diplomatic)	Highly adaptable to diverse scenarios, such as online transactions, IoT, and secure communications
Historical Impact	Laid the foundation for automated cryptographic methods and influenced early computer science	Integral to global cybersecurity, protecting data integrity, privacy, and authenticity in modern systems
Notable Examples	Enigma, Lorenz cipher, and SIGABA	AES, RSA, ECC, and post-quantum algorithms such as Kyber and Dilithium.

***Table 2.2**: Comparison Between Mechanical and Modern Encryption Techniques*

The Enigma of World War II

In the history of cryptography, the Enigma machine stands as a testament to human ingenuity and the relentless quest for secrecy. Born in the turbulent years of the early 20th century, it owes its existence to the visionary efforts of Arthur Scherbius, a German engineer who sought to create a device that could revolutionize secure communication. Scherbius' vision was rooted in the volatile geopolitical climate of the time, where nations were racing to protect their classified information. Little did he know that his creation would become an iconic symbol of cryptography's evolution.

Mechanical Mastery: Inside the Enigma

At the heart of the Enigma machine lay a mechanical masterpiece, intricately designed to encode messages with mathematical precision. Its intricate components included a series of rotors, a plugboard, and a lamp board. Each rotor, meticulously calibrated and mounted on an axle, played a vital role in the encryption process. The plugboard, ingeniously integrated into the military version of the Enigma, allowed for additional permutations of letters. These mechanical intricacies transformed the Enigma into a cryptographic juggernaut, generating an astronomical number of possible letter combinations with each keystroke.

Cryptographic Strength and Complexity: A Cipher Unsolved

The Enigma machine's cryptographic strength lay in its bewildering complexity. With multiple rotors whose positions could be adjusted and daily key settings, it generated a staggering number of possible letter combinations. This cryptographic complexity made it an extraordinarily secure system for its time, defying the efforts of codebreakers and ensuring the confidentiality of the most sensitive military communications. Attempts to decipher its encoded messages would prove to be a monumental challenge.

World War II and the Enigma: A Tactical Advantage

During World War II, the Enigma machine took center stage as a linchpin in securing German military communications. It played an indispensable role in safeguarding everything from strategic plans to battlefield orders. The German military's reliance on the Enigma machine underscored its significance in ensuring the secrecy of their wartime operations. Yet, the machine's brilliance would be challenged by the relentless determination of Allied codebreakers, including Alan Turing, whose groundbreaking work at Bletchley Park led to the decryption of Enigma-encoded messages.

Enduring Legacy: Beyond Wartime Secrets

The legacy of the Enigma machine transcends its wartime usage. It resonates not only in the history of cryptography but also in the realm of modern computer science. Alan Turing's code-breaking efforts, stemming from the Enigma challenge, laid the foundation for early computers and the digital age. Beyond its historical importance, surviving Enigma machines have become sought-after collector's items, celebrated for their rarity and cultural significance. In popular media and literature, the Enigma machine continues to captivate as a symbol of intrigue, espionage, and the timeless human endeavor to unlock secrets hidden within the cryptic realm of cryptography.

Digital Dawn and Modern Cryptography

As humanity stood on the threshold of the digital age, the world underwent a seismic transformation. The advent of computers, the internet's global embrace, and the relentless surge of digital data redefined nearly every facet of human existence. This epochal shift in how we processed, communicated, and stored information revolutionized our lives, spawning a digital renaissance that offered unparalleled connectivity and convenience. Yet, amidst this digital dawn, new challenges emerged, and the need to safeguard our digital realm became increasingly evident.

In the wake of this digital revolution, the world found itself in a delicate balance, where the boundless opportunities for communication and commerce coexisted with the looming specter of cyber threats. The conveniences of instant global communication and data sharing were juxtaposed with the vulnerabilities of data breaches, identity theft, and digital espionage. It was within this crucible of opportunity and peril that the role of cryptography evolved, adapting to secure our digital lives.

This section delves into the intricate dance between the digital age and modern cryptography. It explores how the very essence of securing information was reshaped by this new digital frontier. From the evolution of cryptographic algorithms to the birth of concepts such as public key cryptography, we navigate the fascinating journey of safeguarding our digital world in an age where information knows no bounds. As we embark on this exploration, we discover how cryptography emerged as the guardian of our digital realms, enabling secure communication, protecting our data, and preserving the sanctity of the digital dawn.

Introducing the Digital Age: Transforming Information in the Digital Era

The dawn of the digital age marked an epochal shift in the way society processed, communicated, and safeguarded information. It emerged as a period defined by the proliferation of computers, the inexorable rise of the internet, and the profound transformation of everyday life. This era, which began to take root in the latter half of the 20th century, brought with it unprecedented opportunities for connectivity, knowledge exchange, and economic growth but also presented a new set of challenges, particularly in the realm of information security.

As computers became increasingly accessible and integral to various facets of human existence, the sheer volume of digital data grew exponentially. Tasks that once required manual effort—calculations, communication, record-keeping—were now executed with unprecedented speed and efficiency. The internet, acting as a global nervous system, facilitated the near-instantaneous transmission of data across continents, connecting people and organizations as never before. This digital metamorphosis fundamentally altered the landscape of information, rendering it ephemeral, easily replicable, and susceptible to theft or manipulation.

Challenges of the Digital Era: Complexities of the Digital Frontier

The advent of the digital era ushered in a time of profound change, where the power of computers, the internet, and digital communication reshaped the world. However, amidst the transformative opportunities, an array of formidable challenges emerged. In this new landscape, data became an omnipresent force, continuously generated and stored. Yet, this proliferation posed a pressing concern: how to safeguard the privacy of individuals and the security of sensitive information in an age of unparalleled connectivity.

Cybersecurity threats have become an omnipresent concern, evolving alongside digital advancements. Malware, ransomware, and hacking became household terms, threatening everyone from individuals to global corporations. As data became more interconnected, the vulnerabilities of the digital realm became apparent. Critical infrastructure, financial systems, and government networks were suddenly exposed to potential cyberattacks from anywhere in the world, necessitating international collaboration to address the shared challenge of cybersecurity.

The need for secure encryption became paramount. While digital communication flourished, managing encryption keys, ensuring secure key exchange, and reconciling security with user-friendly interfaces proved complex. Furthermore, the integrity of digital data has become a concern across various industries. In fields such as finance, healthcare, and law, verifying the authenticity of digital documents and transactions has become vital for maintaining trust in the digital age.

Balancing security with accessibility was another intricate challenge. As society became increasingly reliant on digital services, finding the equilibrium between safeguarding sensitive data and ensuring access for legitimate purposes became a topic of intense debate. The question of whether encryption should include backdoors for government access to encrypted data highlighted the complexities inherent in this balance.

The digital era also presented a continually evolving threat landscape. Cybercriminals adapted rapidly, necessitating ongoing innovation in cybersecurity and cryptographic methods to stay one step ahead. The challenges posed by this dynamic environment spurred the development of modern cryptography, as experts sought solutions to protect digital communication and data in a world teeming with opportunities and threats alike. This journey of navigating the complexities of the digital frontier continues, reflecting the intricate tapestry of challenges that define the digital era.

Birth of Modern Cryptography

Modern cryptography emerged as a direct response to the unique challenges posed by the digital era, addressing the pressing need to secure information in an increasingly interconnected and data-centric world. As the digital age dawned, traditional methods of encryption faced inherent limitations, particularly in the realm of digital communication and data protection. Here, we explore how modern cryptography was born to mitigate these challenges and redefine the landscape of information security.

The digital era ushered in an unprecedented surge in the volume of data generated, transmitted, and stored digitally. This proliferation presented a fundamental dilemma: how to protect sensitive information from unauthorized access, eavesdropping, or tampering. Traditional cryptographic methods, which had served well in the analog world, struggled to scale up to the demands of this new digital landscape. Modern cryptography emerged as a response to this dilemma, offering innovative solutions that could safeguard data in this digital deluge.

One of the primary challenges of the digital era was secure key management and distribution. In a world where digital communication and transactions occur on a global scale, the secure exchange of encryption keys has become a complex undertaking. Modern cryptography introduced the concept of public key encryption, where a pair of keys—a public key and a private key—could be used to encrypt and decrypt data. The public key could be freely shared, allowing for secure communication, while the private key remained securely held by the owner. This revolutionary approach solved the key distribution challenge and enabled secure digital communication on an unprecedented scale.

Moreover, modern cryptography recognized the need for data integrity and authentication. In an interconnected world, ensuring that data remained unaltered during transmission and verifying the authenticity of digital documents became paramount. Cryptographic techniques such as digital signatures, which leveraged public key cryptography, were introduced to tackle these issues. They allowed individuals and organizations to sign digital documents, providing a level of trust and assurance in the digital realm.

In essence, modern cryptography was born to bridge the gap between the possibilities and vulnerabilities of the digital era. It revolutionized the way information was secured, making digital communication, e-commerce, and online transactions safe and trustworthy. As the digital landscape continues to evolve, modern cryptography remains at the forefront of information security, adapting and innovating to meet the ever-changing challenges posed by the relentless march of technology in our interconnected world.

Symmetric and Asymmetric Encryption

Modern cryptography was born to meet these ever-changing challenges head-on. Two foundational approaches emerged: symmetric encryption and asymmetric encryption. Symmetric encryption relies on a single, shared secret key for both encrypting and decrypting data. It excels in terms of speed and efficiency but necessitates secure key distribution, making it suitable for scenarios where key management is feasible.

On the other hand, asymmetric encryption, often referred to as public key cryptography, introduced a revolutionary concept: pairs of keys—a public key and a private key. The public key is openly distributed and used for encryption, while the private key, closely guarded by the owner, is employed for decryption. Asymmetric encryption elegantly solved the key distribution challenge that had hampered symmetric encryption, making it ideal for securing communication over untrusted networks, such as the

Internet. It also played a pivotal role in digital signatures, verifying the authenticity and integrity of digital documents.

Modern Cryptographic Algorithms

In the realm of modern cryptography, a diverse array of cryptographic algorithms has emerged, each designed to address specific security requirements and challenges. These algorithms serve as the mathematical underpinnings of secure digital communication, data protection, and information integrity.

- **Advanced Encryption Standard (AES)**

  AES is one of the most widely used symmetric encryption algorithms. It employs a variable key length (128, 192, or 256 bits) and operates through multiple rounds of substitution, permutation, and mixing operations. AES is renowned for its security and efficiency, making it a cornerstone of data encryption in various applications, including securing sensitive files and communications.

- **Rivest-Shamir-Adleman (RSA)**

  RSA is a pioneering asymmetric encryption algorithm, named after its inventors. It relies on the mathematical properties of large prime numbers for encryption and decryption. RSA is primarily used for secure key exchange, digital signatures, and securing sensitive data in public key infrastructure (PKI) systems. It remains a fundamental component of secure communication over the Internet.

- **Elliptic Curve Cryptography (ECC)**

  ECC is another asymmetric encryption technique that leverages the mathematics of elliptic curves. It offers strong security with shorter key lengths compared to RSA, making it efficient for resource-constrained devices. ECC is integral to secure communication in applications such as mobile devices and IoT devices.

- **Secure Hash Algorithm (SHA) Family**

  The SHA family includes cryptographic hash functions such as SHA-256 and SHA-3. These algorithms take input data and produce fixed-length hash values, ensuring data integrity and authentication. They are extensively used for password storage, digital signatures, and data verification.

- **Diffie-Hellman Key Exchange**

  Although not an encryption algorithm per se, Diffie-Hellman is a vital asymmetric key exchange protocol. It allows two parties to securely exchange encryption keys over an untrusted network. It forms the basis for secure connections in protocols such as SSL/TLS used in web browsing.

These cryptographic algorithms represent the building blocks of modern security in the digital age. They have evolved to meet the ever-changing landscape of threats and technologies, ensuring that data remains confidential, tamper-proof, and trustworthy. As technology advances and new challenges arise, the field of cryptography continues to innovate, adapting to safeguard the digital frontier. In the quest for secure digital communication, cryptography remains an essential and dynamic component, driving the secure exchange of information in our interconnected world.

Secure Communication Protocols

In the dynamic landscape of modern cryptography, securing data at rest is only part of the equation. Equally crucial is ensuring the confidentiality and integrity of data while it's in transit. This is where secure channel protocols come into play, forming the bedrock of secure communication across the digital realm.

- **Transport Layer Security (TLS)**

  TLS, formerly known as SSL (Secure Sockets Layer), is perhaps the most recognizable secure channel protocol. It provides a secure and encrypted connection between a client and a server over the Internet. TLS ensures that data exchanged during online interactions, such as web browsing, email communication, and online transactions, remains confidential and protected from eavesdropping or tampering.

- **Internet Protocol Security (IPsec)**

  IPsec is a suite of protocols used to secure internet communications at the network layer. It enables the creation of virtual private networks (VPNs) and ensures that data transmitted between networks, remote offices, or individual devices remains private and authenticated. IPsec is vital for securing corporate data across distributed networks.

- **Secure Shell (SSH)**

  SSH is a cryptographic network protocol used for secure remote access and file transfer. It authenticates users and encrypts data, making it a go-to choice for administrators and developers when accessing remote servers or managing cloud infrastructure securely.

- **Signal Protocol**

  Signal Protocol is an open-source encryption protocol used in secure messaging applications, such as Signal, WhatsApp, and others. It provides end-to-end encryption, ensuring that only the intended recipient can decipher the messages. Signal Protocol exemplifies the importance of privacy in digital communication.

- **Encrypted Email Protocols**

  Secure email protocols such as Pretty Good Privacy (PGP) and Secure/Multipurpose Internet Mail Extensions (S/MIME) enable the encryption of email messages, ensuring that sensitive content remains private and protected from unauthorized access.

Continuing the Pursuit of Security

Secure channel protocols are the digital highways on which our information travels securely. They uphold the principles of confidentiality, integrity, and authenticity, ensuring that sensitive data remains safeguarded from interception or manipulation during transmission.

As we forge ahead in the digital age, the pursuit of security remains relentless. Cryptographers and cybersecurity experts continue to refine existing protocols, develop new ones, and adapt to emerging threats. The synergy between modern cryptography, secure channel protocols, and evolving technologies forms the backbone of trust in our interconnected world.

The Role of Cryptography Today

In the rapidly evolving landscape of the 21st century, cryptography stands as a formidable sentinel, safeguarding the digital realm that has become integral to our daily lives. Its multifaceted role, underpinned by the principles of security, privacy, and trust, extends across various domains, shaping the way we interact, transact, and communicate in the modern world.

- **Data Protection and Privacy**

  Cryptography serves as the bedrock of data protection and privacy in our digital age. It ensures that our personal, financial, and sensitive information remains confidential, whether stored on remote servers, transmitted across networks, or housed in the cloud. This foundational security is vital in sectors such as healthcare, finance, and e-commerce.

- **Secure Communication**

  The secure transmission of data over the internet is made possible by cryptographic protocols, exemplified by SSL/TLS. This is the cornerstone of secure online activities, including online banking, shopping, and confidential communications, reassuring us that our interactions remain private and invulnerable to prying eyes.

- **Digital Signatures and Authentication**

  Cryptographic signatures provide a means of authenticating the origin and integrity of digital documents and transactions. They underpin the trust in e-commerce transactions, ensuring that buyers and sellers can engage confidently, free from the specter of fraud.

- **Password Security**

  In an era marked by cyber threats, cryptographic hashing algorithms shield user passwords in databases. This means that even if databases are compromised, hackers can't access plaintext passwords, fortifying our online identities.

- **Secure Mobile Devices**

  Cryptography secures our indispensable mobile devices, from encryption that protects our data to secure communications between apps. This assurance is pivotal in a world where smartphones and tablets have become extensions of our lives.

- **Cloud Security**

  Our reliance on cloud storage and services is enabled by cryptography. It ensures that data stored in the cloud remains confidential and intact, immune to unauthorized access.

- **Digital Currencies and Blockchain**

  Cryptocurrencies such as Bitcoin rely on cryptographic principles to enable secure transactions and verify ownership. The underlying technology, blockchain, uses cryptographic hashes to guarantee the integrity and immutability of transaction records.

- **IoT Security**

  The burgeoning Internet of Things (IoT) is grounded in cryptography, securing devices ranging from smart thermostats to industrial sensors. This security prevents unauthorized control and data breaches in an increasingly interconnected world.

- **National Security and Government Operations**

  Governments worldwide depend on cryptography for national security. Secure communication, protection of classified information, and the development of encryption standards are vital components of defense and intelligence operations.

In essence, cryptography has assumed a central role in modern society, empowering individuals, businesses, and governments to navigate the digital age with confidence. Its significance extends far beyond encryption; it signifies the assurance of trust, privacy, and security in our interconnected world. Cryptography's enduring evolution ensures its place as an indispensable guardian, preserving the principles of confidentiality, integrity, and authenticity that underpin our information age.

Ethical and Legal Considerations

Now that we have covered many aspects of cryptography, we should enlighten ourselves with the ethical and legal considerations.

Ethical Considerations:

- **Privacy vs. Accountability**: Encryption is a powerful tool that safeguards individuals' privacy by securing their digital communications and data. Ethical concerns arise when this privacy protection is exploited for illicit purposes such as conducting illegal activities online or hiding evidence of criminal behavior. Striking a balance between protecting individual privacy rights and holding individuals accountable for unlawful actions poses a significant ethical challenge.
- **Dual-Use Technology**: Cryptographic technologies are considered dual-use, meaning they can be used for both beneficial and harmful purposes. While encryption ensures the confidentiality of sensitive data, it can also be used to encrypt malicious software or communication in cyberattacks. Ethical debates center on how to manage the dual-use nature of cryptography while promoting its legitimate uses.
- **User Consent and Data Protection**: Ethical cryptographic practices involve obtaining informed consent from users when their data is encrypted and stored. This ensures transparency and respects individuals' autonomy over their data. Additionally, data encryption is closely tied to ethical principles of data protection, particularly in fields such as healthcare and finance, where sensitive personal information must be secured.

Legal Considerations:

- **Export Controls**: Many countries have regulations governing the export of cryptographic technology. These laws are intended to prevent the proliferation of strong encryption to unauthorized entities, such as criminal organizations or hostile governments. Legal frameworks aim to strike a balance between facilitating international commerce and safeguarding national security interests.
- **Lawful Interception**: Governments worldwide assert the need for lawful interception capabilities to combat criminal activities and ensure national security. Legal frameworks in various jurisdictions dictate the circumstances under which law enforcement agencies can access encrypted communications and data. Balancing the right to privacy with the necessity of lawful access remains a contentious legal issue.
- **Data Protection and Privacy Laws**: Data protection regulations, such as the European Union's General Data Protection Regulation (GDPR), govern the use

of encryption in safeguarding individuals' personal data. Legal considerations include the requirements for data encryption, data breach notification, and the right to be forgotten, ensuring that encryption aligns with the principles of data protection.

- **International Agreements**: International agreements and treaties influence the legal landscape of cryptography, particularly in cases involving cross-border data sharing and law enforcement cooperation. These agreements seek to harmonize legal approaches to encryption while respecting the sovereignty of individual nations.

The ethical and legal dimensions of cryptography remain dynamic and evolving. Striking the right balance between protecting individual rights, preserving security, and enabling lawful access is an ongoing challenge. Cryptographers, legal experts, policymakers, and privacy advocates continue to engage in discourse, seeking solutions that uphold both ethical principles and the rule of law in an increasingly interconnected digital world.

Ongoing Evolution

The ongoing evolution of ethical and legal considerations in cryptography is a complex and dynamic process. Here are some key points to discuss in this context:

- **Technological Advancements**

  The relentless advancement of technology continually reshapes the ethical and legal landscape of cryptography. As encryption techniques become more robust and widely available, policymakers and legal authorities must adapt to new capabilities and challenges, such as the rise of quantum computing and its potential impact on encryption.

- **Emerging Threats**

  The evolving nature of cybersecurity threats introduces new ethical and legal dilemmas. As cyberattacks become increasingly sophisticated, governments and organizations must weigh the need for strong encryption against the imperative of protecting critical infrastructure and national security interests.

- **Legislative Responses**

  The GDPR (General Data Protection Regulation) protects the EU citizens' data and their privacy, within EU territory, likewise, the Digital Personal Data Protection Act, 2023 (DPDP) protects the personal information and data of Indian citizens. Governments around the world are continuously reviewing and updating legislation related to cryptography. This includes enacting data protection laws, revising export controls, and debating the boundaries of lawful access. The legal framework must remain flexible to address emerging challenges and technological advancements.

- **Public Awareness and Education**

  As encryption becomes increasingly accessible to the public, ethical considerations extend to issues of digital literacy and responsible encryption use. Promoting public awareness and education on encryption's benefits and limitations is essential.

Recent Developments in Cryptography

Now we will discuss about the recent developments in cryptography, which are much more important than ever before:

- **Post-Quantum Cryptography**

  Post-quantum cryptography focuses on creating encryption algorithms that are resistant to attacks from quantum computers. As quantum computing power grows, traditional cryptographic methods may become vulnerable, making the development of quantum-resistant algorithms crucial for future security.

- **Homomorphic Encryption**

  Homomorphic encryption allows computation on encrypted data without the need to decrypt it. This breakthrough enables secure and private computation in cloud environments and is particularly valuable for industries such as healthcare and finance, where sensitive data is involved.

- **Blockchain and Cryptocurrency**

  Blockchain technology has revolutionized digital transactions by providing a decentralized and tamper-resistant ledger. Cryptocurrencies such as Bitcoin and Ethereum rely on cryptographic techniques for secure transactions and have spurred further research into distributed ledger technology.

- **Zero-Knowledge Proofs**

  Zero-knowledge proofs enable one party to prove to another party that they know a specific piece of information without revealing the actual information itself. This cryptographic technique enhances privacy and security in various applications, including authentication and digital identity.

- **Multi-Party Computation**

  Multi-party computation allows multiple parties to jointly compute a function over their inputs while keeping those inputs private. This technique is essential for secure collaborative tasks such as secure voting systems and confidential data analysis.

- **Secure Hardware**

  The development of secure hardware, such as Trusted Platform Modules (TPMs) and Hardware Security Modules (HSMs), plays a crucial role in safeguarding cryptographic keys and ensuring the integrity of computing environments, particularly in IoT and cloud computing.

- **Continuous Cryptanalysis**

  As cryptographic techniques evolve, so do the methods of attackers. Ongoing cryptanalysis efforts seek to identify vulnerabilities in existing cryptographic algorithms and protocols, prompting the development of stronger and more resilient encryption methods.

These ongoing developments in cryptography are instrumental in addressing the evolving challenges of cybersecurity and privacy in our increasingly digital world.

Conclusion

Our exploration of cryptography, from its ancient roots to its pivotal role in the digital age, has revealed a remarkable journey. This journey, marked by innovation, adaptation, and ethical complexities, underscores the enduring significance of cryptography in shaping the course of human history and the digital world we inhabit today.

As we've traversed the historical aspects, examined ancient ciphers, and witnessed the transformation of cryptographic methods from paper to machine, we've gained insights into the profound impact of cryptography on civilizations past and present. The Enigma machine and the digital dawn have unveiled the power of cryptographic technologies in shaping events and securing information.

In our discussions on the role of cryptography in the modern era, we have explored the multifaceted dimensions of data protection, secure communication, and the ethical and legal considerations that define the digital landscape. Yet, our journey through cryptography is far from complete.

In the chapters to come, we will delve deeper into the intricacies of cryptographic algorithms, exploring their inner workings and practical applications. We will unravel the mysteries of encryption and decryption, revealing the mathematical underpinnings of security in the digital age. We will also examine the challenges and innovations that lie ahead, including quantum computing, post-quantum cryptography, and the ever-evolving landscape of cyber threats.

Join us in the chapters that follow as we continue our exploration of cryptography, delving into its technical depths, practical implications, and its role in securing a future where trust, privacy, and security remain paramount in our interconnected world. The journey is far from over, and together, we will navigate the intricate paths of this fascinating field, uncovering the secrets that lie within the art and science of cryptography.

CHAPTER 3
Symmetric Key Cryptography

Introduction

In the previous chapter, we embarked on an exciting journey into the fascinating world of cryptography. We uncovered the basic principles and concepts that underpin this ancient and ever-evolving field, offering a broad perspective on the art and science of securing information. Now, in this chapter, we delve deeper into one of the most fundamental aspects of cryptography: symmetric key cryptography.

Symmetric key cryptography serves as a cornerstone of modern encryption techniques, building upon the cryptographic foundations we explored in the introductory chapter. In this chapter, we will focus on the use of a single shared key for both encryption and decryption, which is a concept central to symmetric key cryptography. We will navigate through the intricate details of key management, the operation of various symmetric encryption algorithms, and the security considerations that accompany this approach to securing information.

But first, let us retrace our steps briefly. In *Chapter 2, Introduction to Cryptography*, we learned that cryptography is the art and science of securing information by transforming it into an unreadable format, known as cipher-text, and subsequently decrypting it back into its original form, known as plaintext. We understood the importance of confidentiality, integrity, and authenticity in secure communication and data storage. Furthermore, we delved into the classification of cryptography into two main categories: symmetric key cryptography and public key cryptography.

Symmetric key cryptography, which we are about to explore in this chapter, is the older of the two. It involves the use of a single shared secret key between the sender and the recipient, making it a fascinating subject of study with its roots extending deep into history. This method stands in stark contrast to public key cryptography, which relies on a pair of keys: one public and one private, opening up new possibilities for secure communication, digital signatures, and key exchange.

In our journey through symmetric key cryptography, we will unravel the intricacies of key management, encryption algorithms, and various modes of operation. We will also examine real-world applications and the critical role this approach plays in securing sensitive data. This chapter will empower you to understand, appreciate, and work with symmetric key cryptography to protect your own information.

As we continue this exploration, it is essential to acknowledge the critical interplay between these two cryptographic paradigms. The knowledge gained in our study of symmetric key cryptography will not only deepen your understanding of cryptographic concepts but also lay the groundwork for our later exploration of public key cryptography in subsequent chapters.

So, let us begin our journey through the realm of symmetric key cryptography. By the end of this chapter, you will have a strong grasp of its principles, mechanisms, and applications, and be better prepared to appreciate the broader landscape of cryptographic techniques.

Structure

In this chapter, the following topics will be covered:

- Introducing Symmetric Key Cryptography
- Symmetric Key Management
- Symmetric Encryption Algorithms
- Block Ciphers
- Stream Ciphers
- Modes of Operation
- Security Considerations

Introducing Symmetric Key Cryptography

Symmetric key cryptography is a fundamental branch of cryptography that involves the use of a single shared secret key for both encryption and decryption processes. The main purpose of symmetric key cryptography is to secure the confidentiality and privacy of data during transmission or storage. Encryption, which is a crucial operation in symmetric key cryptography, is the process of converting plaintext (unencrypted data) into ciphertext (encrypted data) using a secret key. Here's a more detailed explanation:

Encryption Process:

1. In symmetric key cryptography, the encryption process begins with a plaintext message that you want to protect. This plaintext could be a message, a file, or any data you wish to keep confidential.

2. The core concept of symmetric key cryptography is that both the sender (encryptor) and the recipient (decryptor) share a single secret key. This secret key is kept confidential between the two parties and is known only to them.

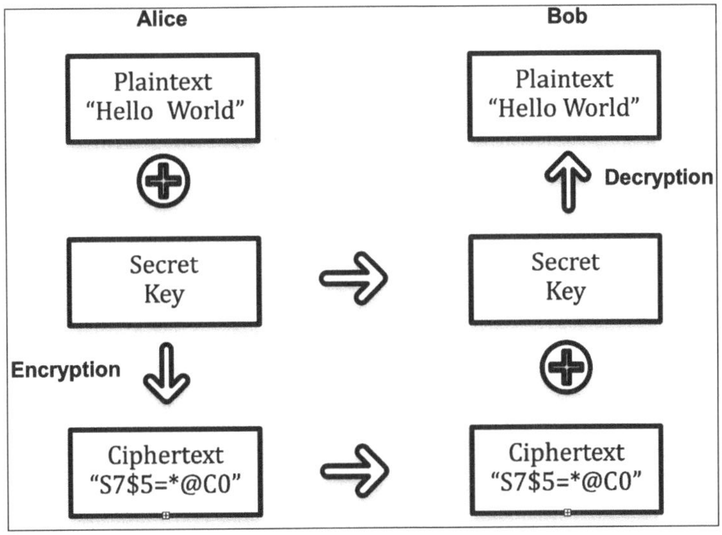

Figure 3.1: *Encryption and Decryption Process*

3. To encrypt the plaintext, the sender uses the shared secret key and an encryption algorithm. The encryption algorithm takes the plaintext and the secret key as input and produces ciphertext as output.
4. The ciphertext is a scrambled and unreadable version of the plaintext. It appears as random data to anyone who intercepts it without the knowledge of the secret key.
5. The encrypted message (ciphertext) is then transmitted over an insecure channel. Even if an adversary intercepts the ciphertext, they should not be able to decipher it without knowledge of the secret key.

Fundamental Concept: Using a Single Shared Key

The fundamental concept of symmetric key cryptography is the use of a single shared key for both encryption and decryption. This shared key serves two primary purposes:

- **Confidentiality**

  By using the same key for both encryption and decryption, only parties with knowledge of the key can read and understand the original message. This shared secret key is the linchpin that ensures the confidentiality of the communication.

- **Efficiency**

  Symmetric key cryptography is computationally efficient because the same key is used for encryption and decryption. This makes it suitable for securing large volumes of data quickly.

However, there are some significant challenges associated with symmetric key cryptography, particularly concerning key management. Key distribution, ensuring that the shared secret key remains confidential, is one of the central issues. If the key is compromised or falls into the wrong hands, the security of the communication is jeopardized.

In summary, symmetric key cryptography encryption relies on a shared secret key and an encryption algorithm to transform plaintext into ciphertext. This fundamental concept of using a single shared key for both encryption and decryption is at the heart of this cryptographic technique, enabling efficient and confidential communication.

Symmetric Key Management

Symmetric key management is a critical aspect of symmetric key cryptography. It involves all the processes and practices associated with generating, distributing, storing, and safeguarding the secret keys used for encryption and decryption. Effective symmetric key management is essential for maintaining the security of encrypted communication and data. Here, we will provide an elaborate explanation of symmetric key management.

Symmetric Key Generation

Effective symmetric key generation is the cornerstone of securing cryptographic systems, ensuring that the keys used provide both confidentiality and robustness against attacks.

Randomness and Entropy

The first step in symmetric key management is the generation of secret keys. Keys should be highly random and unpredictable. This randomness is derived from sources of entropy, such as hardware random number generators or user input. A lack of randomness can make keys vulnerable to brute-force attacks.

Key Length

The length of the key plays a significant role in security. Longer keys generally offer stronger protection. Common key lengths for symmetric algorithms are 128, 192, and 256 bits. The choice of key length should align with the level of security required.

Key Generation Algorithms

Cryptographically secure pseudorandom number generators (CSPRNGs) are used to create symmetric keys. These algorithms are designed to produce keys that are statistically indistinguishable from true randomness.

Symmetric Key Distribution

Ensuring the secure distribution of symmetric keys is critical to maintaining the overall security of cryptographic systems. Without proper safeguards, even the most robust key generation methods can be undermined.

Secure Channel

Distributing symmetric keys securely is one of the most challenging aspects of symmetric key management. Ideally, keys should be exchanged over a secure channel, meaning a communication channel that is already protected using symmetric or asymmetric cryptography. If an attacker intercepts the key during distribution, the security of the system can be compromised.

Key Exchange Protocols

Several key exchange protocols, such as the Diffie-Hellman key exchange, have been developed to facilitate secure key distribution over insecure channels. These protocols allow two parties to agree on a shared secret key without revealing the key during the exchange.

Key Escrow

In some situations, it may be necessary to have a trusted third party hold a copy of the symmetric key for recovery purposes. This is often referred to as key escrow and is used in scenarios where key recovery is crucial.

Symmetric Key Storage

Once the keys are generated and distributed, they must be securely stored. Storing keys on secure hardware modules or within tamper-resistant hardware can help protect them from physical attacks. Robust storage mechanisms are essential to prevent unauthorized access or tampering.

Key Vault Systems

Organizations often use key vault systems to manage the storage and retrieval of symmetric keys. These systems provide secure storage environments for cryptographic keys and support access control policies. Examples of popular key vault systems include:

- **AWS Key Management Service (KMS)**: A managed service that integrates with other AWS offerings to securely create, manage, and control access to encryption keys. It provides audit logs, automatic rotation, and fine-grained permissions using AWS Identity and Access Management (IAM).
- **Azure Key Vault:** A cloud-based solution for securely managing secrets and cryptographic keys. Azure Key Vault offers integration with Azure Active Directory, role-based access control (RBAC), and hardware security modules (HSMs) for enhanced protection.
- **Google Cloud Key Management Service:** It enables secure key generation, storage, and usage across Google Cloud Platform services. It supports automatic key rotation and detailed access logs via Cloud Audit Logging.
- **HashiCorp Vault:** A versatile solution for securely storing and accessing secrets, keys, and certificates. It provides dynamic secret generation, key leasing, and multi-factor authentication for enhanced security.

By leveraging these systems, organizations can ensure centralized and secure management of their cryptographic keys, reducing the risk of breaches and simplifying compliance with security standards.

Key Rotation and Revocation

Effective key management involves not only the secure generation and storage of keys but also their timely rotation and revocation to maintain robust security practices.

Key Rotation

Regularly changing or rotating keys is a security best practice. If a key is compromised, a new key can be used to secure future communications, preventing an attacker from gaining access to past messages.

Key Revocation

In cases where a key is suspected to be compromised or no longer needed, it should be revoked to prevent its use. Revocation lists or mechanisms can be employed to inform parties not to use a specific key.

Backup and Recover

In cryptographic systems, planning for unexpected scenarios is crucial. This involves both maintaining backups of symmetric keys and ensuring readiness for potential disasters.

Key Backup

Backups of symmetric keys should be maintained to ensure data recovery in case of key loss or failure. These backups should be stored securely, preferably in multiple geographically distributed locations, and protected using encryption to prevent unauthorized access. Regular testing of backups is essential to ensure their reliability.

Disaster Recovery

Organizations should have robust disaster recovery plans tailored to key management processes. A comprehensive plan might include:

- **Risk Assessment:** Identifying potential threats to key storage and availability, such as hardware failures, natural disasters, or cyberattacks
- **Key Recovery Procedures:** Establishing clear steps to securely retrieve and reinstate keys from backups without exposing them to additional risks
- **Access Control:** Defining who can initiate recovery procedures and ensuring that access to recovery systems is restricted to authorized personnel
- **Regular Testing and Updates:** Periodically testing the disaster recovery plan and updating it to address new threats, organizational changes, or advancements in cryptographic practices

Implementing such plans ensures continuity and security in cryptographic operations, even during catastrophic events.

Access Control and Auditing

Effective management of symmetric keys requires both restricting access and monitoring their usage. By combining stringent access controls with thorough auditing practices, organizations can enhance the security of their cryptographic systems.

Access Control

Strict access controls should be in place to limit access to the keys. Only authorized personnel should have access to the keys and be protected with strong authentication mechanisms. Role-based access control (RBAC) can be employed to ensure that users only have the permissions necessary for their specific roles.

Auditing

Regular audits and monitoring of key usage and access are critical for detecting unauthorized or suspicious activities. These audits should include detailed logs of who accessed the keys, when, and for what purpose. Employing automated monitoring tools can help identify anomalies in real-time, strengthening the overall security framework.

Lifecycle Management

Symmetric keys have a lifecycle that includes key generation, distribution, usage, rotation, and eventual retirement or deletion. An organized and documented approach to key management throughout its lifecycle is essential. Effective symmetric key management is crucial to maintaining the security of cryptographic systems. It ensures that secret keys remain secret, that they are used properly, and that they are rotated or retired as needed. Careful consideration of the entire key management process is essential to protect sensitive data and communications.

Block Ciphers

A block cipher is a symmetric key encryption algorithm that processes data in fixed-size blocks (for example, 64 or 128 bits), converting the input block into an output block of the same size. The primary purpose of a block cipher is to provide data confidentiality by transforming plaintext data into ciphertext, making it difficult for unauthorized parties to understand the original content without knowledge of the secret key. Block ciphers are a fundamental component of modern cryptography and are commonly used for securing data transmission and storage. Here are various points to consider when elaborating on block ciphers.

Block Size

- Block ciphers are cryptographic algorithms that process data in fixed-size blocks (for example, 64 or 128 bits) and use a secret key for encryption and decryption
- They differ from stream ciphers, which process data bit by bit, and from hash functions, which produce fixed-size outputs without a key

Key Size

- Block ciphers require a secret key for encryption and decryption
- The key size varies among block ciphers, and longer keys often provide better security, for example, AES supports key sizes of 128, 192, and 256 bits

Rounds

- Block ciphers typically operate in multiple rounds, with each round consisting of several transformation functions
- The number of rounds varies, with more rounds generally increasing security but also impacting performance

Design Architectures

Block ciphers can be majorly two types of design architecture: Feistel Architecture and Substitution Permutation Network model. Many block ciphers, including DES, use a Feistel network structure. This design splits the data block into two halves and performs multiple rounds of processing on each half before combining them. AES, on the other hand, uses a substitution-permutation network. It involves substitution and permutation layers to scramble the data.

Substitution Boxes (S-Boxes)

- Substitution boxes (S-boxes) are an integral part of block ciphers and are used to substitute values in the data block with other values
- S-boxes introduce non-linearity into the encryption process, enhancing security

Permutation

- Permutation mechanisms are used to rearrange the bits within the data block
- Permutation contributes to the diffusion property, where changes in one part of the input affect the entire output
- S-Boxes and permutation mechanisms together help to achieve confusion and diffusion; Block ciphers aim to achieve confusion (making the relationship between the key and ciphertext complex) and diffusion (spreading changes in the plaintext across the ciphertext).

There are several block cipher algorithms such as AES (Advanced Encryption Standard) and DES (Data Encryption Standard) which are Substitution Permutation Network and Feistel Network architectures, respectively. Whatever underlying architecture the block cipher possesses, it has some common operations. It achieves non-linearity (substitution) and linear transformation (permutation) and performs these operations for n number of times eventually generating the ciphertext. Using the base key, the key scheduling algorithm generates different keys for each encryption round, which is EX-ORed as a round operation. The round operations can also have a constant but different value addition in each encryption round to widen the round dis-similarity. Later in this chapter, we will discuss AES and DES in detail.

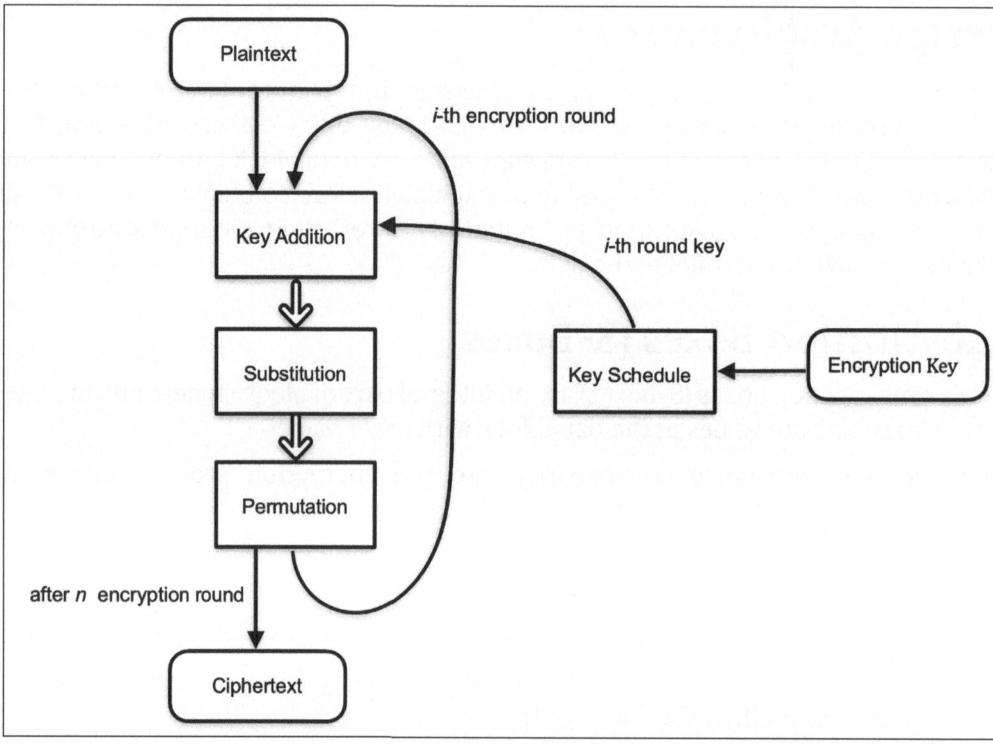

***Figure 3.2**: General Design Structure of a Block Cipher*

AES (Advanced Encryption Standard)

The Advanced Encryption Standard (AES) stands as a beacon of security in the realm of modern cryptography, replacing the aging Data Encryption Standard (DES) to meet the growing demand for robust encryption in our digital age. AES is built upon the foundation of the Rijndael cipher, a creation of Belgian cryptographers Vincent Rijmen and Joan Daemen, who designed it to be secure, efficient, and adaptable. Chosen as the AES standard through an extensive international competition organized by the US National Institute of Standards and Technology (NIST), Rijndael excelled in security and performance.

AES operates using a substitution-permutation network (SPN) structure, incorporating elements, such as substitution boxes (S-boxes), permutation layers, and round keys. It supports three standard key sizes: 128 bits, 192 bits, and 256 bits, with AES-128, AES-192, and AES-256 being the three standard variants. The encryption process involves multiple rounds, with the number of rounds contingent on the key size, and includes operations, such as byte substitution, shifting rows, mixing columns, and key mixing. Decrypting AES is the reverse of encryption, using inverse operations to retrieve the original plaintext from the ciphertext. AES finds widespread application in securing digital communication, data storage, and various industries due to its proven security, withstanding rigorous cryptographic scrutiny. As a beacon of data security in an interconnected world, AES continues to evolve to meet the challenges posed by emerging technologies, ensuring the confidentiality and integrity of data in the digital landscape.

Encryption Steps of AES

AES (Advanced Encryption Standard) follows a series of encryption and decryption steps, which vary in number depending on the key size. Here's an outline of the steps involved in both encryption and decryption for AES.

1. **Key Expansion**: The AES secret key is expanded into a set of round keys for using in each encryption round, and this involves creating a key schedule by applying key expansion algorithms, such as the Rijndael key schedule
2. **Initial Round (Round 0)**: In the initial round, the plaintext is XORed with the first round key
3. **Rounds (Rounds 1 to n-1)**: For AES-128, there are 9 rounds; for AES-192, there are 11 rounds; and for AES-256, there are 13 rounds; each round consists of the following operations:
    a. **`ShiftRows`**: Shifts the rows of the data block to the left
    b. **`MixColumns`**: Mixes the columns of the data block to introduce diffusion
    c. **`AddRoundKey`**: XORs the data block with the round key for the current round
4. **Final Round (Round n)**: In the final round, there are no **`MixColumns`** operation; it consists of **`SubBytes`**, **`ShiftRows`**, and **`AddRoundKey`**
5. **Ciphertext:** After the final round, the ciphertext is produced, which represents the encrypted data

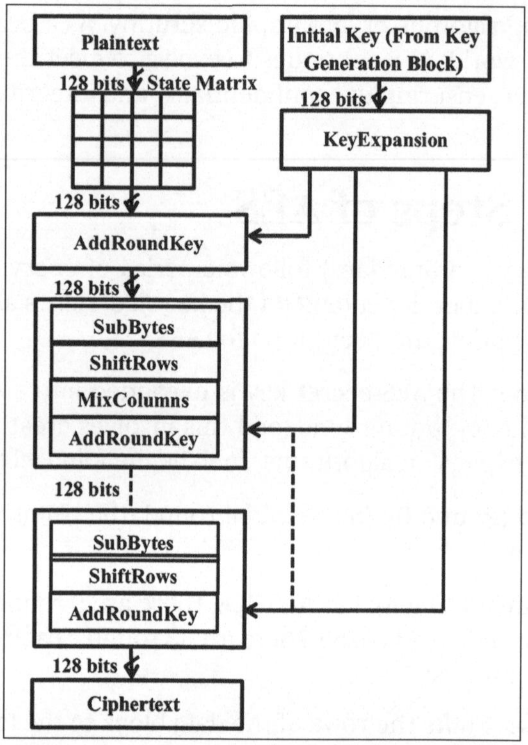

***Figure* 3.3**: *AES Encryption Block Diagram*

Decryption Steps of AES

The decryption process is essentially the reverse of encryption, with operations applied in the reverse order:

1. **Key Expansion**: The same key expansion process is applied to generate the round keys.
2. **Initial Round (Round 0)**: In the initial round of decryption, the ciphertext is XORed with the last round key used in encryption.
3. **Rounds (Rounds 1 to n-1)**: Similar to encryption, rounds consist of the following operations, applied in reverse order:
    a. **`AddRoundKey`**: XOR the data block with the round key for the current round
    b. **`InvMixColumns`**: Reverse the **`MixColumns`** operation from encryption to unmix the columns
    c. **`InvShiftRows`**: Reverse the **`ShiftRows`** operation to shift rows to the right
    d. **`InvSubBytes`**: Reverse the **`SubBytes`** operation to substitute bytes using the inverse S-box

4. **Final Round (Round n)**: In the final round of decryption, there is no **`InvMixColumns`** operation, and it consists of **`InvShiftRows`**, **`InvSubBytes`**, and **`AddRoundKey`**.
5. **Plaintext**: After the final decryption round, the plaintext is retrieved, representing the original, unencrypted data.

Implementation Code of AES

Now we will implement Python code for AES encryption and decryption using the '**`pycryptodome`**' library, which is a widely-used library for cryptography in Python. Ensure that the library is installed using '**`pip install pycryptodome`**'. Here we provide code for both encryption and decryption.

AES Encryption in Python:

```
from Crypto.Cipher import AES
from Crypto.Random import get_random_bytes
from Crypto.Util.Padding import pad, unpad

# Sample plaintext and secret key
plaintext = b'This is a secret message'
secret_key = get_random_bytes(16)  # AES-128 key

# Create an AES cipher object in ECB mode
cipher = AES.new(secret_key, AES.MODE_ECB)

# Encrypt the plaintext
cipher_text = cipher.encrypt(pad(plaintext, AES.block_size))

# Print the ciphertext
print("Ciphertext:", cipher_text)
```

AES Decryption in Python:

```
# Using the same secret key, create a new AES cipher object for
decryption
cipher_decrypt = AES.new(secret_key, AES.MODE_ECB)

# Decrypt the ciphertext
decrypted_text = unpad(cipher_decrypt.decrypt(cipher_text), AES.
block_size)

# Convert bytes to string for human-readable output
decrypted_text_str = decrypted_text.decode('utf-8')

# Print the decrypted plaintext
print("Decrypted Text:", decrypted_text_str)
```

Please note that this example uses AES in Electronic Codebook (ECB) mode for simplicity. In practice, it's recommended to use more secure modes such as Cipher Block Chaining (CBC) or Galois/Counter Mode (GCM) for better security, especially when dealing with larger data and multiple blocks. We will discuss the different modes of operations and their implementations in later chapters.

Data Encryption Standard (DES)

The Data Encryption Standard (DES) stands as a crucial milestone in the history of encryption, developing as a response to the need for a standardized encryption method. Established in the 1970s by IBM in partnership with the National Institute of Standards and Technology (NIST), DES was designed by an IBM team under the leadership of Horst Feistel. It was based on the Lucifer cipher, an earlier IBM project, and emerged as a federal standard in 1977.

Utilizing a symmetric key block cipher structure, DES operated on fixed-size blocks of 64 bits, employing a 56-bit key and executing 16 rounds of encryption. The Feistel network, a central aspect of its design, underwent multiple transformation rounds involving substitution and permutation. Its Substitution-Permutation Network (SPN) structure incorporated substitution boxes (S-boxes) and key expansion, ensuring confusion and diffusion within the encryption process. Over time, as technology advanced, the 56-bit key size proved vulnerable to brute-force attacks, leading to its eventual replacement by more secure encryption standards. Nevertheless, DES's impact remained profound, laying the groundwork for modern cryptography and influencing subsequent encryption algorithms, thereby shaping our understanding of block ciphers, key expansion, and substitution-permutation networks. AES, developed as a successor to DES, addressed many of the vulnerabilities present in DES, becoming the contemporary benchmark for secure encryption methods.

Encryption Steps of DES

The encryption process in the Data Encryption Standard (DES) involves several distinct steps that collectively transform plaintext into ciphertext.

1. **Initial Permutation (IP)**: The 64-bit plaintext block is subjected to an initial permutation using a predefined table. This permutation shuffles the bits of the plaintext, providing an initial obfuscation of the input data.
2. **Key Generation**: From the 56-bit key, a set of sixteen 48-bit subkeys are generated using the key schedule. These subkeys, one for each round of the encryption process, are derived through a series of permutations and shifts from the original key.

3. **Feistel Network Rounds**: The Feistel network structure, the core of DES, consists of 16 rounds. Each round includes several key operations:
   a. **Expansion**: The 32-bit half-block is expanded to 48 bits using a predefined expansion table. This step enhances the diffusion of the data.
   b. **Subkey Mixing**: The expanded block is XORed with the current round's 48-bit subkey derived from the key schedule.
   c. **S-box Substitution**: The XOR result is divided into six 4-bit blocks. Each block is substituted using eight S-boxes, each providing a 4-bit output based on the 6-bit input.
   d. **Permutation**: The outputs from the S-boxes are rearranged according to a fixed permutation table, shuffling the bits further.
   e. **Swap Halves**: The processed block is divided into two 32-bit halves. The right half becomes the left half for the next round.
4. **Final Permutation (FP)**: After the 16 rounds of the Feistel network, a final permutation, the inverse of the initial permutation, is applied to the data block. This permutation rearranges the bits of the block based on a predefined table.

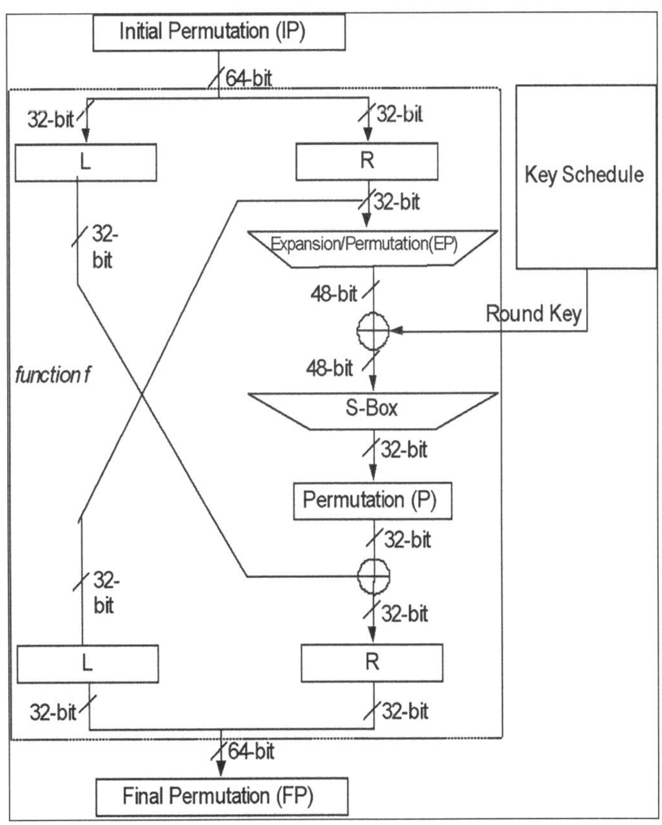

Figure 3.4: *DES Encryption Block Diagram*

5. **Ciphertext Generation**: The final 64-bit block resulting from the final permutation represents the ciphertext. This block is the result of the multiple transformations applied during the Feistel rounds, the initial and final permutations, and represents the encrypted form of the original plaintext. This detailed process encompasses the intricate steps involved in DES encryption, where permutations, expansions, substitutions, and permutations are applied iteratively to transform plaintext into ciphertext. Despite its historical significance, DES's limited key length made it vulnerable to evolving computational capabilities, eventually leading to its replacement by more secure encryption standards.

Implementation Code of DES

Implementing DES from scratch in most programming languages can be quite complex due to the intricacies of the algorithm. However, 'pycryptodome' library provides a convenient way to use DES. Here's a simple code snippet for DES encryption and decryption using 'pycryptodome'. It generates a random 8-byte (64-bit) key, encrypts a sample plaintext, and then decrypts the ciphertext back to the original plaintext.

Encryption and Decryption of DES in Python:

```
from Crypto.Cipher import DES
from Crypto.Random import get_random_bytes

def des_encrypt(plaintext, key):
    cipher = DES.new(key, DES.MODE_ECB)
    ciphertext = cipher.encrypt(plaintext)
    return ciphertext

def des_decrypt(ciphertext, key):
    cipher = DES.new(key, DES.MODE_ECB)
    plaintext = cipher.decrypt(ciphertext)
    return plaintext

# Sample plaintext and key
plaintext = b'This is a secret'
key = get_random_bytes(8)  # 8 bytes key for DES

# Encryption
encrypted = des_encrypt(plaintext, key)
print("Encrypted:", encrypted)

# Decryption
decrypted = des_decrypt(encrypted, key)
print("Decrypted:", decrypted)
```

In conclusion, block ciphers, exemplified by standards such as DES and AES, play a critical role in securing digital communication and data integrity. Their symmetric key design, where the same key is used for both encryption and decryption, offers efficiency and simplicity. AES, in particular, has become the *de facto* standard due to its robust security features, key flexibility, and widespread adoption in various applications.

In real-life scenarios, block ciphers find applications in securing sensitive data at rest and in transit. They are the foundation of cryptographic protocols such as SSL/TLS for secure communication on the internet, disk encryption for safeguarding stored data, and file-level encryption in various operating systems. AES, with its various key sizes, provides a versatile solution catering to different security requirements.

Having explored the realm of block ciphers, it's valuable to extend our understanding to another category of cryptographic algorithms: stream ciphers. While block ciphers operate on fixed-size blocks of data, stream ciphers focus on encrypting individual bits or bytes in a continuous stream. This distinction leads to different use cases and considerations in the design and implementation of stream ciphers. Let's delve into the principles, characteristics, and practical applications of stream ciphers in the subsequent discussion.

Stream Cipher

A stream cipher is a type of symmetric-key encryption algorithm designed to encrypt continuous streams of data bit by bit or byte by byte. Unlike block ciphers, which operate on fixed-size blocks of data, stream ciphers dynamically generate a key stream based on an initial secret key and, in some cases, an initialization vector (IV). This key stream is then combined with the plaintext using bitwise XOR (exclusive OR) to produce the ciphertext. Stream ciphers are particularly well-suited for real-time communication scenarios, continuous data streams, and applications where the length of the encrypted data is not predetermined. The efficiency and simplicity of stream ciphers make them valuable in situations requiring lightweight encryption and where data is generated or consumed in a continuous and sequential manner. This chapter delves into the architecture, use cases, and design principles of stream ciphers. We explore the fundamental structures, discussing synchronous and asynchronous stream ciphers, key stream generation methods, and the pivotal role of structures such as Linear Feedback Shift Registers (LFSRs) and Nonlinear Feedback Shift Registers (NLFSRs). Examples of stream cipher algorithms, including the well-known RC4 and modern alternatives such as Salsa20 and ChaCha, are explored, shedding light on their applications and security considerations. As we navigate through practical implementation aspects, security considerations, and comparisons with block ciphers, we aim to provide a comprehensive understanding of stream ciphers in the contemporary cryptographic landscape.

Characteristics	Block Cipher	Stream Cipher
Data Processing	Operates on fixed-size blocks of data	Processes data bit by bit or byte by byte
Key Usage	Uses the same secret key for each block	Generates a continuous key stream based on a secret key
Mode of Operation	Utilizes different modes of operation	Doesn't inherently require modes of operation
Use Cases	Common in scenarios with fixed-size data blocks	Suited for continuous data streams, real-time communication
Efficiency	Generally more computationally intensive	More efficient for streaming applications
Example Algorithms	AES, DES, 3DES, Ascon	RC4, A5/1, Salsa20, ChaCha

***Table 3.1**: Comparison Table Between Block Cipher and Stream Cipher*

The practical applications of stream ciphers underscore their significance in contemporary cryptography. In real-time communication scenarios, stream ciphers such as swift maestros, encrypt data on the fly, securing voice-over-IP communication and video conferencing. They excel in the secure transmission of continuous data streams, safeguarding streaming media content with efficiency and immediacy. The wireless communication landscape, including mobile networks, benefits from stream ciphers' prowess, as exemplified by their use in protocols such as GSM. Additionally, stream ciphers play a crucial role in securing internet protocols, ensuring the confidentiality and integrity of data exchanged in dynamic web sessions.

Architecture Structures of Stream Ciphers

Stream ciphers employ a distinctive architecture tailored for encrypting data bit by bit or byte by byte, emphasizing efficiency and speed in processing continuous streams. The fundamental architecture typically revolves around the key stream generation and its integration with the plaintext. Here's an overview of the key components:

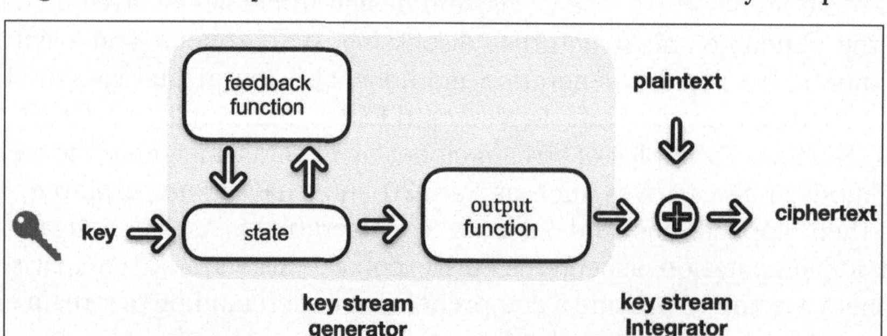

***Figure 3.5**: Generalized Block Diagram of Stream Cipher*

At the core of a stream cipher's architecture is the generation of a key stream. The key stream is a sequence of random or pseudo-random bits that are generated based on a secret key and, in some cases, an initialization vector (IV). Various algorithms and structures are used to create this key stream, ensuring unpredictability and randomness. Common methods include feedback shift registers (FSRs), linear feedback shift registers (LFSRs), and nonlinear feedback shift registers (NLFSRs).

Stream ciphers are broadly categorized into synchronous and asynchronous types based on how the key stream is generated and synchronized with the plaintext. In synchronous stream ciphers, the key stream generator is synchronized with the data stream, processing bits simultaneously. Asynchronous stream ciphers, on the other hand, may vary the timing of key stream generation, providing more flexibility.

Once the key stream is generated, it is combined with the plaintext using a bitwise XOR (exclusive OR) operation. This simple operation ensures that each bit of the key stream influences the corresponding bit of the plaintext, providing encryption. The XOR operation is reversible, allowing the ciphertext to be decrypted by reapplying the key stream.

Some stream ciphers incorporate feedback mechanisms to enhance security. Feedback mechanisms introduce dependencies between successive bits or bytes of the key stream, adding complexity to the encryption process. Linear feedback shift registers (LFSRs) and nonlinear feedback shift registers (NLFSRs) are common components that introduce feedback in the key stream generation process.

An initialization vector is often used in stream ciphers to ensure that the same plaintext encrypted with the same key does not produce identical ciphertext. The IV is typically combined with the secret key in the key stream generation process, providing additional variability.

Understanding the architecture structures of stream ciphers involves exploring the interplay between key stream generation, synchronization mechanisms, and integration with the plaintext. In the subsequent sections, we will delve deeper into the specific structures, design principles, and examples of stream cipher algorithms that exemplify these architectural components.

Feedback Shift Registers in Stream Ciphers

In the realm of stream ciphers, Feedback Shift Registers (FSRs) play a pivotal role in generating pseudorandom key streams that are fundamental to the encryption process. These registers introduce an element of dynamism and unpredictability, contributing to the cryptographic strength of the cipher.

Definition: A Feedback Shift Register is a shift register whose state evolves over time based on feedback from certain positions in the register. The feedback is typically determined by Boolean functions, creating a cyclic and pseudorandom sequence of bits. In stream ciphers, FSRs are employed to generate key streams used for bitwise XOR operations with the plaintext, thereby achieving encryption. Feedback Shift Registers are of two types: LFSRs and NLFSRs.

Characteristics	Linear Feedback Shift Registers (LFSRs)	Nonlinear Feedback Shift Registers (NLFSRs)
Feedback Mechanism	Linear combination of current state bits	Nonlinear Boolean functions applied to current state bits
Cryptographic Strength	Vulnerable to certain linear cryptanalysis techniques	Enhanced resistance to linear cryptanalysis
Complexity	Simple and computationally efficient	Potentially more complex due to nonlinear functions
Security Considerations	Potential vulnerabilities due to linearity	Greater resistance to certain cryptanalysis methods

Table 3.2*: Differences Between LFSR and NLFSR*

Linear Feedback Shift Registers (LFSRs):

LFSRs are a class of FSRs where the next state of the register is a linear combination of its current state bits. The linearity of LFSRs provides simplicity and efficiency in generating pseudorandom sequences. However, their linear nature can make them vulnerable to certain cryptanalysis techniques.

Nonlinear Feedback Shift Registers (NLFSRs):

NLFSRs address the vulnerability of linearity in LFSRs by introducing nonlinear Boolean functions in the feedback mechanism. The next stage of the register is determined through nonlinear operations, enhancing the cryptographic strength of the generated key stream. NLFSRs are employed to mitigate vulnerabilities associated with linear shift registers.

Let's examine the distinctions between Linear Feedback Shift Registers (LFSRs) and Nonlinear Feedback Shift Registers (NLFSRs) in the context of stream cipher construction.

In the construction of stream ciphers, the choice between LFSRs and NLFSRs involves a trade-off between simplicity and security. While LFSRs offer efficiency, NLFSRs provide an additional layer of cryptographic strength, making them suitable for scenarios where heightened security is paramount.

Synchronous and Asynchronous Stream Cipher

Synchronous stream ciphers represent a class of encryption algorithms where the generation of the key stream is tightly synchronized with the data stream. In this framework, each bit of the key stream corresponds directly to a specific bit in the plaintext, and the encryption and decryption processes progress in lockstep. This synchronization simplifies the cryptographic operations, as the sender and receiver are precisely aligned in their use of the key stream. However, rigid synchronization also introduces potential vulnerabilities. Any disruption or loss of synchronization can lead to errors in decryption, making synchronous stream ciphers susceptible to certain types of attacks. Despite these considerations, synchronous stream ciphers are widely employed in scenarios where a reliable synchronization mechanism can be maintained.

In contrast, asynchronous stream ciphers offer a more flexible approach to key stream generation and synchronization. The key stream generator may not be perfectly aligned with the data stream, allowing for variations in the timing and generation of the key stream. This flexibility enhances the security of the cipher, as disruptions or variations in the synchronization are less likely to lead to decryption errors. Asynchronous stream ciphers are particularly well-suited for scenarios where maintaining strict synchronization is challenging, such as in environments with variable transmission delays or when the cryptographic system needs to adapt to changing conditions. The increased flexibility comes at the cost of added complexity, as the cryptographic processes need to handle potential variations in the timing of the key stream.

In practical applications, the choice between synchronous and asynchronous stream ciphers depends on the specific requirements of the system and the nature of the data being encrypted. Synchronous stream ciphers are often favored in scenarios where precise synchronization can be maintained while asynchronous stream ciphers provide a more adaptable solution for situations where maintaining strict synchronization is challenging or impractical. The selection of a synchronous or asynchronous approach is a crucial aspect of designing stream ciphers that meet the diverse needs of real-world applications.

Characteristics	**Synchronous Stream Ciphers**	**Asynchronous Stream Ciphers**
Key Stream Generation	Synchronized with the data stream	Generated independently of the data stream timing
Synchronization Requirement	Strict synchronization is crucial	Allows for variations in synchronization
Error Propagation	Errors in synchronization can propagate	Tolerance to variations, minimizing error propagation
Adaptability	Less adaptable to changes in transmission delays	More adaptable to variable transmission conditions
Complexity	Generally simpler due to fixed synchronization	Potentially more complex to handle variable synchronization
Security Considerations	Vulnerable to certain timing-related attacks	Greater resilience to timing-related attacks

***Table 3.3**: Differences between Synchronous and Asynchronous Stream Cipher*

RC4 (Rivest Cipher 4)

The RC4 (Rivest Cipher 4) cipher was developed by Ronald Rivest in 1987, one of the three co-founders of RSA Data Security, Inc. Initially, RC4 was a proprietary algorithm held by RSA; its simplicity, efficiency, and quick adoption in various cryptographic applications led to its popularity.

RC4 operates as a stream cipher, generating a pseudorandom key stream based on a secret key. The key stream is then bitwise XORed with the plaintext to produce the ciphertext. The key stream generation process is dynamic and involves permutations of the internal state of the cipher. This simplicity and speed made RC4 a favorable choice for various applications, including wireless networks, internet protocols, and TLS encryption.

In the early 2000s, vulnerabilities in RC4 started to emerge. The Fluhrer, Mantin, and Shamir (FMS) attack, discovered in 2001, allowed attackers to distinguish the keystream and recover portions of the plaintext. Despite attempts to address these vulnerabilities, subsequent research revealed additional weaknesses in the algorithm. Notably, biases in the keystream were discovered, enabling attackers to exploit statistical patterns and compromise the confidentiality of encrypted data.

By 2015, researchers demonstrated practical attacks against RC4 in real-world scenarios. These attacks exploited biases in the key stream to recover sensitive information, rendering RC4 unsuitable for secure communications. The cryptographic community, including major browser vendors and standards organizations, acknowledged the severity of these vulnerabilities.

The impact of RC4's vulnerabilities reverberated across the cybersecurity landscape. Leading cryptographic standards, including TLS and WPA, deprecated the use of RC4 due to the demonstrated vulnerabilities. Browser vendors, such as Mozilla, Google, and Microsoft, phased out support for RC4 in their products to protect users from potential attacks.

The deprecation of RC4 highlighted the dynamic nature of cryptographic security. As vulnerabilities are discovered, the cryptographic community must adapt swiftly to maintain the integrity of encrypted communications. The deprecation of RC4 reinforced the importance of transitioning to more secure cryptographic algorithms to address emerging threats and evolving cryptanalysis techniques.

The following is a simple implementation of the RC4 cipher in Python. Keep in mind that for real-world usage, it's essential to use established and well-reviewed cryptographic libraries rather than implementing cryptographic algorithms from scratch.

This code includes functions for key scheduling, encryption, and decryption using the RC4 algorithm. Again, it's important to emphasize that implementing cryptographic algorithms requires a deep understanding of cryptography, and for practical purposes, using established libraries like cryptography in Python is highly recommended. This example serves educational purposes and may not be suitable for production use.

Encryption and Decryption of RC4 Cipher in Python:

```
def rc4_key_schedule(key):
    key_len = len(key)
    S = list(range(256))
    j = 0

    for i in range(256):
        j = (j + S[i] + key[i % key_len]) % 256
        S[i], S[j] = S[j], S[i]

    return S

def rc4_encrypt(plaintext, key):
    S = rc4_key_schedule(key)
    i = j = 0
    ciphertext = []

    for char in plaintext:
        i = (i + 1) % 256
        j = (j + S[i]) % 256
        S[i], S[j] = S[j], S[i]
        k = S[(S[i] + S[j]) % 256]
        ciphertext.append(ord(char) ^ k)

    return bytes(ciphertext)

def rc4_decrypt(ciphertext, key):
    # Decryption is the same as encryption in RC4
    return rc4_encrypt(ciphertext, key)

# Example Usage:
plaintext = "Hello, RC4!"
key = "SecretKey"

encrypted_text = rc4_encrypt(plaintext, key)
decrypted_text = rc4_decrypt(encrypted_text, key)

print("Plaintext:", plaintext)
print("Encrypted:", encrypted_text)
print("Decrypted:", decrypted_text.decode('utf-8'))
```

A5/1 Cipher: Stream Cipher for GSM Networks

A5/1 is a stream cipher used for encrypting voice and data communications in GSM cellular networks. Developed in the late 1980s, A5/1 was designed to provide confidentiality and security for mobile communications. It is part of the A5 family of algorithms, with A5/2 being a simpler alternative introduced later.

Structure

A5/1 operates as a synchronous stream cipher, generating a key stream based on a 64-bit secret key and a 22-bit frame number. The key stream is then XORed with the plaintext to produce the ciphertext. A5/1 employs a combination of linear feedback shift registers (LFSRs) and nonlinear combining functions to create a complex pseudorandom sequence.

The primary components of A5/1 include three LFSRs, denoted as LFSR1, LFSR2, and LFSR3. These LFSRs have feedback functions and clocking mechanisms that contribute to the generation of the key stream. The 64-bit secret key, along with the 22-bit frame number, determines the initial state of the LFSRs.

Key Generation

The key generation process in A5/1 involves the initialization of the LFSRs with the secret key and frame number. The clocking mechanism iteratively advances the state of the LFSRs, generating a key stream bit by bit. The key stream is then combined with the plaintext using XOR operations, providing the encrypted output.

Despite the seemingly robust structure, A5/1 has faced scrutiny due to vulnerabilities in its key generation process. The small key space and certain characteristics of the LFSRs have made A5/1 susceptible to cryptographic attacks, including the well-known "time-memory trade-off" attack.

Security Considerations

Over the years, security researchers have identified weaknesses in A5/1, leading to concerns about its cryptographic strength. One notable vulnerability is the susceptibility to the "known-plaintext attack," where an attacker can recover parts of the secret key if they have knowledge of the plaintext and corresponding ciphertext.

The limited key length (64 bits) makes A5/1 vulnerable to brute-force attacks. In practice, the computational resources required for a successful brute-force attack on A5/1 have become more attainable, emphasizing the need for stronger encryption standards in modern mobile networks.

Impact and Future Developments

Despite its vulnerabilities, A5/1 has been widely used in GSM networks for an extended period. However, as security concerns mounted, efforts were made to transition to more secure algorithms. The subsequent generations of mobile networks, such as 3G and 4G, introduced stronger encryption standards to address the shortcomings of A5/1.

In conclusion, A5/1 played a crucial role in securing mobile communications during its era. However, its vulnerabilities have necessitated the adoption of more robust encryption algorithms such as A5/2 in modern mobile networks to ensure the continued confidentiality and integrity of voice and data transmissions.

A5/2 Cipher: A Simplified Variant in GSM Networks

In the evolution of GSM network encryption, A5/1, despite its initial adoption, faced increasing scrutiny due to identified vulnerabilities. As a response to security concerns and the need for a simpler alternative, A5/2 was introduced. A5/2 was intended to provide a balance between security and computational efficiency, addressing some of the flaws of its predecessor.

Background

A5/2 is a stream cipher designed for GSM cellular networks, serving as an alternative to A5/1. Introduced as a simplified version, A5/2 was envisioned to be a lightweight solution for scenarios where computational resources were limited. However, the design choices made in A5/2 eventually led to its rejection as a secure encryption standard.

Structure

A5/2 shares some similarities with A5/1, employing linear feedback shift registers (LFSRs) in its structure. However, A5/2 simplifies certain aspects to reduce computational overhead. Notably, A5/2 utilizes a single LFSR, as opposed to the three LFSRs employed in A5/1. This reduction in complexity was aimed at making A5/2 more efficient in terms of hardware implementation.

Key Generation

The key generation process in A5/2 involves the initialization of the LFSR with a 64-bit secret key, similar to A5/1. The clocking mechanism advances the state of the LFSR, generating a key stream that is XORed with the plaintext for encryption. Despite its attempts to simplify the process, A5/2's design choices ultimately led to vulnerabilities that undermined its security.

Security Considerations

Contrary to its intended purpose, A5/2 was found to be significantly weaker than A5/1. The reduction in complexity made it more susceptible to cryptographic attacks, and its security flaws were exposed. A5/2 was quickly deprecated due to its vulnerabilities, prompting the GSM community to discourage its use in favor of stronger alternatives.

Impact and Deprecation

The adoption of A5/2 was short-lived, and its impact on GSM networks was marked by concerns over its compromised security. Recognizing the need for more robust encryption standards, the GSM community moved away from A5/2. Its deprecation underscored the importance of not only efficiency but also the paramount need for security in cryptographic algorithms.

Transition to Modern Standards

The vulnerabilities in both A5/1 and A5/2 prompted a paradigm shift in mobile network security. Subsequent generations of mobile networks, including 3G and 4G, introduced more advanced encryption standards such as A5/3 (KASUMI), aiming to provide enhanced security against evolving threats.

In conclusion, the brief era of A5/2 highlighted the delicate balance between efficiency and security in cryptographic design. As mobile networks continue to advance, the lessons learned from the vulnerabilities of A5/2 contribute to the ongoing efforts to secure voice and data communications in the ever-evolving landscape of wireless communication.

In the rapidly evolving landscape of cryptography and information security, it's acknowledged that the A5/1 and A5/2 algorithms, once pivotal components in GSM network encryption, may not be considered suitable for application in modern scenarios. These algorithms, designed several decades ago, have since been scrutinized for vulnerabilities and cryptographic weaknesses. However, understanding the historical implementation of classical cryptographic modules, such as A5/1 and A5/2, contributes significantly to strengthening the foundational knowledge in cryptography. Insights gained from the study of these algorithms not only provide a historical perspective on the evolution of encryption standards but also offer valuable lessons in designing and evaluating robust cryptographic solutions. While the use of A5/1 and A5/2 in contemporary applications may be limited, their examination remains instrumental in building a comprehensive understanding of cryptographic principles, paving the way for the development and deployment of more secure and resilient encryption techniques in today's advanced digital landscape.

Encryption and Decryption of A5/2 Cipher in Python:

```
class A52Cipher:
    def __init__(self, key):
        # Convert the key to a list of bits
        self.key = [int(bit) for bit in bin(key)[2:].zfill(64)]

        # Initialize the LFSR
        self.lfsr = self.key[:19]

    def clock(self):
        # Perform one clock cycle on the LFSR
        feedback = self.lfsr[17] ^ self.lfsr[16] ^ self.lfsr[13]
^ self.lfsr[11] ^ self.lfsr[10] ^ self.lfsr[7] ^ self.lfsr[5] ^
self.lfsr[4] ^ self.lfsr[2] ^ self.lfsr[1] ^ self.lfsr[0]

        # Shift the bits in the LFSR
        self.lfsr = [feedback] + self.lfsr[:-1]

    def generate_keystream(self, length):
        # Generate keystream of specified length
        keystream = []

        for _ in range(length):
            output_bit = self.lfsr[18] ^ self.lfsr[16] ^ self.
lfsr[13] ^ self.lfsr[11] ^ self.lfsr[10] ^ self.lfsr[7] ^ self.
lfsr[5] ^ self.lfsr[4] ^ self.lfsr[2] ^ self.lfsr[1] ^ self.
lfsr[0]
            keystream.append(output_bit)

            # Clock the LFSR
            self.clock()

        return keystream

    def encrypt(self, plaintext):
        # Convert the plaintext to a list of bits
        plaintext_bits = [int(bit) for bit in bin(plaintext)[2:].
zfill(64)]

        # Generate keystream
        keystream = self.generate_keystream(len(plaintext_bits))

        # XOR the plaintext with the keystream to get the
ciphertext
        ciphertext = [plaintext_bit ^ keystream_bit for
plaintext_bit, keystream_bit in zip(plaintext_bits, keystream)]
```

```
        # Convert the ciphertext back to an integer
        ciphertext_int = int(''.join(map(str, ciphertext)), 2)

        return ciphertext_int

    def decrypt(self, ciphertext):
        # Decryption is the same as encryption in A5/2
        return self.encrypt(ciphertext)


# Example Usage:
key_a5_2 = 0x0123456789ABCDEF  # 64-bit key
plaintext_a5_2 = 0x123456789ABCDEF0  # 64-bit plaintext

a52_cipher = A52Cipher(key_a5_2)
ciphertext_a5_2 = a52_cipher.encrypt(plaintext_a5_2)
decrypted_text_a5_2 = a52_cipher.decrypt(ciphertext_a5_2)

print("Plaintext:", hex(plaintext_a5_2))
print("Encrypted:", hex(ciphertext_a5_2))
print("Decrypted:", hex(decrypted_text_a5_2))
```

```
Plaintext: 0x123456789abcdef0
Encrypted: 0x24465c9175d898e5
Decrypted: 0x247a07c73f9a0837
```

Salsa20 and ChaCha

ChaCha and Salsa20, both modern stream ciphers, share a common design philosophy rooted in the ARX (Addition, Rotation, and XOR) architecture. This innovative approach represents a departure from traditional cryptographic designs, introducing a streamlined structure that combines simplicity with formidable security. Their ARX-based design emphasizes the use of simple and efficient bitwise operations, contributing to both the clarity of the algorithms and their adaptability to various computing platforms. As two pillars of contemporary symmetric-key cryptography, ChaCha and Salsa20 exemplify the evolution towards ARX architectures, showcasing the ongoing pursuit of cryptographic solutions that excel in both security and computational efficiency.

Salsa20

Salsa20, created by Daniel J. Bernstein in 2005, stands as a prominent member of the Salsa family of stream ciphers. The algorithm operates on 32-bit words and employs a series of quarter-round operations and diffusion steps to generate a key stream. The key components include a 256-bit key, a 64-bit nonce, and a 64-bit counter. Salsa20's strength lies in its ability to produce a secure pseudorandom stream, striking a balance between cryptographic security and computational efficiency. With 20 rounds of operations, Salsa20 has become a widely adopted choice for various cryptographic applications, providing reliable confidentiality.

ChaCha

ChaCha, introduced by Daniel J. Bernstein in 2008, can be considered an evolution of Salsa20. While retaining the 32-bit word size and the core components of a 256-bit key, a 64-bit nonce, and a 64-bit counter, ChaCha brings modifications to enhance its diffusion properties. These changes aim to bolster resistance against specific cryptographic attacks, making ChaCha a compelling alternative, particularly in scenarios where certain implementation vulnerabilities may be a concern. Similar to Salsa20, ChaCha operates by performing quarter-round operations and diffusion steps, albeit with a different arrangement. Its design improvements underscore the ongoing commitment to refining cryptographic primitives for heightened security and efficiency.

Shared Design Principles

1. **Stream Cipher Structure**: Both Salsa20 and ChaCha belong to the stream cipher category, generating a pseudo random stream of bits for encryption.
2. **Key Components**: The core components of these ciphers include a 256-bit key, a 64-bit nonce, and a 64-bit counter. These elements contribute to the generation of a unique key stream for each encryption session.
3. **Quarter-Round Operations**: Both algorithms employ quarter-round operations, a set of bitwise operations that ensure the diffusion and mixing of input data.
4. **Diffusion Steps**: Through diffusion steps, Salsa20 and ChaCha spread the influence of input bits across the entire state, contributing to the creation of a well-distributed and unpredictable key stream.
5. **Round Count**: Salsa20 and ChaCha both utilize multiple rounds of operations (20 rounds for Salsa20), providing a trade-off between computational efficiency and cryptographic security.

Understanding the nuanced evolution from Salsa20 to ChaCha underscores the commitment to continuous improvement in cryptographic algorithms, addressing potential vulnerabilities and adapting to the dynamic landscape of information security.

Modes of Operation

As we delve deeper into the realm of symmetric key cryptography, we transition our focus from individual block and stream ciphers to their broader applications through various modes of operation. While block ciphers, such as the Advanced Encryption Standard (AES) and Data Encryption Standard (DES), provide a foundation for secure data transformation in fixed-size blocks, modes of operation play a pivotal role in determining how these blocks are processed and encrypted. These modes introduce versatility and efficiency, addressing the challenges of encrypting large datasets and supporting diverse cryptographic requirements. Building on our understanding of symmetric key cryptography, we now embark on an exploration of block cipher modes, unveiling their distinctive characteristics, use cases, and cryptographic implications. There are several types of modes of operations based on the use cases, such as Electronic Codebook (ECB), Cipher Block Chaining (CBC), Cipher Feedback (CFB), Output Feedback (OFB), Counter (CTR), Galois/Counter Mode (GCM), XEX-based Tweaked CodeBook (XTS), and so on. We will discuss a few of them in this section.

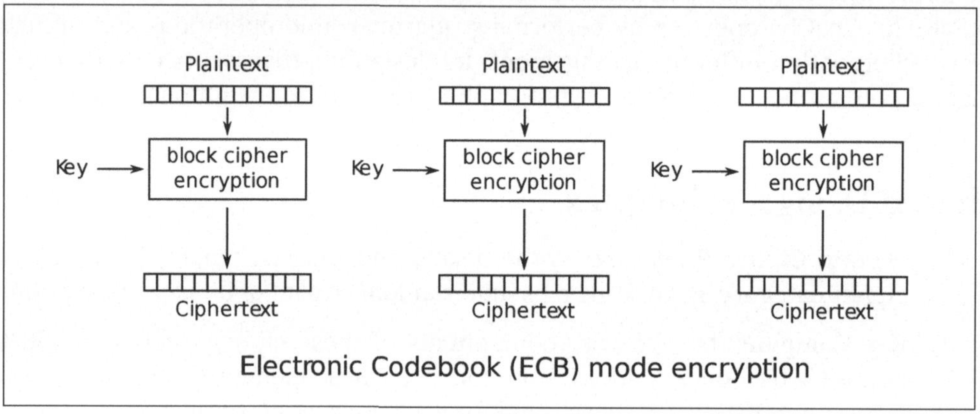

***Figure 3.6**: Electronic Codebook (ECB) mode encryption*

Electronic Codebook (ECB) Mode

ECB is one of the simplest and most straightforward modes of operation for block ciphers. In this mode, each block of plaintext is independently encrypted using the same key, resulting in a corresponding block of ciphertext. The independence of blocks makes ECB easy to understand and parallelize, as each block is processed in isolation.

Encryption Process

1. The plaintext message is divided into fixed-size blocks, typically 64 or 128 bits, depending on the block cipher used (for example, AES).
2. Each block of plaintext is individually encrypted using the same encryption key. This means that identical plaintext blocks will produce identical ciphertext blocks, introducing a vulnerability known as pattern recognition.
3. The resulting ciphertext blocks are concatenated to form the final encrypted message.

Decryption Process

1. The ciphertext is divided into blocks of the same size as used during encryption.
2. Each ciphertext block is decrypted independently using the same decryption key.
3. The resulting decrypted blocks are concatenated to reconstruct the original plaintext message.

Advantages

- ECB is straightforward to implement and parallelize, making it computationally efficient.
- Each block can be decrypted independently, allowing for random access to specific parts of the message.

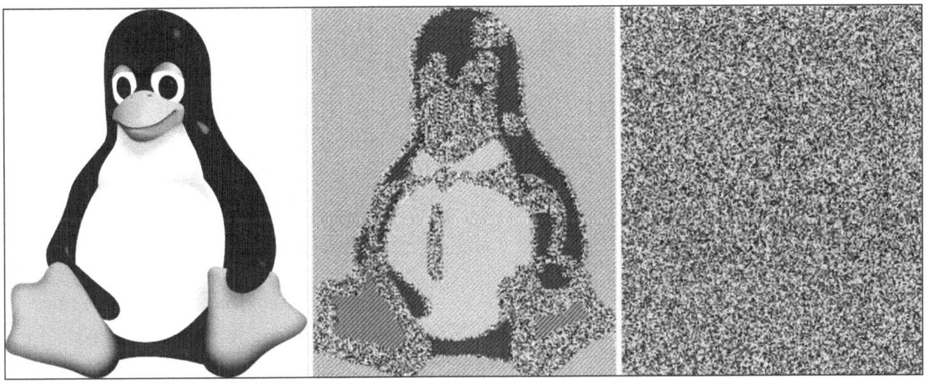

Figure 3.7: *Original Image vs Encrypted with ECB modes vs encrypted with other modes of operations*

Disadvantages

- Identical plaintext blocks result in identical ciphertext blocks, which can reveal patterns in the data. This lack of diffusion and pattern recognition vulnerability makes ECB unsuitable for encrypting large amounts of data or sensitive information.
- Due to the deterministic nature, ECB is not suitable for securing data with certain characteristics, such as images or data with repeating patterns.

In practice, ECB is rarely used for encrypting sensitive data alone, but it may find application in situations where individual block independence is desired or when combined with other cryptographic techniques to address its limitations. Understanding its characteristics is crucial for making informed decisions about its usage in specific scenarios.

Cipher Block Chaining (CBC) Mode

CBC is a widely used mode of operation for block ciphers, adding an element of feedback and chaining to the encryption process. In CBC mode, each plaintext block is combined with the ciphertext of the previous block before encryption. This introduces dependencies between blocks, enhancing security by eliminating the deterministic patterns present in ECB mode.

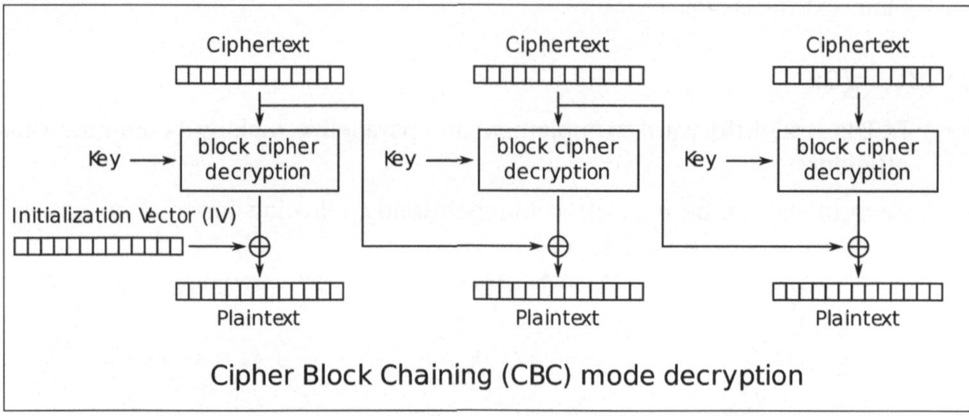

Figure 3.8: *Cipher Block (CBC) mode decryption*

Encryption Process

1. A unique random value, known as the Initialization Vector (IV), is XORed with the first block of plaintext before encryption. The IV ensures that even identical plaintext blocks produce different ciphertext blocks.
2. The result of the XOR operation in the first step becomes the input for the encryption of the current plaintext block. For subsequent blocks, the ciphertext of the previous block is XORed with the current plaintext block before encryption.
3. Each modified block is encrypted using the chosen block cipher, for example, AES.
4. The resulting ciphertext blocks are concatenated to form the final encrypted message.

Decryption Process

1. The same IV used for encryption is XORed with the first block of ciphertext.
2. The result of the XOR operation in the first step becomes the input for the decryption of the current ciphertext block. For subsequent blocks, the

ciphertext of the previous block is XORed with the current ciphertext block before decryption.

3. Each modified block is decrypted using the same block cipher.
4. The resulting decrypted blocks are concatenated to reconstruct the original plaintext message.

Advantages

- CBC introduces inter-block dependencies, causing changes in one part of the plaintext to affect the entire ciphertext, enhancing diffusion and the avalanche effect.
- The use of an IV helps ensure that identical plaintext blocks result in different ciphertext blocks.

Disadvantages

- CBC requires sequential processing of blocks, making parallelization more challenging than in ECB.
- Padding schemes need to be carefully chosen to handle messages that are not a multiple of the block size.

Counter (CTR) Mode of Operation

Counter (CTR) mode is a versatile mode of operation for block ciphers that transforms them into stream ciphers. It stands out for its efficiency, parallelizability, and suitability for random access to encrypted data, making it superior in certain aspects compared to other modes of operation.

Superiority of CTR Mode

One key advantage of CTR mode lies in its parallelizability. Unlike Cipher Block Chaining (CBC), which requires the sequential processing of blocks, CTR allows for the concurrent encryption of multiple blocks. This is particularly advantageous in modern computing environments with multiple processing units or scenarios where computational efficiency is paramount.

In CTR mode, a unique counter value is used for each block, and the encryption of blocks is independent. This allows for random access to any part of the message without needing to decrypt the entire preceding portion. This property makes CTR mode well-suited for applications where efficient data retrieval or manipulation is crucial.

Encryption Process

1. A unique IV is chosen, and a counter value is initialized.
2. The IV and counter value are combined to form the counter block.
3. The counter block is encrypted using the block cipher, producing a pseudorandom key stream.
4. The key stream is XORed with the plaintext to produce the ciphertext.
5. The counter is incremented for the next block, and the process is repeated.

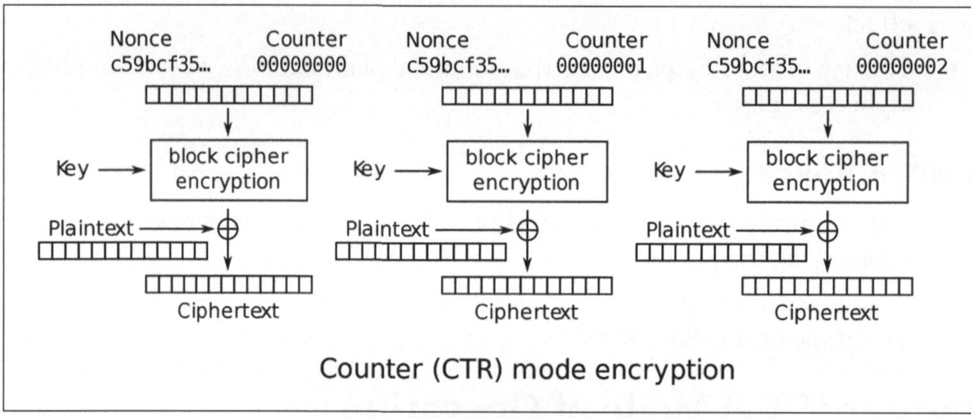

Figure 3.9: *Counter (CTR) mode encryption*

Decryption Process

The decryption process for CTR mode is identical to the encryption process, as XORing the ciphertext with the same key stream produces the original plaintext.

Advantages

- CTR allows for parallel processing of blocks, improving overall performance in modern computing environments.
- CTR supports random access to encrypted data, allowing for efficient retrieval and manipulation.
- Like other block cipher modes, CTR provides deterministic encryption, ensuring the same plaintext produces the same ciphertext.

Disadvantages

- Unlike CBC, transmission errors are not contained to specific blocks, potentially impacting the entire message.
- Care must be taken in choosing unique nonces to avoid key stream reuse, which could compromise security.

Practical Use Cases of Block Cipher Modes of Operation

As we explore the diverse landscape of block cipher modes of operation, it becomes evident that each mode brings its unique set of characteristics and applications to the table. The practical implementations and use cases of these modes play a crucial role in securing information in various scenarios. Let's delve into the specifics of how these modes are practically applied and the real-world problems are addressed.

- **Electronic Codebook (ECB) Mode**

  Image Encryption: Despite its vulnerabilities, ECB finds application in encrypting images where individual blocks correspond to pixels. While not suitable for sensitive data, it provides a simple and efficient solution for image encryption.

- **Cipher Block Chaining (CBC) Mode**

  CBC mode is a cornerstone in securing internet communications through protocols, such as SSL/TLS. By chaining blocks and introducing an Initialization Vector (IV), CBC effectively mitigates the deterministic patterns observed in ECB, providing a robust solution for secure data transfer over the web.

- **Cipher Feedback (CFB) Mode**

  CFB mode's ability to transform block ciphers into self-synchronizing stream ciphers makes it suitable for streaming encryption scenarios. Real-time communication applications benefit from CFB's ability to process data on the fly without requiring the entire message for decryption.

- **Counter (CTR) Mode**

  CTR mode shines in scenarios such as disk encryption, where parallel processing and random access are paramount. Encrypting and decrypting data blocks independently allows for efficient access to specific parts of the disk without decrypting the entire volume.

- **Galois/Counter Mode (GCM)**

  GCM combines counter mode with Galois field multiplication to provide not only confidentiality but also authenticity through authentication tags. This makes it a popular choice for securing communications and ensuring data integrity.

- **XEX-based Tweaked CodeBook (XTS) Mode**

  XTS mode is specifically designed for encrypting data on storage devices such as hard drives. Its tweakable nature allows for the encryption of multiple sectors without revealing patterns, making it suitable for full disk encryption scenarios.

Practical Considerations and Security Implications

- **Nonce Management**: Many modes, especially those with streaming capabilities, require nonces or initialization vectors. Proper management of these values is crucial to prevent key stream reuse and maintain the security of the encrypted data.
- **Padding Schemes**: The choice of padding schemes is essential, especially in block-oriented modes. The padding ensures that the plaintext fits into complete blocks and is crucial for maintaining the security and integrity of the encrypted data.
- **Error Handling**: Understanding how each mode handles errors during transmission is vital. While some modes contain errors to specific blocks (for example, CBC), others may propagate errors throughout the entire message.

The practical implementations and use cases of block cipher modes of operation extend across a wide range of applications, from securing internet communication to encrypting disk drives. The choice of a specific mode depends on the unique requirements of each scenario, balancing factors such as parallelizability, random access, and resistance to specific vulnerabilities. As technology evolves, so does the importance of selecting the right mode to address the ever-growing challenges of securing sensitive information.

Security Considerations in Symmetric Key Cryptography

As we navigate the intricate landscape of symmetric key cryptography, with its emphasis on shared secret keys for encryption and decryption, it becomes imperative to delve into the critical realm of security considerations. Symmetric key cryptography, while robust and widely adopted, demands a meticulous examination of various facets to fortify its defenses and safeguard sensitive information. In the journey so far, we've explored symmetric key algorithms, block ciphers, modes of operation, and practical implementations. Now, at this pivotal stage, let's focus our attention on the essential security considerations that underpin the reliability and resilience of symmetric key cryptographic systems.

Key Management

In the realm of symmetric key cryptography, managing cryptographic keys is a cornerstone of maintaining secure communication and data protection. Proper key management encompasses a variety of practices, from secure key generation to storage, ensuring the confidentiality, integrity, and availability of cryptographic material. With evolving cyber threats, a well-structured approach to key management becomes indispensable in safeguarding sensitive information.

Key Generation and Distribution

The secure and reliable generation and distribution of cryptographic keys stand as foundational pillars within the realm of symmetric key cryptography. This process plays a pivotal role in determining the overall security posture of a cryptographic system. It is essential to comprehend that if an adversary were to gain unauthorized access to the cryptographic key, it would lead to the complete compromise of the system's security. Therefore, establishing and adhering to robust key generation mechanisms and deploying secure key distribution protocols become essential in fortifying the overall security posture of a cryptographic system. The resilience of the entire cryptographic infrastructure hinges upon the meticulous execution of these key management practices, ensuring that cryptographic keys remain confidential, protected, and resistant to adversarial threats throughout their lifecycle.

Key Storage

Safeguarding cryptographic keys emerges as a paramount imperative within the intricate landscape of symmetric key cryptography. Recognizing the critical role these keys play in upholding the confidentiality and integrity of sensitive information, it becomes imperative to implement robust measures to protect them from potential compromise. The storage of keys in plaintext or susceptible locations introduces a substantial risk, leaving them vulnerable to unauthorized access or malicious exploitation. To mitigate these risks effectively, a multifaceted approach is essential. Techniques such as key wrapping, which involves adding an additional layer of protection to the keys before storage, contribute significantly to bolstering their resilience against unauthorized access. Embracing hardware security modules (HSMs), specialized devices designed to secure cryptographic material serve as an additional layer of defense by providing a physically isolated environment for key storage. Furthermore, adopting secure key storage practices, including encryption of key repositories and adherence to stringent access controls, further fortifies the protective shield around cryptographic keys. These comprehensive measures collectively contribute to the creation of a robust and layered defense mechanism, ensuring that cryptographic keys remain shielded from potential threats and vulnerabilities throughout their lifecycle.

Algorithmic Strength

The robustness of a cryptographic system relies on the algorithm's strength, often assessed by key length. This factor significantly impacts the system's resistance to brute force attacks. Longer keys expand the key space, making it computationally infeasible for attackers to systematically test all possible keys. This strategic use of longer keys acts as a formidable deterrent, enhancing the system's resilience against brute force attacks and bolstering its overall security.

Initialization Vectors (IVs) and Nonces

Initialization Vectors (IVs) and nonces are crucial for ensuring randomness and uniqueness in symmetric encryption. They prevent identical ciphertext for the same plaintext, reducing the risk of exposing patterns that could lead to vulnerabilities.

Uniqueness and Randomness

Initialization vectors (IVs) and nonces assume pivotal roles in specific modes of operation within cryptographic systems, holding paramount significance in guaranteeing the uniqueness of ciphertext for identical plaintext. The meticulous orchestration of nonces is imperative, necessitating uniqueness for each encryption session to avert any potential risks associated with key reuse. This uniqueness is inherently tied to their random generation, a process carefully designed to eliminate any discernible patterns within the resulting ciphertext. Through this intricate dance of randomness and uniqueness, nonces emerge as guardians against predictability, fortifying the cryptographic system against potential vulnerabilities arising from repeated encryption sessions. The dual commitment to both uniqueness and randomness in the generation and utilization of nonces stands as a formidable defense mechanism, elevating the integrity and security of the ciphertext while navigating the intricacies of cryptographic operations.

Secure Storage and Transmission

IVs and nonces merit a security level akin to cryptographic keys in symmetric key cryptography. Ensuring their protection is crucial for the integrity of encryption processes. Robust storage and transmission practices are essential to ward off vulnerabilities stemming from predictability or inadvertent reuse of IVs. Treating IVs and nonces with the same security as cryptographic keys establishes a comprehensive defense, minimizing risks and enhancing the overall resilience of the cryptographic system.

Cryptographic Modes of Operation

In cryptography, the choice of a mode of operation is just as crucial as the underlying algorithm. Modes define how blocks of plaintext are processed and encrypted, shaping the overall security properties of the system. Each mode introduces unique functionalities and trade-offs, influencing its suitability for specific applications.

Understanding Mode Characteristics

Various modes of operation present diverse security properties, each contributing distinct advantages and considerations. For instance, the Electronic Codebook (ECB), due to its deterministic nature, may inadvertently unveil patterns in the data, rendering it less suitable for specific applications. Acquiring a comprehensive understanding of the characteristics inherent to each mode becomes paramount. This profound comprehension is instrumental in judiciously selecting the most fitting mode for a given scenario, navigating the nuanced landscape of cryptographic requirements with precision and foresight.

Authenticated Encryption

In contexts where safeguarding both data confidentiality and integrity is of utmost importance, sophisticated modes such as Galois/Counter Mode (GCM) emerge as indispensable. GCM goes beyond mere encryption; it delivers authenticated encryption, a comprehensive security layer. This dual functionality guarantees not just the confidentiality of data but also actively safeguards against tampering during transmission. The meticulous orchestration of GCM in cryptographic operations represents a sophisticated approach that harmonizes the imperatives of confidentiality and integrity. By incorporating GCM into the cryptographic arsenal, a robust and versatile defense mechanism is established, assuring the preservation of data privacy and thwarting potential malicious alterations throughout the transmission process. The nuanced and multifaceted protection afforded by GCM sets the stage for elevated standards in cryptographic protocols, where the imperative of both confidentiality and integrity is seamlessly and comprehensively addressed. Side-Channel Attacks

Protecting Against Information Leakage

Symmetric key cryptographic systems face vulnerability to side-channel attacks, a category where sensitive information is exposed through channels, such as timing, power consumption, or electromagnetic radiation. The threat landscape introduces a pressing need for robust countermeasures embedded within implementations. Incorporating strategic measures, including the deployment of constant-time algorithms and fortified hardware protections, becomes imperative to effectively mitigate the risks posed by these insidious side-channel attacks. By diligently integrating these countermeasures, cryptographic systems elevate their resilience, ensuring that sensitive information remains shielded against potential leaks through various covert channels, and fortifying the overall security posture against a spectrum of sophisticated threats.

Operational Security

Operational security in symmetric key cryptography focuses on bridging the gap between theoretical robustness and practical resilience. Effective measures ensure that cryptographic systems withstand real-world threats, from implementation vulnerabilities to evolving attack vectors.

Secure Implementation Practices

The implementation of cryptographic algorithms must adhere to secure coding practices. Common vulnerabilities, such as buffer overflows or injection attacks, can compromise the security of the entire system.

Secure Communication Channels

The exchange of symmetric keys in the initial stages of key establishment demands meticulous attention to the security of communication channels. This exchange must transpire over channels fortified with robust security measures. Any inadequacies in shielding key exchange mechanisms could expose the keys to interception or manipulation by adversaries, compromising the very foundation of the cryptographic system. The criticality of secure key exchange cannot be overstated, as it forms the bedrock upon which the confidentiality and integrity of subsequent communication rely. By prioritizing and fortifying the security of these key establishment phases, organizations can erect a formidable defense against potential threats and adversarial interference in the intricate dance of symmetric keys.

Periodic Security Audits

Cryptographic systems are foundational to modern security, but their robustness depends on more than just initial design and implementation. Ongoing vigilance is critical, as evolving threats and emerging vulnerabilities demand continuous reassessment and adaptation. Regular evaluations ensure that cryptographic defenses remain resilient, proactive, and aligned with the latest advancements in security.

Regular Evaluation

Regular and systematic security audits and evaluations of cryptographic systems stand as crucial practices in ensuring sustained robustness. Given the dynamic nature of security threats, the periodic scrutiny of a system's design, implementation, and operational practices is indispensable. These comprehensive reviews serve as proactive measures, adeptly identifying and addressing potential vulnerabilities before they can be exploited. The continuous evolution of security threats necessitates a vigilant and iterative approach to system evaluation, affirming that cryptographic infrastructures remain resilient in the face of emerging challenges. Through these recurrent assessments, organizations fortify their security posture, creating a proactive shield against potential exploits and fortifying the longevity and effectiveness of their cryptographic defenses.

Adaptability to Emerging Threats

The cryptographic landscape operates within a dynamic framework, characterized by the continuous emergence of new attack vectors and vulnerabilities over time. In response to this ever-evolving threat landscape, cryptographic systems must be thoughtfully designed with adaptability as a foundational principle. This entails the ability to seamlessly integrate updated algorithms or protocols that can effectively counter and mitigate the evolving array of threats. The forward-looking design philosophy of cryptographic systems, emphasizing adaptability, serves as a proactive strategy to ensure their resilience against the relentless evolution of cyber threats. By fostering a system that can readily embrace advancements and innovations, organizations can position themselves to navigate the complexities of the cryptographic terrain, staying ahead of potential vulnerabilities and effectively safeguarding sensitive information.

The security considerations within symmetric key cryptography extend far beyond mere algorithmic choices. They encompass a holistic approach, covering key management, algorithmic strength, operational security, and adaptability to emerging threats. As we chart the course forward, these considerations will serve as a compass, guiding the design, implementation, and maintenance of cryptographic systems toward enhanced resilience and robust security.

Conclusion

In this chapter, we embarked on a comprehensive journey, traversing the intricate landscape of symmetric key cryptography and delving into the core principles and multifaceted elements that define this fundamental branch of cryptography. Beginning with an exploration of symmetric ciphers, the cornerstone of secure communication, we unraveled the intricate dance of encryption and decryption using a shared key. The discussion then pivoted towards the realm of block ciphers, where the robust design principles and historical significance of stalwarts such as AES (Advanced Encryption Standard) and DES (Data Encryption Standard) were unveiled. From the algorithmic intricacies to practical implementations, the exploration of these block ciphers provided a nuanced understanding of their pivotal role in securing digital communications.

Venturing further, the chapter navigated the dynamic terrain of stream ciphers, exploring their real-world applications and illustrating their functionality through code snippets. The exploration extended to modes of operation, dissecting Electronic Codebook (ECB), Cipher Block Chaining (CBC), and other mechanisms that orchestrate the symphony of cryptographic processes. As the cryptographic symposium unfolded, security considerations emerged as the unsung heroes, underlining the imperative of meticulous key management, algorithmic robustness, and the safeguarding of initialization vectors and nonces.

In concluding this chapter, we reflect on the holistic exploration of symmetric key cryptography, a journey that commenced with the fundamentals and evolved into an in-depth analysis of encryption algorithms, modes of operation, and the intricate dance of securing keys. From the timeless elegance of block ciphers to the dynamic versatility of stream ciphers, each element we explored contributes to the resilient tapestry that safeguards our digital interactions. As we bid farewell to this chapter, we carry forward not just an understanding of cryptographic mechanisms but a profound appreciation for the craftsmanship that underlies secure communication in the digital realm. Symmetric key cryptography stands not merely as a set of algorithms but as an evolving testament to our collective commitment to fortifying the digital landscapes we traverse.

As we draw the curtains on this chapter, unlocking the intricacies of symmetric key cryptography, our journey through the cryptographic realm continues to unfold. In our next chapter, we will embark on a compelling exploration into the world of asymmetric key cryptography. The symmetrical dance of shared secrets has paved the way, laying a robust foundation for our cryptographic understanding. Now, we eagerly anticipate delving into the asymmetric counterpart, where public and private keys engage in a choreography of secure communication. Join us in the upcoming chapters as we unravel the complexities of asymmetric encryption, decipher the elegance of key pairs, and explore the transformative landscapes of public-key cryptography. The cryptographic saga unfolds, inviting you to traverse the realms of security, privacy, and the captivating dance between keys in the ever-evolving symphony of cryptography.

CHAPTER 4
Asymmetric Key Cryptography

Introduction

As we seamlessly transition from the rhythmic harmonies of symmetric key cryptography, where shared secrets perform a delicate dance, our exploration now ventures into the avant-garde realm of asymmetric key cryptography. In this chapter, we witness a captivating shift in the cryptographic narrative–a transition from shared secrets to an intricate duet between public and private keys–adding a layer of complexity and elegance to our cryptographic ballet. This chapter unfurls the captivating narrative of asymmetric key cryptography, a paradigm that introduces a captivating duet: the dance of public and private key pairs.

In our cryptographic journey, where the language of security is spoken through algorithms and keys, the curtain rises on asymmetric key cryptography–a stage where the orchestration of keys is a nuanced ballet. This chapter commences with an introduction to the mesmerizing world of asymmetric encryption, a realm where cryptographic partners engage in a dance that defies the conventions of traditional cryptography.

Fundamental concepts unfold as we explore the intricacies of asymmetric key encryption. Here, the protagonists are not merely keys but key pairs–public and private– each playing a distinct role in a dance of encryption and decryption that adds a layer of complexity and security. This duet introduces us to a cryptographic waltz where the elegance lies in the asymmetry of power, where the public key disseminates knowledge while the private key guards secrets.

Key generation becomes our next act, and we delve into the meticulous process of creating these cryptographic duets. Randomness takes center stage, and entropy becomes the choreographer, ensuring the unpredictability and uniqueness of each key pair. The audience is introduced to the artistry behind generating secure keys that form the backbone of cryptographic security.

As our narrative unfolds, the concept of Public-Key Infrastructure (PKI) emerges as a supporting ensemble. Certification Authorities (CAs) and digital certificates take their places, contributing to the establishment of trust in the cryptographic ecosystem. We explore the trust model and its pivotal role in maintaining the integrity of asymmetric key systems.

Common asymmetric key algorithms, akin to masterful compositions, become the focal point of our exploration. RSA, ElGamal, and Elliptic Curve Cryptography (ECC) take center stage, each showcasing its unique strengths, applications, and mathematical beauty. The algorithms become the notes in our cryptographic symphony, creating melodies of security and resilience.

In this chapter, we navigate through the historical echoes of RSA, the versatility of ElGamal, and the elegance of ECC, unraveling the narratives behind these cryptographic compositions. Join us in this captivating exploration of asymmetric key cryptography, where the dance of keys transcends the traditional boundaries of encryption, forging a new path toward enhanced security and cryptographic sophistication.

Structure

In this chapter, the following topics will be covered:

- Introduction to Asymmetric Key Cryptography
- Fundamental Concepts of Asymmetric Key Encryption
- Common Asymmetric Key Algorithms
- RSA Algorithm - History, Design, and Operation
- Elliptic Curve Cryptography (ECC)
- Elliptic Curve Digital Signature Algorithm
- Public-Key Infrastructure (PKI)
- Future Trends in Asymmetric Key Cryptography

Introduction to Asymmetric Key Cryptography

Asymmetric key cryptography, also known as public-key cryptography, represents a revolutionary paradigm in secure communication. Unlike its symmetric counterpart, which relies on a shared secret for both encryption and decryption, asymmetric cryptography employs a distinctive pair of keys, an intricate dance between the public and private keys.

In this cryptographic ballet, the public key serves as an open invitation, disseminated freely to facilitate secure communication. Messages encrypted with the public key can only be decrypted by its corresponding private key, and vice versa. This unique duality forms the bedrock of asymmetric key cryptography, adding a layer of sophistication and versatility to cryptographic protocols.

The Historical Odyssey

The inception of asymmetric key cryptography is interwoven with a historical narrative that challenges traditional cryptographic norms. The seeds of this cryptographic evolution were sown in the early 1970s when Whitfield Diffie and Martin Hellman, in their seminal paper *New Directions in Cryptography*, introduced the concept of public-key cryptography. Prior to this groundbreaking revelation, cryptographic systems predominantly relied on symmetric key algorithms, where a shared secret needed to be securely exchanged between communicating parties. The Diffie-Hellman paper laid the groundwork for a paradigm shift, presenting the notion of key pairs—a public key for encryption and a private key for decryption. This transformative idea paved the way for a more secure, scalable, and flexible approach to cryptographic communications.

The RSA Breakthrough

Furthering the evolution of asymmetric key cryptography, the discovery of the RSA algorithm by Ron Rivest, Adi Shamir, and Leonard Adleman in 1977 marked a significant milestone. RSA, named after the initials of its inventors, introduced the use of a mathematical trapdoor function based on the difficulty of factoring the product of two large prime numbers. This breakthrough not only solidified the legitimacy of asymmetric cryptography but also opened new avenues for secure digital communication.

Widespread Adoption and Modern Significance

Over the decades, asymmetric key cryptography has become the cornerstone of secure digital communication, underpinning technologies, such as secure sockets layer (SSL), Transport Layer Security (TLS), and digital signatures. Its significance extends to securing email communication, online transactions, and the very fabric of the internet. The inherent security and versatility of asymmetric key algorithms have made them indispensable in modern cryptographic frameworks. As we delve into the complexities of key pairs, digital certificates, and the mathematical underpinnings of algorithms, such as RSA, ElGamal, and Elliptic Curve Cryptography (ECC), we unravel a rich tapestry that continues to shape the landscape of secure communication in our digital age.

Fundamental Concepts of Asymmetric Key Encryption

As we embark on a journey to understand the fundamental concepts, we encounter mathematical principles that underpin the security, uniqueness, and versatility of asymmetric key algorithms.

Key Pairs

At the core of asymmetric cryptography lies the concept of key pairs, two distinct yet interrelated keys: the public key and the private key. The public key, shared openly, serves as an invitation for secure communication. The private key, known only to its possessor, guards the secrets encoded with the corresponding public key. The security of this relationship relies on the mathematical intricacies embedded in the key pair generation process.

Central to the creation of secure key pairs is the canvas of modular arithmetic. This mathematical discipline provides a framework for performing calculations within a finite set or modulus. In the context of key pair generation, modular arithmetic introduces an essential layer of security by confining operations to a manageable range. The modulus acts as a mathematical boundary, ensuring that calculations wrap around within a predefined scope. The security of asymmetric cryptography hinges on the computational complexity of certain mathematical operations, particularly the difficulty of factoring the modulus into its prime components. The use of modular arithmetic ensures that even if adversaries intercept the public key and modulus, deciphering the private key remains a formidable task due to the mathematical intricacies involved in modular exponentiation.

In essence, the marriage of key pairs and modular arithmetic establishes the mathematical ballet that defines asymmetric key cryptography. This nuanced dance, grounded in the principles of number theory and mathematical elegance, forms the bedrock of secure communication in the digital realm.

Key Generation

Key generation in asymmetric cryptography is the initial step in establishing secure communication channels. It involves creating a pair of cryptographic keys, one public and one private. The public key is shared openly and is used for encryption, while the private key is kept confidential and utilized for decryption. This dual-key system forms the foundation of asymmetric encryption, enabling secure and authenticated data exchange.

Random Number Generation

Random number generation is a crucial aspect of key generation to introduce unpredictability. The entropy required for generating secure keys is sourced from various factors, including user interactions such as mouse movements and keyboard inputs and external environmental elements such as atmospheric noise. The quality of the randomness directly impacts the strength of the resulting keys, making the process a critical component of cryptographic security.

Prime Number Generation

Asymmetric key algorithms often rely on prime numbers. These primes are carefully selected to enhance the complexity of the cryptographic system. Advanced algorithms, coupled with primality tests such as Miller-Rabin, are employed to ensure the chosen numbers meet the necessary criteria for primality. Using prime numbers contributes to the security and robustness of the key pairs generated.

Key Length Considerations

The length of cryptographic keys is a critical factor influencing the security of cryptographic systems. Longer keys provide a larger key space, making it computationally infeasible for adversaries to perform brute-force attacks. Industry standards recommend key lengths based on the current understanding of computational capabilities and potential threats, ensuring a balance between security and efficiency.

For example, the National Institute of Standards and Technology (NIST) recommends using 2048-bit RSA keys for most applications, as they offer a strong level of security against current computational capabilities. Similarly, in elliptic curve cryptography (ECC), a 256-bit key provides comparable security to a 3072-bit RSA key due to the inherent strength of elliptic curve mathematics. These recommendations evolve as advancements in computational power, such as quantum computing, become a more significant factor.

By adhering to these recommended key lengths, cryptographic systems can achieve robust security while maintaining acceptable levels of performance.

RSA Key Generation

The RSA algorithm, a widely used asymmetric encryption method, involves a detailed key generation process. This includes the selection of two large prime numbers, the computation of the modulus and totient, and the determination of the public and private exponents. The resulting public key comprises the modulus and the public exponent, while the private key consists of the modulus and the private exponent.

Elliptic Curve Key Generation

Elliptic Curve Cryptography (ECC) introduces a different approach to key generation, leveraging elliptic curves. ECC provides the advantage of shorter key lengths while maintaining equivalent security compared to traditional methods. The parameters of the elliptic curve, including the base point and curve equation, are chosen carefully to ensure security. ECC key generation is computationally efficient and well-suited for resource-constrained environments.

Key Generation Protocols

Key generation protocols such as Diffie-Hellman and Elliptic Curve Diffie-Hellman enable secure key exchange without directly transmitting the keys. Diffie-Hellman involves the selection of a base and modulus, and parties independently compute a shared secret. Elliptic Curve Diffie-Hellman employs elliptic curves for key exchange, contributing to the establishment of a shared secret between communicating parties. These protocols play a crucial role in securing communication over insecure channels.

Security Considerations

Key generation is not a one-time event; it involves careful planning and management throughout the entire lifecycle of cryptographic keys. This life cycle includes generation, storage, usage, rotation, and eventual retirement or destruction. Properly managing these stages is critical to maintaining the integrity and security of cryptographic systems. Periodic key updates are essential to counter potential attacks that exploit advancements in computing power or newly discovered vulnerabilities. Regular key rotation reduces the risk of long-term key exposure and strengthens the overall security posture. Secure key storage practices play an equally vital role in preventing unauthorized access and potential compromises. Using hardware security modules (HSMs) and secure key vaults is strongly recommended to ensure keys are stored in tamper-resistant environments, safeguarding them against physical and digital attacks.

Avoid hardcoding private keys directly into software or configuration files, as this practice exposes them to significant risk. Hardcoded keys can be easily discovered through reverse engineering, code inspection, or other exploitation techniques, making them highly vulnerable to theft and misuse. Instead, private keys should be securely stored and accessed only through controlled mechanisms, such as secure APIs or dedicated cryptographic hardware. By implementing these practices, organizations can mitigate risks and establish a strong foundation for cryptographic security, ensuring that keys remain protected against evolving threats.

Quantum-Safe Key Generation

The advent of quantum computing has prompted research into post-quantum cryptography to develop key generation methods resistant to quantum attacks. "Quantum-safe" refers to cryptographic algorithms designed to resist potential attacks from quantum computers, which could otherwise break many classical cryptographic schemes. Algorithms and protocols are under exploration to safeguard cryptographic systems against this emerging threat. This forward-looking approach is essential for ensuring the long-term security of asymmetric key cryptography.

Real-World Implementations

In real-world scenarios, asymmetric key generation plays a pivotal role in securing digital communication. In SSL/TLS protocols, public and private keys are used for key exchange, ensuring encrypted communication over the internet. Additionally, key generation is integral to creating digital signatures for authentication purposes, contributing to the overall security of online transactions and communications.

Challenges and Best Practices

The computational complexity associated with key generation poses challenges, especially with larger key sizes. Ongoing research addresses these challenges, exploring efficient algorithms and optimizations to streamline the key generation process. Secure key storage practices, including using hardware security modules (HSMs) and secure key vaults, are vital for preventing unauthorized access and potential compromises. Continuous advancements in cryptographic research and adherence to best practices are essential for maintaining the security of key generation processes.

Mathematics in the Asymmetric Key Cryptography

Asymmetric key cryptography relies heavily on the principles of advanced mathematics, ensuring the security and efficiency of its operations. Among these mathematical foundations, modular arithmetic plays a pivotal role, providing the tools necessary for encryption, decryption, and key generation processes.

Modular Arithmetic Unveiled: A Deep Dive into Fundamental Concepts

At the heart of number theory lies the fascinating realm of modular arithmetic, a mathematical discipline that unveils its elegance through the manipulation of remainders and cyclical patterns. In the intricate dance of integers, modular arithmetic introduces the concept of a modulus, a positive integer that serves as the boundary defining the "wrapping" behavior of numbers. In equations, the expression "a mod m" signifies the remainder when integer "a" is divided by modulus "m."

The Modulus (m) is the guiding force, determining the range of possible remainders. Congruence relations, denoted as "$a \equiv b \pmod{m}$," signify that two integers "a" and "b" share the same remainder when divided by "m," creating an equivalence class of numbers with identical residue properties.

Modular arithmetic gracefully extends its influence across fundamental arithmetic operations. Addition and Subtraction in the modular realm involve performing the standard operation and then wrapping the result within the modulus, ensuring that the outcome stays within the defined range. The expression "(a + b) mod m" encapsulates this cyclic arithmetic dance.

Similarly, Multiplication in modular arithmetic is a two-step process: multiply the numbers and then find the remainder when divided by the modulus. This operation is denoted as "(a * b) mod m," where the final result is constrained within the boundaries set by the modulus.

In the quest for completeness, modular arithmetic introduces a critical concept, the Modular Inverse or the inverse modulo operation. Finding a number "x" such that "(a * x) mod m ≡ 1" is akin to discovering a key to unlock a cryptographic vault. This operation holds immense significance, especially in asymmetric key cryptography, where it forms the foundation for key generation and certain decryption processes.

The beauty of modular arithmetic lies in its simplicity and versatility, transcending mathematical abstractions to permeate practical applications. From the safeguarding of cryptographic keys to the generation of secure prime numbers, modular arithmetic provides a robust framework for computational elegance. As we delve deeper into the intricacies of asymmetric key cryptography, the significance of modular arithmetic becomes increasingly apparent, showcasing its pivotal role in the secure exchange of digital information.

Group Theory Unveiled: Navigating the Algebraic Landscape of Cryptography

In the enchanting realm of abstract algebra, Group Theory emerges as a guiding star, illuminating the mathematical structures that underpin the intricacies of cryptographic operations. At its core, Group Theory explores the properties and interactions of sets endowed with a binary operation, setting the stage for a profound understanding of cryptographic algorithms, particularly within the domain of Elliptic Curve Cryptography (ECC).

A Group is a mathematical entity defined by four fundamental properties: closure, associativity, the existence of an identity element, and the presence of inverses. Within this algebraic framework, elements combine under a specified operation, forming a coherent structure that showcases both symmetry and mathematical elegance.

In the cryptographic saga, Elliptic Curve Cryptography (ECC) takes center stage, leveraging the rich tapestry of Group Theory for its cryptographic dance. Elliptic curves, defined by cubic equations, serve as the mathematical landscape upon which cryptographic operations unfold. The group structure on elliptic curves introduces two fundamental operations: Point Addition and Point Doubling.

Point Addition encapsulates the essence of group operations on elliptic curves. Given two points on the curve, this operation yields a third point, forming a unique dance that respects the underlying group structure. Meanwhile, Point Doubling becomes a special case of point addition when both input points coincide, resulting in a tangent line to the curve.

Central to ECC is the concept of a Generator Point (G), a fixed point on the elliptic curve that generates all other points through repeated application of group operations. The efficiency and security of ECC hinge on the mathematical principles of Group Theory, providing a robust foundation for cryptographic endeavors. The Order of the Group stands as a pivotal parameter, representing the number of points on the elliptic curve. This parameter ensures the effectiveness of ECC operations and becomes a cornerstone for cryptographic key management.

As we navigate the captivating landscape of Group Theory, its relevance becomes increasingly apparent in the secure exchange of digital information. The symmetry, invertibility, and mathematical structure offered by groups lay the groundwork for the cryptographic symphony, where algebraic elegance meets the practical demands of secure communication.

Probabilistic Primality Testing: Navigating the Realm of Secure Prime Number Generation

In the cryptographic quest for secure prime numbers, the spotlight turns to probabilistic primality testing, a sophisticated method that blends mathematical probability with the crucial task of identifying prime numbers. As the building blocks of asymmetric key cryptography rely on the robustness of primes, this testing approach becomes a pivotal step in ensuring the integrity and security of cryptographic systems.

Defining Probabilistic Primality Testing

Probabilistic primality testing involves employing algorithms that provide a high probability (not absolute certainty) of determining whether a given number is prime. Unlike deterministic tests that guarantee a definite answer, probabilistic tests offer an efficient and often quicker means of assessing primality with a small probability of error.

Key Concepts:

- **Fermat's Little Theorem:** At the heart of many probabilistic primality tests lies Fermat's Little Theorem, which states that if "p" is a prime number and "a" is an integer not divisible by "p," then a^(p−1) ≡ 1(mod p). In other words, certain properties hold for prime numbers, allowing tests to exploit these patterns probabilistically.

- **Miller-Rabin Algorithm:** A prominent example of a probabilistic primality test is the Miller-Rabin algorithm. This algorithm, based on Fermat's Little Theorem, repeatedly tests the primality of a given number with different witness values. While not infallible, the Miller-Rabin algorithm provides a high degree of confidence in identifying primes.

Efficiency and Confidence:

Probabilistic primality testing strikes a delicate balance between efficiency and confidence. It offers a rapid means of checking whether a number is likely prime, making it suitable for the generation of large prime numbers required in cryptographic applications. However, the slight chance of error necessitates careful consideration and validation, especially in scenarios where absolute certainty is paramount.

Applications in Cryptography:

The application of probabilistic primality testing extends to cryptographic protocols, key generation, and secure communication. Cryptographic systems often demand the generation of large prime numbers, and probabilistic tests provide a pragmatic approach to achieving this while maintaining computational efficiency. As we venture into the probabilistic realm of primality testing, the fusion of mathematical elegance and computational pragmatism becomes evident. While not devoid of a minute margin of error, probabilistic primality testing stands as a powerful tool in the cryptographic toolkit, ensuring the robustness of prime numbers that form the bedrock of secure digital communication.

Trapdoor Functions: Unlocking Security through Mathematical Elegance

At the heart of asymmetric key cryptography lies the concept of trapdoor functions, an elegant mathematical construct that forms the bedrock of secure communication. A trapdoor function is a one-way mathematical operation that is easy to compute in one direction but computationally infeasible to reverse without specific knowledge, often referred to as the "trapdoor." This inherent one-way property is fundamental to the security of asymmetric key algorithms.

Significance of Trapdoor Functions:

The significance of trapdoor functions lies in their ability to establish a computational asymmetry between two operations: the ease of going in one direction and the difficulty of retracing the steps in the opposite direction. This asymmetry ensures that encrypting information with the public key is a relatively straightforward process while decrypting the same information without the corresponding private key becomes a computationally formidable challenge.

Computational Complexity and Security:

The security of asymmetric key cryptography hinges on the computational complexity introduced by trapdoor functions. The mathematical operations involved, whether based on factoring large numbers (as in RSA) or solving discrete logarithm problems (as in Diffie-Hellman and ElGamal), present a barrier to adversaries attempting to reverse the encryption process. The sheer difficulty of undoing these operations without possessing the trapdoor knowledge renders the system resistant to attacks, ensuring the confidentiality and integrity of communicated information.

Examples of One-Way Functions:

Several one-way functions contribute to the one-way operation of trapdoor functions in asymmetric cryptography:

- **Integer Factorization (RSA):**

  The difficulty of factoring the product of two large prime numbers serves as the foundation for RSA's one-way operation.

- **Discrete Logarithm (Diffie-Hellman, ElGamal):**

  The challenge of solving the discrete logarithm problem in finite fields or elliptic curves provides the one-way property for algorithms such as Diffie-Hellman and ElGamal.

- **Elliptic Curve Discrete Logarithm (ECC):**

  In ECC, the difficulty of solving the discrete logarithm problem on elliptic curves contributes to the one-way nature of the cryptographic operations.

Understanding these one-way functions illuminates the intricate dance of keys in asymmetric cryptography. The reliance on mathematical properties that permit easy-forward computation and defy efficient reverse computation exemplifies the beauty and security inherent in trapdoor functions–a cornerstone of secure digital communication.

Common Asymmetric Key Algorithms

In this section, we embark on a deeper exploration of the fascinating world of asymmetric key cryptography. Our journey will delve into the core principles and structures that underpin various asymmetric key algorithms, offering a nuanced understanding of their inner workings. We will illuminate the cryptographic landscape by examining notable algorithms, such as RSA, ECC, and DH, each wielding unique mathematical constructs to achieve security objectives.

Beyond theoretical considerations, we will provide practical insights into the implementation of these algorithms, demonstrating their application in real-world scenarios. The intricate dance of public and private keys will unfold, showcasing how these algorithms enable secure data transmission, digital signatures, and key exchange protocols. The discussion will extend to the establishment of trust through Public Key Infrastructures (PKI) and the meticulous management of cryptographic keys.

This comprehensive exploration serves as a gateway to a deeper understanding of asymmetric key cryptography, setting the stage for a detailed examination of key algorithms, their structures, and practical implementations. Join us as we unravel the complexities of this cryptographic realm, unlocking the secrets behind secure communication in the digital age.

RSA Algorithm

The RSA algorithm, an acronym derived from the surnames of its inventors Ron Rivest, Adi Shamir, and Leonard Adleman, stands as a cornerstone in modern cryptography. Introduced in 1977, RSA revolutionized the landscape by introducing a novel asymmetric key encryption system that laid the foundation for secure digital communication.

At its core, RSA relies on the mathematical complexity of factoring the product of two large prime numbers, an operation believed to be computationally infeasible within a reasonable timeframe. The algorithm employs a pair of keys—a public key for encryption and a private key for decryption—intricately linked by mathematical relationships. This distinctive approach addresses the challenges posed by key distribution in symmetric key cryptography, offering a secure means for parties to communicate over untrusted networks.

Historical Significance

The historical significance of RSA is profound, rooted in its transformative role as the first practical public-key cryptosystem. Its introduction marked a turning point, challenging established cryptographic norms that predominantly relied on shared secret keys. Before RSA, secure communication often involved the cumbersome task of physically exchanging secret keys, limiting the scalability and efficiency of cryptographic systems. RSA's emergence heralded a new era where secure communication became not only feasible but also scalable, efficient, and adaptable to the evolving demands of a rapidly advancing digital landscape.

With RSA, the field of cryptography witnessed a paradigmatic shift, opening up avenues for secure communication without the constraints of pre-established secrets. The mathematical elegance of RSA's design, grounded in number theory and modular arithmetic, not only showcased the potential of harnessing mathematical complexity for practical cryptographic applications but also laid the groundwork for subsequent developments in public-key cryptography. Over the decades, RSA has become a linchpin in the foundation of secure communication protocols, fortifying the security of digital interactions and exemplifying the enduring impact of visionary cryptographic innovations. As we delve into the historical evolution of RSA, we recognize it not merely as a cryptographic algorithm but as a catalyst that propelled the field into a new epoch, shaping the digital landscape and empowering secure communication worldwide.

Encryption and Decryption steps

In RSA, two essential operations define its functionality: encryption and decryption. The encryption process involves using a public key to secure messages, while decryption requires the corresponding private key to retrieve the original information. Let's delve into the intricate steps of RSA encryption and decryption, unraveling the mathematical intricacies that form the basis of this enduring cryptographic scheme.

RSA Encryption Steps:

1. **Key Generation**:
   a. Select two large prime numbers, p and q.
   b. Compute $n = p*q$ and $phi(n) = (p-1)*(q-1)$.
   c. Choose a public exponent e such that $1< e < phi(n)$ and $gcd(e, phi(n)) = 1$.
2. **Public Key Formation:**
   a. The public key is represented as (e, n).
3. **Private Key Calculation**:
   a. Compute the private exponent d as the modular multiplicative inverse of e modulo $phi(n)$.
4. **Key Distribution**:
   a. Share the public key (e, n) openly, while keeping the private key d secret.
5. **Message Encryption**:
   a. Represent the plaintext message as M where $0 < M < n$.
   b. Calculate the ciphertext C using the encryption formula: $C \equiv M^e \bmod n$.

RSA Decryption Steps:

1. Received Ciphertext:
   a. Received Ciphertext is C.

2. Use of Private Key and Message retrieval:
   a. Utilize the private key d to decrypt the ciphertext: M ≡ C^d mod n. Here M is the underlying message.

Implementation Code of RSA

Here is a simple implementation of the RSA algorithm in Python. This code includes key generation, encryption, and decryption functions.

```
import random
from sympy import mod_inverse, isprime

def generate_keypair(bits):
    # Step 1: Choose two large prime numbers
    p = generate_prime(bits)
    q = generate_prime(bits)

    # Step 2: Compute n and Euler's totient function
    n = p * q
    phi_n = (p - 1) * (q - 1)

    # Step 3: Choose a public exponent e
    e = choose_public_exponent(phi_n)

    # Step 4: Compute the private exponent d
    d = mod_inverse(e, phi_n)

    # Public key (e, n), Private key (d, n)
    return ((e, n), (d, n))

def generate_prime(bits):
    while True:
        num = random.getrandbits(bits)
        if isprime(num):
            return num

def choose_public_exponent(phi_n):
    # Common choices for e include 65537 or a randomly selected prime
    e = 65537
    while True:
        if isprime(e) and 1 < e < phi_n and mod_inverse(e, phi_n):
            return e
        e = generate_prime(16)  # Choose a random prime if 65537 is not
suitable
```

```
def encrypt(public_key, plaintext):
    e, n = public_key
    cipher_text = [pow(ord(char), e, n) for char in plaintext]
    return cipher_text

def decrypt(private_key, cipher_text):
    d, n = private_key
    decrypted_text = [chr(pow(char, d, n)) for char in cipher_text]
    return ''.join(decrypted_text)

def main():
    bits = 1024
    public_key, private_key = generate_keypair(bits)

    message = "Hello, RSA!"
    print(f"Original Message: {message}")

    cipher_text = encrypt(public_key, message)
    print(f"Ciphertext: {cipher_text}")

    decrypted_text = decrypt(private_key, cipher_text)
    print(f"Decrypted Message: {decrypted_text}")

if __name__ == "__main__":
    main()
```

Please note that for practical applications, it's advisable to use established libraries such as `**cryptography**` for security and efficiency. Ensure that the '**sympy**' library is installed. This implementation uses a bit size of 1024 for demonstration purposes; in practice, larger bit sizes are recommended for increased security.

Elliptic Curve Cryptography (ECC)

As we advance into the realms of modern cryptographic methodologies, Elliptic Curve Cryptography (ECC) emerges as a pivotal paradigm, standing in stark contrast to traditional approaches such as RSA. ECC, recognized for its efficiency and robust security, revolves around the mathematical elegance of elliptic curves. Its journey from mathematical curiosity to cryptographic cornerstone marks a significant chapter in the evolution of secure communication. One of the key advantages of ECC is its ability to provide strong security with shorter key lengths compared to traditional algorithms. For instance, a 256-bit ECC key offers a level of security comparable to a 3072-bit RSA key. This efficiency in key size not only enhances performance but also reduces computational overhead, making ECC an attractive choice for modern cryptographic applications.

Historical Significance

While RSA, with its reliance on prime factorization, paved the way for public-key cryptography, ECC introduced a transformative shift. The roots of ECC can be traced back to the mid-1980s, gaining traction as researchers explored alternative mathematical structures. Its inception is often attributed to the work of Neal Koblitz and Victor Miller, who independently proposed the concept of elliptic curves as a foundation for cryptographic operations.

ECC's historical significance lies in its ability to offer equivalent security with shorter key lengths compared to traditional systems such as RSA. The elegance of elliptic curves provides a unique blend of efficiency and strength, making ECC particularly well-suited for resource-constrained environments, such as mobile devices and the Internet of Things (IoT). The adoption of ECC in standards such as the Digital Signature Algorithm (DSA) and the Elliptic Curve Diffie-Hellman (ECDH) key exchange protocol underscores its vital role in contemporary cryptographic systems.

As we delve into the intricacies of ECC, it becomes apparent that its historical journey mirrors the continual quest for cryptographic solutions that balance security and efficiency. ECC's rise exemplifies the dynamic nature of cryptographic evolution, where mathematical innovation converges with real-world applicability, shaping the landscape of secure communication for the digital age.

Encryption and Decryption steps

In Elliptic Curve Cryptography (ECC), the encryption and decryption steps unfold through the intricacies of elliptic curves, introducing a paradigm where the security foundation relies on the elusive nature of the elliptic curve discrete logarithm problem. The key generation, encryption, and decryption processes collectively contribute to ECC's efficiency and robustness in securing digital communication.

ECC Key Generation:

1. Select an elliptic curve E defined over a finite field F_p with a base point G and the order n of the cyclic subgroup generated by G.
2. Choose a private key randomly from the range [1, n-1].
3. Compute the public key Q as Q = d x G, where x denotes elliptic curve point multiplication.

ECC Encryption:

1. Choose a random ephemeral private key k from the range [1, n-1].
2. Compute the ephemeral public key K as K = k x G.

3. Compute the shared secret point S as S = $d \times$ K.
4. Calculate the x-coordinate of S to derive a symmetric key K_s for data encryption.
5. Choose a suitable symmetric encryption algorithm (for example, AES) and use K_s to encrypt the plaintext message.
6. Transmit the ciphertext along with the ephemeral public key K.

ECC Decryption:

1. Receive the ciphertext and the ephemeral public key K.
2. Compute the shared secret point S as S = $d \times$ K.
3. Calculate the x-coordinate of S to derive the symmetric key K_s.
4. Use K_s to decrypt the ciphertext, revealing the original plaintext message.

Implementation Code of ECC

In this section, we will delve into the intricacies of Elliptic Curve Cryptography (ECC) for encryption and decryption. The provided Python program showcases a simplified example of ECC in action. It begins by generating key pairs for both parties, Alice and Bob. The program then performs an Elliptic Curve Diffie-Hellman (ECDH) key exchange between the two parties, enabling them to derive a shared secret key. Subsequently, this shared key is employed for encrypting and decrypting a message using the AES-GCM symmetric encryption algorithm. The example demonstrates the fundamental principles of ECC, showcasing its role in secure communication through key exchange and symmetric encryption.

```
import os
from cryptography.hazmat.primitives import serialization
from cryptography.hazmat.primitives.asymmetric import ec
from cryptography.hazmat.primitives.ciphers import Cipher, algorithms,
modes
from cryptography.hazmat.backends import default_backend


def generate_keypair():
    """
    Generate an ECC key pair using the SECP256k1 curve.
    """
    private_key = ec.generate_private_key(ec.SECP256K1(), default_
backend())
    public_key = private_key.public_key()
    return private_key, public_key
```

```
def perform_ecdh_key_exchange(private_key, other_public_key):
    """
    Perform ECDH key exchange.
    """
    shared_key = private_key.exchange(ec.ECDH(), other_public_key)
    return shared_key

def aes_encrypt(plaintext, key):
    """
    Encrypt plaintext using AES-GCM.
    """
    nonce = os.urandom(16)
    backend = default_backend()
    cipher = Cipher(algorithms.AES(key), modes.GCM(nonce), backend=
backend)
    encryptor = cipher.encryptor()
    ciphertext = encryptor.update(plaintext.encode()) + encryptor.
finalize()
    tag = encryptor.tag
    return ciphertext, nonce, tag

def aes_decrypt(ciphertext, key, nonce, tag):
    """
    Decrypt ciphertext using AES-GCM.
    """
    backend = default_backend()
    cipher = Cipher(algorithms.AES(key), modes.GCM(nonce, tag),
backend=backend)
    decryptor = cipher.decryptor()
    plaintext = decryptor.update(ciphertext) + decryptor.finalize()
    return plaintext.decode()

def main():
    # Alice generates key pair
    alice_private_key, alice_public_key = generate_keypair()

    # Bob generates key pair
    bob_private_key, bob_public_key = generate_keypair()

    # Alice performs ECDH key exchange with Bob's public key
    alice_shared_key = perform_ecdh_key_exchange(alice_private_key, bob_
public_key)

    # Bob performs ECDH key exchange with Alice's public key
    bob_shared_key = perform_ecdh_key_exchange(bob_private_key, alice_
public_key)
```

```
    # Both Alice and Bob now share the same secret key
    assert alice_shared_key == bob_shared_key

    # Example message
    message = "Hello, ECC Key Exchange!"

    # Encrypt message using shared key
    ciphertext, nonce, tag = aes_encrypt(message, alice_shared_key)

    # Decrypt message using shared key
    decrypted_message = aes_decrypt(ciphertext, bob_shared_key, nonce,
tag)

    print(f"Original Message: {message}")
    print(f"Encrypted Message: {ciphertext.hex()}")
    print(f"Decrypted Message: {decrypted_message}")

if __name__ == "__main__":
    main()
```

Elliptic Curve Digital Signature Algorithm

The Elliptic Curve Digital Signature Algorithm (ECDSA) stands as a cornerstone in modern cryptographic systems, providing a robust and efficient means of ensuring the authenticity and integrity of digital messages. Building upon the principles of elliptic curve cryptography, ECDSA operates within the framework of public-key cryptography. Its distinctive feature lies in leveraging the mathematical properties of elliptic curves over finite fields, offering security comparable to traditional algorithms such as RSA but with shorter key lengths. ECDSA plays a pivotal role in securing digital communication, digital signatures, and cryptographic key exchanges, making it a cornerstone in the landscape of secure and efficient cryptographic protocols.

Historical Significance

The inception of ECDSA can be traced back to the late 20th century when the need for more efficient public-key cryptographic algorithms became apparent. In the early 1990s, elliptic curve cryptography emerged as a promising area of study, demonstrating the potential for robust security with shorter key lengths compared to other asymmetric algorithms. In 1999, the National Institute of Standards and Technology (NIST) standardized ECDSA, solidifying its place as a key cryptographic algorithm. Since then, ECDSA has gained widespread adoption, particularly in resource-constrained environments such as embedded systems and mobile devices, where its efficiency shines. Its historical significance lies in offering a powerful tool for digital signatures, ensuring data integrity, and contributing to the evolution of cryptographic practices.

Working Principles

The Elliptic Curve Digital Signature Algorithm (ECDSA) involves several steps to generate and verify digital signatures. Here are the key working steps of the ECDSA algorithm:

1. **Key Generation:**
   a. Select an elliptic curve and a base point on the curve.
   b. Choose a private key (random number) as a secret.
   c. Compute the corresponding public key by multiplying the base point by the private key using elliptic curve point multiplication.
2. **Signing a Message:**
   a. Hash the message using a cryptographic hash function (for example, SHA-256) to generate a fixed-size digest.
   b. Generate a random number (nonce) as a temporary private key.
   c. Compute a temporary public key by multiplying the base point by the nonce.
   d. Compute the signature parameters:
      i. r is the x-coordinate of the temporary public key modulo the order of the base point.
      ii. s is the modular inverse of the nonce times the sum of the private key and the product of the digest and the actual private key.
3. **Verification of a Signature:**
   a. Hash the received message to generate the digest.
   b. Compute the modular inverse of s.
   c. Compute two values, u_1 and u_2, as the product of the digest and the inverses of s and *r* respectively, modulo the order of the base point.
   d. Compute a point on the elliptic curve by adding u_1 times the base point and u_2 times the public key.
   e. Verify that the x-coordinate of the computed point is equal to *r*. If true, the signature is valid.

The security of ECDSA relies on the difficulty of solving the elliptic curve discrete logarithm problem. The algorithm provides a secure and efficient way to generate and verify digital signatures, making it widely used in various cryptographic applications.

Implementation code of ECDSA

In this section, we present a Python implementation of the Elliptic Curve Digital Signature Algorithm (ECDSA) using the cryptography library. ECDSA is a widely used cryptographic algorithm for generating and verifying digital signatures. The provided code showcases the signing and verification process, highlighting the key steps involved in utilizing elliptic curves for secure digital communication. It begins by generating a private and public key pair using the SECP256R1 elliptic curve. The `ecdsa_sign` function is employed to sign a sample message, and the `ecdsa_verify` function checks the validity of the generated signature using the corresponding public key. The example usage includes a simple message, and the code can be adapted for various applications requiring secure digital signatures.

```
from cryptography.hazmat.backends import default_backend
from cryptography.hazmat.primitives import hashes
from cryptography.hazmat.primitives.asymmetric import ec

def ecdsa_sign(private_key, message):
    # Generate a signature for the message using the private key
    signature = private_key.sign(
        message,
        ec.ECDSA(hashes.SHA256())
    )
    return signature

def ecdsa_verify(public_key, message, signature):
    # Verify the signature for the given message using the public key
    try:
        public_key.verify(
            signature,
            message,
            ec.ECDSA(hashes.SHA256())
        )
        return True  # Signature is valid
    except Exception:
        return False  # Signature is invalid

# Example Usage:
# Generate private and public keys
private_key = ec.generate_private_key(ec.SECP256R1(), default_backend())
public_key = private_key.public_key()

# Sign a message
message_to_sign = b"Hello, ECDSA!"
signature = ecdsa_sign(private_key, message_to_sign)
```

```
# Verify the signature
is_signature_valid = ecdsa_verify(public_key, message_to_sign, signature)

# Output results
print("Original Message:", message_to_sign.decode())
print("Signature:", signature.hex())
print("Is Signature Valid?", is_signature_valid)
```

Public-Key Infrastructure (PKI)

In our exploration of the cryptographic landscape, we've traversed the realms of symmetric and asymmetric key cryptography, unraveling the intricacies that safeguard our digital interactions. Now, we venture into the sophisticated domain of Public Key Infrastructure (PKI), a linchpin orchestrating the secure management of cryptographic keys and digital certificates. Asymmetric cryptography, with its dual-key dance, opened avenues for secure communication, yet the need for a systematic framework to manage these cryptographic keys becomes evident. PKI steps onto the stage as the guardian of trust in the digital realm, ensuring that our exchanges of sensitive information or online authentication are executed with confidence. Connecting the dots from our previous chapters, we transition seamlessly into PKI, enhancing our understanding of how cryptographic keys are meticulously managed, authenticated, and utilized. PKI is not merely a technological infrastructure; it's a framework for building trust, encompassing Certificate Authorities (CAs), Registration Authorities (RAs), end entities, and digital certificates. This section embarks on a journey through the various components of PKI, exploring the lifecycle of digital certificates, mechanisms of secure key distribution, and complexities of key management. Join us as we navigate the PKI landscape, unraveling the web of trust that underlies secure communication in the digital age and bringing us closer to a holistic understanding of cryptographic systems.

Introduction to PKI

PKI is a comprehensive framework designed to manage the generation, distribution, and verification of cryptographic keys in a secure manner. At its core, PKI establishes a trust infrastructure that facilitates secure communication over digital networks. It achieves this by employing a system of digital certificates and key pairs, allowing users and systems to authenticate each other and encrypt sensitive information. PKI plays a pivotal role in establishing and maintaining trust in online transactions, communication, and data exchanges, ensuring the confidentiality, integrity, and authenticity of digital interactions.

Highlighting the Fundamental Principles of PKI

The fundamental principles of PKI revolve around the secure management of cryptographic keys, particularly leveraging asymmetric cryptography. Asymmetric cryptography, also known as public-key cryptography, involves the use of key pairs–a public key for encryption and a private key for decryption. PKI leverages this dual-key approach to address the challenges of secure key exchange and authentication. The public key is openly shared and used for encryption, while the private key, kept confidential, is used for decryption. This asymmetric key pair forms the foundation of trust in PKI, enabling secure communication and digital signatures. Emphasizing the use of asymmetric cryptography underscores the importance of robust key management practices in ensuring the security of the entire PKI ecosystem.

Key Components of PKI

Let's delve into the key components of Public Key Infrastructure (PKI) by exploring the roles of Certificate Authorities (CAs), Registration Authorities (RAs), and end entities.

Certificate Authority (CA)

At the heart of PKI lies the Certificate Authority (CA), a trusted entity responsible for issuing and managing digital certificates. CAs play a crucial role in establishing trust within the system. They verify the identity of entities, such as individuals, organizations, or devices and validate their ownership of public-private key pairs. CAs are hierarchically structured, with root CAs at the top and subordinate CAs beneath them. The root CA's digital signature is used to sign the certificates of subordinate CAs, forming a chain of trust. This hierarchical structure ensures the integrity of the entire PKI.

Registration Authority (RA)

Working in tandem with CAs, the Registration Authority (RA) acts as an intermediary that verifies the identities of entities requesting digital certificates. RAs play a pivotal role in the certificate issuance process by confirming the authenticity of the information provided by end entities. While CAs focus on the overall trust establishment and management, RAs serve as a crucial step in the validation process, ensuring that entities are who they claim to be before receiving digital certificates.

End Entities

End entities represent the ultimate users or systems within the PKI. These can be individuals, devices, servers, or any entity requiring a digital certificate to engage in secure communication. End entities possess a key pair–an associated public key for encryption and a private key for decryption. Digital certificates, verified by RAs and issued by CAs, bind these public keys to the identity of the end entities. The certificates serve as a trust anchor, allowing others to securely communicate, verify, or exchange information with the respective end entity.

Digital Certificates

Digital Certificates are fundamental components of Public Key Infrastructure (PKI), playing a crucial role in establishing trust and securing online communication. At their core, digital certificates serve as electronic credentials that bind cryptographic keys to the identity of individuals, devices, or services. This binding is essential for authentication and data integrity, ensuring that parties involved in a digital interaction can be verified and trusted.

Structure of Digital Certificates

The structure of a digital certificate is designed to encapsulate key information required for secure communication. A typical digital certificate includes several components, such as the public key, the identity details of the entity (subject), information about the entity issuing the certificate (issuer), a digital signature, and a validity period. These elements collectively form a comprehensive representation of the certificate holder, allowing others to securely communicate and validate the authenticity of the provided information.

Certificate Formats

Digital certificates adhere to specific formats to ensure interoperability across different systems and applications. One widely adopted format is X.509, a standard defined by the International Telecommunication Union (ITU). X.509 provides a standardized structure for digital certificates, facilitating their use in diverse cryptographic applications. The format specifies how information is organized within the certificate, ensuring consistency and compatibility in the digital realm.

X.509 Certificate Field

Within the X.509 format, digital certificates consist of various fields, each serving a specific purpose. The Subject field contains information about the entity associated with the public key, while the Issuer field identifies the entity that issued the certificate. The Public Key field holds the cryptographic key associated with the certificate, and the Validity Period field indicates the time during which the certificate is considered valid. The digital signature ensures the integrity of the certificate. Understanding these fields is crucial for interpreting the information conveyed by a digital certificate.

Certificate Lifecycle

The lifecycle of a digital certificate encompasses several stages, starting with issuance and progressing through renewal, revocation, and expiration. During the issuance process, a Certificate Authority (CA) verifies the identity of the certificate holder, and upon successful validation, issues the certificate. Renewal ensures that certificates remain valid beyond their original expiration date, while revocation addresses instances where a certificate's trustworthiness is compromised. The lifecycle management of digital certificates is essential for maintaining the security and reliability of cryptographic systems.

Certificate Revocation

Revocation of digital certificates becomes necessary when a certificate is compromised or when the associated private key is lost. Various mechanisms are employed for certificate revocation, including Certificate Revocation Lists (CRLs) and the Online Certificate Status Protocol (OCSP). CRLs provide a list of certificates that have been revoked, allowing relying parties to check the revocation status periodically. OCSP offers a real-time alternative, enabling immediate verification of a certificate's validity.

Public and Private Key Pair Generation in PKI

Public Key Infrastructure (PKI) forms the bedrock of secure communication, relying on the generation and distribution of public and private key pairs. This intricate process ensures cryptographic strength, confidentiality, and authentication within digital transactions.

Generation and Distribution of Keys in PKI Infrastructure

The generation and distribution of public and private key pairs form the cornerstone of secure communication. At its core, PKI relies on the principles of asymmetric cryptography, employing a pair of keys; a public key, openly shared, and a private key, held confidentially. This dual-key system facilitates secure transactions, with the public key encrypting messages and the private key decrypting them, ensuring both confidentiality and authentication.

The process of key generation is a meticulous one, requiring true randomness to enhance the unpredictability of keys. Robust algorithms utilize methods such as modular exponentiation in RSA or elliptic curve-based cryptography in ECC to create mathematically linked yet computationally challenging key pairs. Key length considerations are crucial, striking a balance between heightened security and computational efficiency. For instance, RSA involves selecting large prime numbers, forming the basis of the key's security, while ECC leverages points on elliptic curves for efficient yet robust key pairs.

Security extends beyond key generation to encompass practices such as entropy sources, safeguarding private keys through hardware security modules, and aligning key generation with the requisite cryptographic strength. This intricate process ensures the cryptographic foundation of PKI, fostering a secure environment for digital communication.

Public Keys and Identities Association by Certificate Authority

In the orchestration of PKI, the Certificate Authority (CA) assumes a pivotal role in validating and attesting to the association between public keys and the identities of entities engaged in digital transactions. The CA's responsibilities span the issuance, management, and revocation of digital certificates, crucial components that vouch for the authenticity and trustworthiness of cryptographic communication.

During the issuance process, CAs diligently verify the identities of entities requesting digital certificates. Successful validation results in the issuance of a digital certificate, effectively binding the public key to the entity's identity. CAs play a central role in managing the lifecycle of digital certificates, overseeing processes such as renewal to maintain continuous trust and revocation when a certificate's integrity is compromised.

CAs operate in a hierarchical structure, with root CAs authenticating subordinate CAs, forming a chain of trust integral to PKI's integrity. Their verification processes extend beyond mere key issuance, encompassing thorough identity verification to prevent unauthorized entities from obtaining digital certificates. Additionally, CAs manage cryptographic keys, ensuring robust key management practices that contribute to the overall security and reliability of the PKI infrastructure. In essence, the CA's role is instrumental in attesting and maintaining the secure association between public keys and the verified identities of entities in the digital landscape.

Secure Key Distribution

Secure key distribution is a critical facet of cryptographic systems, ensuring the confidential and reliable delivery of public keys and digital certificates to end entities. This process lays the foundation for secure communication, establishing trust and integrity within a digital ecosystem. In this discussion, we will delve into the intricacies of securely distributing public keys and digital certificates, exploring the mechanisms that underpin this crucial aspect of cryptographic infrastructure. Additionally, we will examine the role of secure channels, such as HTTPS or secure email, in fortifying the security of key distribution processes.

Securely Distributing Public Keys and Digital Certificates

The process of securely distributing public keys and digital certificates involves meticulous steps to safeguard against interception or tampering. When an entity requests a digital certificate, a Certificate Authority (CA) rigorously verifies its identity before issuing a certificate binding the public key to that identity. To ensure secure distribution, these digital certificates are often delivered through encrypted channels, preventing unauthorized access during transmission.

Public keys, integral for encryption and authentication, are disseminated securely to intended recipients. Cryptographic protocols such as Transport Layer Security (TLS) or its predecessor, Secure Sockets Layer (SSL), play a crucial role in this distribution process. When entities connect to a server or a network, these protocols facilitate the exchange of public keys securely. Using digital signatures in certificates further ensures the authenticity of the distributed public keys.

Explaining How Secure Channels are Used for Key Distribution

Secure channels, exemplified by protocols such as HTTPS or secure email, enhance the security of key distribution mechanisms. In the context of HTTPS, web servers and clients establish a secure connection through the exchange of digital certificates and public keys. This process, often known as the TLS Handshake, ensures the confidentiality and integrity of the exchanged keys, thwarting potential man-in-the-middle attacks.

Secure email, employing protocols such as S/MIME or PGP, similarly leverages encryption to protect the distribution of public keys and digital certificates. Recipients can be confident in the authenticity of received keys, thanks to the cryptographic signatures embedded in digital certificates. These secure channels serve as trust anchors, mitigating risks associated with key interception or substitution, thereby bolstering the overall security of cryptographic key distribution.

Key Management and Storage

Effective key management and secure storage are pivotal components of cryptographic systems, ensuring the integrity, confidentiality, and reliability of cryptographic keys. In this section, we will explore best practices for key management, focusing on the secure storage and protection of private keys. Additionally, we will delve into the use of Hardware Security Modules (HSMs) as a specialized solution to enhance the security of cryptographic keys, providing a fortified layer of protection against potential threats.

Best Practices for Key Management

Robust key management practices are foundational to the security of cryptographic systems. Implementing best practices involves a combination of procedural and technological measures to safeguard cryptographic keys.

- **Key Rotation**: Regularly updating cryptographic keys through key rotation practices is a fundamental security measure. This minimizes the risk associated with prolonged key usage, reducing the window of vulnerability in case of a compromise.

- **Secure Storage**: Ensuring secure storage of cryptographic keys is paramount. Employing secure key storage practices, such as encryption of stored keys and access controls, safeguards against unauthorized access or data breaches.
- **Access Controls**: Implementing stringent access controls is essential for restricting key access to authorized personnel only. Role-based access and least privilege principles help mitigate the risk of internal threats.
- **Auditing and Monitoring**: Regularly auditing key usage and monitoring key-related activities contribute to detecting anomalous behavior or potential security breaches. This proactive approach enhances the overall security posture.

Hardware Security Modules (HSMs) for Enhanced Key Security

Hardware Security Modules (HSMs) provide an added layer of security for cryptographic keys by offering a dedicated, tamper-resistant hardware environment. HSMs are specialized devices designed to securely generate, store, and manage cryptographic keys.

- **Physical Security**: HSMs are designed with physical security in mind, often housed in tamper-evident casings. This physical layer of protection prevents unauthorized access to the internal components of the module.
- **Key Generation and Storage**: HSMs excel in secure key generation and storage. The cryptographic keys never leave the HSM, ensuring that they remain protected against both physical and software-based attacks.
- **Secure Key Operations**: HSMs perform cryptographic operations within their secure boundary, preventing exposure of sensitive data during key operations. This ensures the confidentiality and integrity of cryptographic processes.
- **Compliance and Certification**: Many HSMs adhere to industry standards and undergo rigorous certification processes, assuring that they meet stringent security requirements. Compliance with standards enhances the credibility of the key management infrastructure.

PKI in Practice

This section delves into the real-world implementations of PKI, showcasing its pivotal role in securing various domains. We will explore how PKI is seamlessly integrated into protocols such as Secure Sockets Layer (SSL)/Transport Layer Security (TLS) for secure web communication and examine its widespread use in applications such as email encryption and code signing.

Real-world Examples of PKI Implementation

One of the most prevalent real-world implementations of PKI is witnessed in the realm of secure web communication through protocols such as SSL/TLS. When you navigate to a secure website, PKI plays a central role in establishing a secure connection. Digital certificates, issued by Certificate Authorities (CAs), authenticate the identity of the website, while public and private keys facilitate the encryption and decryption of data exchanged between the user's browser and the web server. This robust application ensures the confidentiality and integrity of online transactions, safeguarding sensitive information such as login credentials and payment details.

Furthermore, PKI finds widespread use in email encryption, a critical requirement for securing electronic communication. Through standards such as S/MIME (Secure/Multipurpose Internet Mail Extensions), PKI enables the encryption and digital signing of emails. Recipients can trust the sender's identity and ensure the confidentiality of the message content. This not only protects sensitive information but also verifies the authenticity of the sender.

Use of PKI in Email Encryption, Code Signing, and Other Applications

Beyond secure web communication, PKI plays a pivotal role in various applications, including email encryption and code signing. In the context of email encryption, PKI ensures the secure exchange of sensitive information. By digitally signing and encrypting emails, PKI provides end-to-end security, bolstering the confidentiality and authenticity of communication.

Code signing is another domain where PKI's influence is pronounced. Software developers utilize digital signatures generated through PKI to sign their code. This not only verifies the authenticity of the code but also ensures that it has not been tampered with during distribution. Users can trust the source and integrity of the software, mitigating the risks associated with malicious modifications.

Moreover, PKI finds applications in Virtual Private Networks (VPNs), document signing, and other secure communication channels, exemplifying its versatility across various domains. In practice, PKI's robust security mechanisms and versatility continue to make it a cornerstone in ensuring the trustworthiness and security of digital transactions and communications.

Challenges and Considerations

While PKI is a robust framework for securing digital communication, its implementation comes with its share of challenges and considerations. This section delves into the intricacies of PKI, addressing challenges related to implementation and exploring key considerations for scalability, interoperability, and compliance with industry standards. Understanding and mitigating these challenges is crucial for maintaining the effectiveness and security of PKI in diverse and dynamic digital landscapes.

Addressing Challenges in PKI Implementation

PKI implementation presents various challenges, and one of the foremost is the complexity associated with certificate management. The growing number of digital certificates, each requiring proper issuance, renewal, and revocation, can lead to management overhead. Effective management demands a clear understanding of certificate lifecycle processes to prevent issues such as expired certificates, which can compromise security.

Potential vulnerabilities also pose a challenge in PKI. A compromised Certificate Authority (CA) or a private key can undermine the entire infrastructure's trust. Regular audits, secure key storage practices, and stringent access controls are essential to mitigate these vulnerabilities. Additionally, the challenge of ensuring the secure distribution of public keys and digital certificates, especially in large-scale systems, requires careful consideration of secure channels and encryption mechanisms.

Considering Scalability, Interoperability, and Compliance

Scalability is a significant consideration in PKI, particularly as organizations grow and the demand for digital certificates increases. An effective PKI must scale seamlessly to accommodate the growing number of entities and devices without sacrificing performance or security. Strategies such as hierarchical PKI architectures and proper load balancing can enhance scalability.

Interoperability is crucial, especially in heterogeneous environments where different systems and applications coexist. Ensuring that digital certificates issued by one PKI can be recognized and trusted by other systems requires adherence to established standards such as X.509. Interoperability considerations extend beyond technology to encompass policy harmonization, enabling seamless collaboration in diverse ecosystems.

Compliance with industry standards is paramount for the effectiveness and trustworthiness of PKI. Adhering to standards such as X.509 ensures compatibility and trust in digital certificates across various platforms. Moreover, complying with regulations such as the General Data Protection Regulation (GDPR) and industry-specific standards is essential for maintaining legal and regulatory compliance.

Future Trends in Asymmetric Key Cryptography

Future trends in asymmetric key cryptography are shaped by advancements in technology, emerging security challenges, and the need for more efficient and secure cryptographic systems. Here are some key trends anticipated in the realm of asymmetric key cryptography:

Post-Quantum Cryptography

As the field of post-quantum cryptography advances, several specific advancements and approaches are being explored to address the potential threat posed by quantum computers. Here are some key areas of focus and advancements:

Lattice-Based Cryptography:

Lattice-based cryptography is one of the most promising approaches in the post-quantum era. It relies on the difficulty of certain lattice problems to provide security. Schemes such as Learning With Errors (LWE) and Ring-LWE form the basis of lattice-based cryptographic protocols.

Code-Based Cryptography:

Code-based cryptography leverages the hardness of decoding random linear codes to provide security against quantum attacks. The McEliece crypto system, based on error-correcting codes, is a notable example of a code-based approach.

Hash-Based Signatures:

Hash-based digital signatures, such as the Merkle Signature Scheme, are being explored as a quantum-resistant alternative. These schemes based on the security of hash functions provide a practical solution for secure digital signatures.

Multivariate Polynomial Cryptography:

Multivariate Polynomial Cryptography relies on the difficulty of solving systems of multivariate polynomial equations. It includes schemes like such as Rainbow digital signature scheme, which is resistant to quantum attacks.

Isogeny-Based Cryptography:

Isogeny-based cryptography is based on the mathematical structure of elliptic curves over finite fields. Schemes such as the Super singular Isogeny Diffie-Hellman (SIDH) key exchange provide quantum-resistant alternatives for secure key exchange.

Quantum Key Distribution (QKD):

Quantum Key Distribution offers a quantum-resistant key exchange method by leveraging the principles of quantum mechanics to secure the key exchange process. While QKD is not a universal replacement for classical public-key cryptography, it can serve as a direct substitute in certain scenarios, particularly when the highest level of security is required. This makes QKD an invaluable tool for environments demanding stringent confidentiality and resilience against future quantum computing threats.

Standardization Efforts:

International standardization efforts, such as those led by NIST (National Institute of Standards and Technology), play a crucial role. NIST's Post-Quantum Cryptography Standardization project aims to identify and standardize quantum-resistant cryptographic algorithms.

Integration with Existing Systems:

Smooth integration of post-quantum cryptographic algorithms with existing systems and protocols is a key consideration. Transition plans and compatibility with current infrastructure are important aspects of the ongoing research.

Quantum-Secure Blockchain:

Blockchain platforms are exploring quantum-resistant cryptographic algorithms to safeguard the security and integrity of transactions in a post-quantum environment. Quantum-safe consensus mechanisms and digital signatures are areas of interest.

Continuous Research and Evaluation:

As quantum algorithms and technologies evolve, continuous research and evaluation of cryptographic schemes are imperative. Ongoing efforts involve monitoring advancements in quantum computing and adapting cryptographic solutions accordingly.

Homomorphic Encryption

Homomorphic Encryption stands as a groundbreaking concept in cryptography, presenting a paradigm where computations can be performed on encrypted data without the need for decryption. This transformative approach addresses the fundamental challenge of preserving data privacy while allowing computations to be executed on encrypted content.

In recent years, Homomorphic Encryption has gained prominence and is positioned as a key player in addressing security and privacy concerns in data processing and cloud computing scenarios. The fundamental idea behind homomorphic encryption is to enable computations directly on encrypted data, ensuring that the confidentiality of sensitive information is maintained throughout the entire computation process.

Privacy-Preserving Computation:

Homomorphic Encryption allows computations on encrypted data, preserving the privacy of sensitive information. This is particularly valuable in scenarios where data needs to be outsourced for processing while maintaining confidentiality.

Secure Cloud Computing:

In the era of cloud computing, where data is often processed on external servers, homomorphic encryption has become a powerful tool. Users can delegate computations to the cloud without exposing the raw data, mitigating the risk of unauthorized access.

Data Confidentiality in Machine Learning:

Homomorphic Encryption finds applications in machine learning environments where privacy is paramount. It enables secure outsourcing of computations for tasks such as predictive modeling and data analysis while keeping the underlying data encrypted.

Homomorphic Encryption in Healthcare and Finance:

Sectors such as healthcare and finance, dealing with sensitive and regulated data, are exploring the potential of homomorphic encryption. It offers a means to perform computations on encrypted medical records or financial transactions without compromising confidentiality.

Blockchain and Cryptocurrencies

Blockchain technology, first introduced as the underlying architecture for Bitcoin, has since evolved into a transformative force with implications across various industries. At its core, a blockchain is a decentralized and distributed ledger that records transactions across a network of computers. This decentralized nature, combined with cryptographic principles, introduces a range of innovations and opportunities.

Decentralization and Trustless Transactions:

The hallmark of blockchain is its decentralization, eliminating the need for a central authority. This feature enhances transparency and trust in transactions, as every participant in the network has access to the same immutable record.

Cryptocurrencies as Digital Assets:

Cryptocurrencies, the most well-known application of blockchain, operate as digital or virtual currencies secured by cryptography. Bitcoin, Ethereum, and other cryptocurrencies utilize blockchain to enable secure, verifiable, and tamper-resistant transactions.

Decentralized Finance (DeFi):

Blockchain has given rise to decentralized finance, a movement aiming to recreate traditional financial systems without central authorities. DeFi platforms enable activities such as lending, borrowing, and trading without relying on traditional banks.

Tokenization of Assets:

Blockchain facilitates the tokenization of real-world assets, transforming physical assets such as real estate or art into digital tokens. This process enhances liquidity and accessibility to a broader range of investors.

Multi-Party Computation (MPC)

Multiparty Computation, a groundbreaking area in cryptography, focuses on enabling secure collaboration among multiple entities without revealing private information. This paradigm allows parties to jointly compute a function over their inputs while keeping those inputs confidential. Here are the key aspects and the significance of Multiparty Computation:

Privacy-Preserving Collaborations:

MPC ensures privacy by allowing multiple parties to jointly compute a function without revealing their individual inputs. This is particularly crucial in scenarios where data privacy is paramount, such as collaborative research, financial transactions, or healthcare applications.

Secure Function Evaluation:

MPC enables secure function evaluation, allowing parties to jointly compute a function while keeping their inputs confidential. This is achieved through cryptographic techniques that ensure each party learns only the output of the computation.

Distributed Trust and No Single Point of Failure:

MPC operates on the principle of distributed trust, eliminating the need for a single trusted party. No single participant has access to the complete input data, ensuring that even if one participant is compromised, the privacy of the entire dataset remains intact.

Applications in Sensitive Domains:

MPC finds applications in sensitive domains where parties need to collaborate on data analysis without revealing individual contributions. Examples include financial analyses, genomic research, and collaborative machine learning where privacy is crucial.

Threshold Cryptography:

Threshold cryptography, a subset of MPC, involves distributing cryptographic keys among multiple parties. It ensures that a certain threshold of parties must collaborate to perform cryptographic operations, adding an extra layer of security.

Zero-Knowledge Proofs

Zero-Knowledge Proofs (ZKPs) mark a revolutionary leap in cryptography, allowing entities to prove the validity of a statement without revealing any additional information. These proofs ensure that the verifier gains confidence in the authenticity of a claim while preserving the utmost confidentiality. ZKPs find extensive applications in diverse domains, from secure authentication to blockchain technology, particularly in decentralized systems where privacy and trust are paramount.

ZKPs are categorized into interactive and non-interactive forms and adhere to three key properties: completeness, soundness, and zero-knowledge. These properties ensure the reliability and privacy-preserving nature of the proof, making ZKPs indispensable for enhancing security and trust in cryptographic systems.

However, while ZKPs are powerful tools, they are not without limitations. Many implementations require interaction between the prover and verifier, which can complicate deployment in certain scenarios. Additionally, the computational and communication efficiency of ZKPs can pose challenges, particularly for resource-constrained environments or applications requiring high performance. Despite these challenges and ongoing research, ZKPs continue to play a crucial role in safeguarding sensitive information and facilitating secure interactions, solidifying their place as a cornerstone in modern cryptography.

Continuous Research in Cryptanalysis

Continuous research in asymmetric cryptanalysis is instrumental in the dynamic realm of cryptography, serving as a cornerstone for the robustness of asymmetric key algorithms. These algorithms play a pivotal role in ensuring secure communication by providing the foundation for confidentiality, integrity, and authenticity across various applications. The relentless commitment to cryptanalysis is driven by the need to identify vulnerabilities and weaknesses in existing algorithms, fostering innovation and the development of more resilient cryptographic techniques. In the face of evolving threats, such as those posed by quantum computing, continuous research becomes a proactive strategy to address potential security breaches.

The dynamism of the field, marked by emerging attack vectors and evolving technologies, underscores the necessity of ongoing research. By scrutinizing the mathematical foundations, implementation flaws, and potential exploits of asymmetric algorithms, researchers contribute invaluable insights that shape the design of cryptographic solutions capable of withstanding sophisticated attacks. This commitment to understanding and mitigating risks ensures that cryptographic systems remain adaptive, resilient, and well-prepared to counter emerging threats. Continuous research in asymmetric cryptanalysis thus plays a pivotal role in upholding the trust and security of digital communication in our ever-changing technological landscape.

Global Regulatory Landscape

The global regulatory landscape of asymmetric key cryptography plays a pivotal role in shaping the use and implementation of cryptographic technologies across various industries and jurisdictions. Regulatory frameworks and policies have a direct impact on the adoption, deployment, and management of asymmetric key algorithms, influencing how organizations approach security and privacy in their digital operations.

Standards and Compliance:

Governments and regulatory bodies often establish standards and compliance requirements for cryptographic practices. These standards may dictate the use of specific algorithms, key lengths, or implementation guidelines to ensure a minimum level of security.

Data Protection and Privacy Laws:

Asymmetric key cryptography is integral to data protection and privacy laws worldwide. Regulations such as the General Data Protection Regulation (GDPR) in the European Union mandate the use of robust cryptographic measures to safeguard sensitive information.

Export Controls:

Some countries impose export controls on cryptographic technologies to prevent the proliferation of strong encryption tools. This can impact the global availability and distribution of certain asymmetric key algorithms.

National Security Considerations:

Governments may enact regulations with national security considerations in mind. This can involve restrictions on using specific cryptographic techniques or implementing backdoors for law enforcement access.

Financial Sector Compliance:

The financial sector is often subject to specific regulations governing the use of cryptographic technologies for securing financial transactions. Compliance requirements may include adherence to certain encryption standards and practices.

Cross-Border Data Transfers:

Regulations surrounding cross-border data transfers may require organizations to implement strong cryptographic measures to protect data during transit. Asymmetric key cryptography is instrumental in securing these data transfers.

Conclusion

Throughout this chapter on asymmetric key cryptography, we embarked on a comprehensive exploration of the fundamental principles, key algorithms, and real-world applications shaping the landscape of secure communication. Beginning with an introduction that delved into the historical significance and evolution of asymmetric key cryptography, we elucidated the foundational concepts underpinning this cryptographic paradigm.

The heart of our discussion revolved around key asymmetric algorithms, such as RSA, ECC, and ECDSA. We dissected their structures, elucidated encryption and decryption processes, and provided implementational insights to offer a nuanced understanding of their practical applications. Furthermore, our exploration extended to the intricate workings of public key infrastructure (PKI), shedding light on the orchestration of digital certificates, key generation, and secure key distribution.

As we delved into the contemporary trends, we addressed the paradigm shift propelled by the advent of quantum computers, necessitating research into post-quantum cryptographic algorithms. We also examined the burgeoning realms of homomorphic encryption, blockchain, multiparty computation, zero-knowledge proofs, and continuous research in asymmetric cryptanalysis, offering glimpses into the evolving frontiers of cryptographic innovation.

In conclusion, this chapter not only demystified the intricacies of asymmetric key cryptography but also provided a roadmap for navigating the complex terrain of modern cryptographic technologies. Armed with foundational knowledge and insights into cutting-edge developments, readers are equipped to navigate the dynamic world of asymmetric key cryptography, poised at the intersection of security, privacy, and technological advancement. Looking ahead, our exploration continues into the realm of hashing algorithms in the next chapter, where we will unravel their significance and explore their applications in securing data integrity.

CHAPTER 5
Hashing

Introduction

Embarking on a new chapter, we delve into the realms of Hashing, a pivotal concept in cryptography that holds the keys to secure information processing. As we navigate through this expansive landscape, we'll explore the multifaceted aspects of hash functions, which distill data into fixed-size hash values. Our journey encompasses an in-depth understanding of the properties that characterize robust hash functions, unraveling the cryptographic and non-cryptographic distinctions.

In the vast tapestry of cryptography, hash functions stand as silent sentinels, transforming variable-length data into fixed-length hash values. This transformation is not arbitrary; it adheres to a set of principles that define the efficacy and reliability of hash functions. As we venture deeper into this chapter, we'll unravel the intricacies of these principles, exploring collision resistance, preimage resistance, and the avalanche effect. These properties form the bedrock of a secure hash function, ensuring that even minor changes in input produce radically different hash outputs.

A key facet of our exploration is the diverse application landscape of hash functions. From bolstering password security through hashing and salting to safeguarding digital signatures in public-key cryptography, hash functions play a pivotal role in fortifying the security infrastructure. Moreover, we'll examine their applications in hash tables, checksums, and data integrity verification, showcasing the versatility that makes hash functions indispensable in modern cryptographic protocols.

Throughout this exploration, our aim is to elucidate the significance of hashing in our digital world, providing insights into the mechanisms that underpin its efficacy. We strive to bridge the theoretical foundations of hashing with its real-world implementations, offering a comprehensive perspective that spans from fundamental principles to practical applications. Join us on this enlightening journey as we dissect and comprehend the power of hashing in securing information and ensuring the integrity of our digital interactions.

Structure

In this chapter, the following topics will be covered:

- Introduction to Hash Functions
- Properties of Hash Functions
- Common Hash Functions
- Applications in Cryptography
- Hash Collision Countermeasures
- Security Considerations and Best Practices

Introduction to Hash Functions

In the realm of cryptography, a hash function stands as a computational algorithm designed with specific attributes to perform a crucial role. At its core, this cryptographic tool functions as a mechanism for transforming input data, which may vary in length, into a standardized and fixed-length hash value. This process is integral for various cryptographic applications, providing a means to represent diverse datasets in a uniform and condensed manner. The significance of hash functions lies in their ability to create a unique "digital fingerprint" for any given input, establishing a consistent and recognizable representation.

Role in Data Transformation

The paramount role of hash functions revolves around their capability to undertake data transformation. Irrespective of the input's original length or complexity, a hash function processes it into a fixed-size output. This transformation serves cryptographic purposes by creating a uniform representation of data. Consequently, hash functions are employed in scenarios where maintaining consistent data formats is essential, such as in digital signatures or ensuring data integrity during transmission.

Deterministic Operation

An essential characteristic defining hash functions is their deterministic nature. Determinism in this context implies that for any specific input, the hash function will unfailingly produce the same hash output. This predictability is foundational for cryptographic protocols, ensuring that verification processes and comparisons remain reliable. The deterministic operation of hash functions provides stability and consistency, vital for their widespread use in cryptographic applications.

Cryptographic and Non-cryptographic Hash Function

Hash algorithms can be categorized into two main types: cryptographic and non-cryptographic. Cryptographic hash functions are specifically designed for use in security applications. They possess certain essential properties, including collision resistance, preimage resistance, and the avalanche effect, making them suitable for applications, such as data integrity verification, digital signatures, and password storage. These hash functions play a critical role in ensuring the security of various cryptographic protocols. On the other hand, non-cryptographic hash functions are designed for efficiency rather than security. They are often used in applications where the main focus is on speed and simplicity rather than resistance to malicious attacks. Examples of non-cryptographic hash functions include those used in hash tables for fast data retrieval. Understanding the distinction between cryptographic and non-cryptographic hash functions is crucial for selecting the appropriate algorithm based on the specific requirements of the application at hand. In this book, we will only discuss cryptographic hash-related concepts.

Property	Cryptographic Hash Function	Non-cryptographic Hash Function
Security Properties	Designed with security in mind, emphasizing, collision resistance, preimage resistance, and the avalanche effect	Primarily designed for efficiency, lacking emphasis on collision and preimage resistance
Use Cases	Commonly used in security-critical applications such as digital signatures and password storage	Used in non-security-critical applications such as hash tables for efficient data retrieval
Performance	Generally slower; optimized for security rather than speed	Typically faster; optimized for speed and simplicity
Algorithm Complexity	More complex algorithms with a focus on cryptographic strength	Simpler algorithms, often sacrificing complexity for performance
Collision Resistance	Strong emphasis on collision resistance, making it computationally infeasible to find two different inputs with the same hash output	Less emphasis on collision resistance

Preimage Resistance	Emphasis on preimage resistance, ensuring it is computationally infeasible to determine the original input from its hash	Less emphasis on preimage resistance
Avalanche Effect	Exhibits a strong avalanche effect, where a small change in input results in a significantly different hash output	May or may not exhibit a strong avalanche effect; this depends on the specific implementation

***Table 5.1**: Comparison between Cryptographic and non-Cryptographic Hash Functions*

Properties of Hash Functions

Hash functions are integral to cryptographic systems, serving as tools for data integrity, authentication, and security. Their effectiveness hinges on specific properties, each addressing a unique aspect of reliability and resilience against attacks.

Collision Resistance

Collision resistance is a fundamental property of hash functions in cryptography, ensuring that it is exceptionally challenging to find two distinct inputs that produce the same hash output. In simpler terms, a hash function is deemed collision-resistant if it effectively prevents the creation of identical hash values for different input data. This property is essential for maintaining the integrity and security of cryptographic applications that rely on hash functions.

Let H be a hash function that takes an input X and produces a fixed-length hash output H(X). The collision resistance property can be defined as:

For any two distinct inputs X_1 and X_2, it should be computationally infeasible to find a pair (X_1, X_2) such that $H(X_1) = H(X_2)$.

In mathematical term, for a given hash function H, there should not exist any feasible algorithm A such that:

$$A(H, X_1, X_2) = (X_1, X_2) \text{ where } H(X_1) = H(X_2).$$

Emphasizing Computational Infeasibility for Collision

The heart of collision resistance lies in the computational infeasibility of discovering two unique inputs that result in identical hash outputs. The complexity of this task grows exponentially with the length of the hash output. While theoretically possible to find collisions through a brute-force search (trying all possible inputs), the astronomical number of potential combinations renders this approach practically impossible within a reasonable timeframe. As such, collision resistance relies on the fact that, even with significant computational resources, finding collisions remains a formidable challenge, ensuring the robustness of hash functions against malicious attacks.

One-to-One Mapping Principle

The one-to-one mapping principle underpins the effectiveness of cryptographic hash functions, ensuring that unique inputs produce unique outputs. This behavior forms the foundation for maintaining data integrity and preventing security risks associated with hash collisions. To achieve this principle, hash functions are designed to ideally exhibit certain characteristics.

Ideal Behavior of Hash Functions:

The one-to-one mapping principle in hash functions refers to the desired property where each unique input (X) results in a distinct hash output (H(X)). Mathematically, this is expressed as:

$$\forall X_1, X_2 \text{ where } X_1 \neq X_2, H(X_1) \neq H(X_2)$$

This property ensures that no two different inputs produce the same hash value, contributing to the uniform distribution of hash outputs across the function's output space.

Importance of One-to-One Mapping:

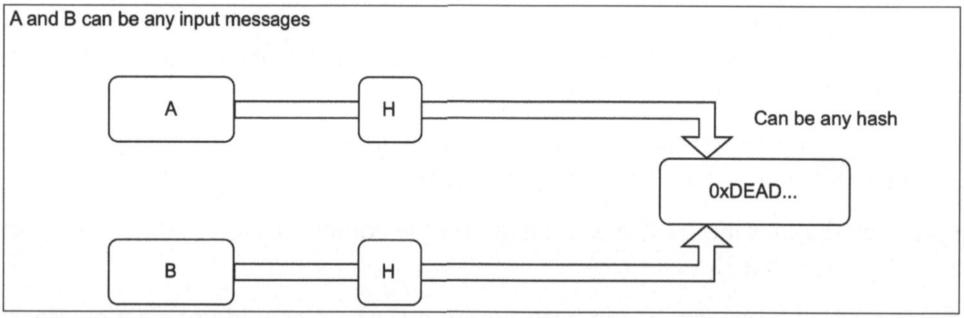

***Figure 5.1**: Hash Collision Attack on Hash Algorithm H*

Maintaining the one-to-one mapping principle is crucial for the reliability and security of hash functions. When each input uniquely maps to a hash value, it minimizes the occurrence of collisions. Collisions, where different inputs produce the same hash output, pose a significant risk to cryptographic applications. The one-to-one mapping principle helps prevent unintended relationships between inputs and ensures the integrity and unpredictability of the hash function. Deviations from this principle could introduce vulnerabilities and compromise the desired cryptographic properties.

Vulnerabilities Introduced by Collisions

Collisions in cryptographic hash functions introduce vulnerabilities that can undermine the security of various protocols. When two different inputs (A, B) produce the same hash output (0xDEAD...), it opens the door to potential attacks. One significant threat is the possibility of attackers creating a malicious input (M_2) that collides with a legitimate input, (M_1) - $H(M_1) = H(M_2)$. This collision can lead to unauthorized activities, such as forged digital signatures, password alterations, or manipulated integrity checks. The computational infeasibility of finding collisions is what provides the security of hash functions, and any compromise to this property poses a serious risk.

Preimage Resistance

In cryptographic hash functions, pre-image resistance is a fundamental property that emphasizes the challenge of deducing the original input (x) from its hash output ($H(x)$). The primary objective is to ensure that, given a hash value, it remains computationally infeasible to reconstruct the precise input that generated it. Pre-image resistance plays a pivotal role in preserving data confidentiality and thwarting reverse engineering attempts.

Mathematical Definition

For a hash function H, pre-image resistance is upheld when, for any given hash value h, finding a specific input x such that $H(x) = h$ is computationally infeasible. The mathematical challenge lies in preventing adversaries from efficiently determining the original data corresponding to a known hash.

Importance of Preimage Resistance

The importance of pre-image resistance extends to numerous cryptographic applications, as it ensures that hashed data remains secure and unrecoverable by malicious actors. By guaranteeing that it is computationally impractical to reverse a hash to its original input, pre-image resistance serves as a crucial safeguard in protecting sensitive information across various security protocols.

Confidentiality Assurance:

Pre-image resistance ensures that hashed data cannot be easily reversed to expose sensitive information, maintaining the confidentiality of the original input.

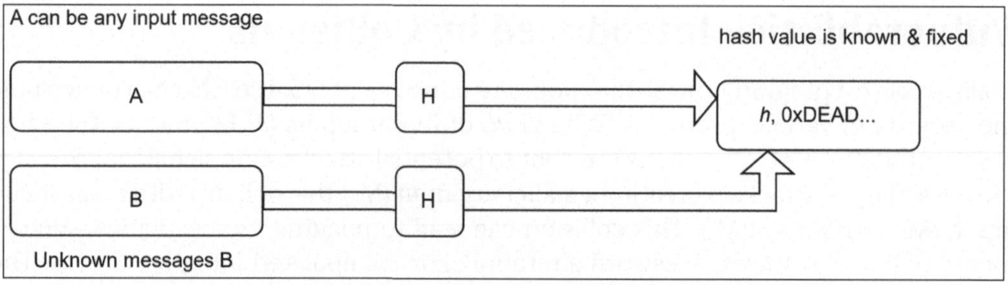

***Figure 5.2**: Preimage Attack on Hash Algorithm H*

Security in Cryptographic Protocols:

Cryptographic protocols often rely on the irreversible nature of hash functions to enhance the security of various operations, such as digital signatures and integrity verification.

Mathematical Challenge

Given $h = H(B)$, the difficulty lies in making it practically impossible for an adversary to find B within a reasonable timeframe. This mathematical hurdle ensures that hash functions remain resilient against reverse engineering attacks.

Exposed Preimage Attacks

While hash functions are designed to be preimage resistant, some well-known algorithms have faced vulnerabilities over time. For instance, certain hash functions such as MD5 and SHA-1 have experienced practical preimage attacks, where researchers demonstrated the ability to find specific inputs corresponding to given hash values, highlighting the importance of using robust hash functions.

Property	**Collision Resistance**	**Preimage Resistance**
Objective	Prevent finding two different inputs producing the same hash	Prevent finding the original input given a hash value
Mathematical Definition	$H(x_1) = H(x_2)$, $x_1 != x_2$, finding such x_1, x_2 is hard	$H(x) = h$, finding x for known h is computationally hard
Common Attacks	Birthday attacks, where the probability of collision increases	Reverse engineering attempts to deduce the original input
Impact on Security	Collisions may compromise integrity but often don't reveal the data	Exposure of the original data may lead to severe security breaches

Applications	Relevant in scenarios where distinct inputs may produce the same outcome	Crucial for maintaining the confidentiality of hashed data

***Table 5.2**: Comparison between Collision Resistance and Pre-image Resistance*

Avalanche Effect

The avalanche effect is a fundamental property of cryptographic hash functions, ensuring that a small change in the input leads to a significantly different hash output. This property plays a crucial role in enhancing the sensitivity of hash functions to even minor alterations in the input data. Let's explore the key aspects of the avalanche effect:

Definition:

The avalanche effect dictates that a minute change in the input should cause a cascade of changes throughout the hash output.

Ideal Behavior:

- It is designed to prevent any patterns or relationships between similar inputs and their corresponding hash outputs.
- In an ideal hash function with the avalanche effect, modifying just one bit of the input should completely alter the resulting hash value.
- The effect ensures unpredictability, making it computationally infeasible for attackers to exploit similarities in the input for information retrieval.
- The avalanche effect adds complexity and uncertainty, making reverse engineering and data retrieval exceptionally challenging.

It is a cornerstone in the design and evaluation of robust cryptographic hash functions. The avalanche effect significantly contributes to the effectiveness of hash functions in protecting data integrity and confidentiality.

Common Hash Functions

In the realm of hashing, where the integrity and security of data are paramount, the discussion naturally extends to specific hash functions with distinct characteristics. Having explored the foundational properties of hash algorithms in the preceding section, we now turn our attention to noteworthy examples. In this chapter, our focus gravitates toward the MD5 algorithm and the SHA family (including SHA-1, SHA-256, and others) family. These algorithms play pivotal roles in various applications, and our exploration will delve into their unique features, applications, and considerations in the cryptographic landscape.

MD5 (Message Digest 5)

MD5 (Message Digest Algorithm 5) stands as one of the earliest and most well-known cryptographic hash functions. Developed by Ronald Rivest in 1991, MD5 was designed to produce a 128-bit hash value (32 hexadecimal characters) and became widely adopted for various applications, including data integrity verification and password storage.

The primary purpose of MD5 is to take an input message and generate a fixed-size hash value, commonly referred to as a digest. The algorithm employs a series of logical functions, bitwise operations, and modular arithmetic to transform the input data into a compact representation. MD5's properties include being deterministic (producing the same output for the same input), quick computation, and producing a fixed-size output.

Working Principle

MD5 processes the input message in 512-bit blocks, breaking it down into smaller segments before applying a series of mathematical operations.

Initialization:

a. Initialize four 32-bit variables (A, B, C, D) with specific constant values

Padding:

a. Append a '1' bit to the input message

b. Append '0' bits until the length of the message is 64 bits less than a multiple of 512

c. Append the length of the original message as a 64-bit integer

Processing:

a. Break the padded message into 512-bit blocks

b. Process each block in four rounds (16 operations per round)

Processing Each Block:

a. For each 512-bit block, perform operations using bitwise functions and logical functions

Update Variables (A, B, C, D):

a. Update A, B, C, and D after each round using specific mathematical operations

Output:

a. Concatenate the final values of A, B, C, and D to obtain the 128-bit hash value

Security Vulnerabilities of MD5

While MD5 was a groundbreaking hash function in its time, it has since become known for its significant security vulnerabilities. These vulnerabilities, particularly around collision resistance, have made MD5 unsuitable for cryptographic applications today. Two main types of attacks–collision attacks and the birthday attack–demonstrate how easily MD5's collision resistance can be broken, compromising its security and reliability.

Collision Attacks

A collision attack is a method of finding two different inputs that produce the same hash value. This directly undermines one of the primary properties of a secure hash function: collision resistance. In MD5, it has become computationally feasible to generate such collisions, due in part to the hash function's 128-bit output size, which does not provide a sufficient level of collision resistance for modern security needs.

In 2004, researchers were able to create two distinct inputs with identical MD5 hashes within a reasonable time frame. This achievement exposed MD5's vulnerability, as it allowed attackers to create malicious files or messages that would pass verification checks if an MD5 hash was used as the integrity measure. For example, in digital signature applications, a malicious actor could craft a fraudulent message that yields the same MD5 hash as a legitimate signed document, undermining the security and trustworthiness of the digital signature.

Birthday Attack

The birthday attack is a specific type of collision attack that exploits the mathematics of probability, particularly in scenarios where the probability of finding a match increases significantly as the number of hashed values grows. In the context of MD5, the birthday paradox highlights that the probability of a collision is much higher than expected due to MD5's 128-bit hash length, which is insufficient to prevent collisions in high-security applications.

The birthday attack on MD5 works by exploiting this probability phenomenon. Given the 128-bit hash size, a collision can typically be found in approximately 2^{64} operations, which, while a large number, is achievable with modern computational power. This attack has become easier as technology advances, making it increasingly feasible for attackers to exploit MD5-based systems through these probabilistic techniques.

Practical Implications of MD5 Vulnerabilities

The practical implications of these vulnerabilities in MD5 are severe, as the algorithm is susceptible to being compromised for purposes such as:

- **Digital Signature Forgery**: By creating a fraudulent document that matches the hash of a legitimate signed document, an attacker can deceive verification systems.
- **Malicious File Tampering**: Attackers can manipulate files or messages to match the hash of an authentic file, allowing malicious payloads to evade detection in systems where MD5 is used for integrity checks.
- **Password Cracking**: Due to MD5's vulnerabilities, it is more susceptible to dictionary and brute-force attacks, making it insecure for password hashing in modern applications.

Depreciation and Replacement

Due to these serious vulnerabilities, MD5 has been deprecated in cryptographic applications where data integrity, authentication, and collision resistance are critical. Security standards and organizations, including NIST, recommend transitioning to more secure hash functions, such as those in the SHA-2 family (for example, SHA-256), which offer stronger collision resistance and longer hash lengths, mitigating the risks associated with collision and birthday attacks.

SHA Algorithm: A Pillar of Cryptography

The SHA (Secure Hash Algorithm) family is a cornerstone of modern cryptographic applications, providing a robust and efficient means of ensuring data integrity and authenticity. Developed by the National Security Agency (NSA) and published by the National Institute of Standards and Technology (NIST), SHA algorithms have become widely adopted and play a crucial role in various security protocols.

History and Significance

The history of the SHA (Secure Hash Algorithm) family is a fascinating journey through the evolution of cryptographic standards, driven by the need for stronger security in the face of emerging threats. Developed by the National Security Agency (NSA) and published by the National Institute of Standards and Technology (NIST), SHA algorithms have become the bedrock of data integrity and digital signatures.

The journey began with the realization of vulnerabilities in earlier hash algorithms such as MD5 and SHA-1. MD5, once considered robust, faced issues related to collision resistance, where distinct inputs produced the same hash output. SHA-1, while an improvement, also exhibited collision vulnerabilities over time. In response to these challenges, the SHA-2 family was introduced in 2001, featuring variants like SHA-224, SHA-256, SHA-384, SHA-512, SHA-512/224, and SHA-512/256. This marked a pivotal moment in the cryptographic landscape, providing a more secure foundation for hashing.

Significance in Cryptography:

The significance of SHA algorithms in cryptography cannot be overstated. These algorithms offer a one-way function that transforms variable-length input into a fixed-length hash value. The resulting hash acts as a digital fingerprint, unique to the input data. This property is fundamental in digital signatures, password hashing, and blockchain technology, where data integrity and authenticity are paramount.

Adoption and Standardization:

Over the years, SHA algorithms have been widely adopted as standard cryptographic primitives. NIST's publication and endorsement have led to their incorporation into various security protocols and applications worldwide. SHA-256, in particular, has become the *de facto* standard in many cryptographic systems, ensuring compatibility and interoperability.

Continuous Evolution and SHA-3:

The cryptographic landscape is dynamic, with researchers and developers constantly striving to stay ahead of potential threats. In 2015, NIST introduced the SHA-3 family as a proactive step to address future vulnerabilities and provide an alternative to SHA-2. SHA-3 employs a different underlying structure known as Keccak, offering diversity in the cryptographic toolkit.

Working Principle

The fundamental working principles are consistent across different members of the SHA family, such as SHA-1, SHA-256, and SHA-3. Here is an overview of the working principles with an example code implementing SHA-256 using hashlib python library,

```
import hashlib

def generate_sha256_hash(data):
    # Use hashlib library to create a SHA-256 hash object
    sha256_hash = hashlib.sha256()

    # Update the hash object with the data to be hashed
    sha256_hash.update(data.encode('utf-8'))

    # Get the hexadecimal representation of the hash
    hashed_data = sha256_hash.hexdigest()
```

```
    return hashed_data

def generate_sha3_hash(data):
    # Use hashlib library to create a SHA-3 (Keccak) hash object
    sha3_hash = hashlib.sha3_256()  # SHA-3 with 256-bit digest size

    # Update the hash object with the data to be hashed
    sha3_hash.update(data.encode('utf-8'))

    # Get the hexadecimal representation of the hash
    hashed_data = sha3_hash.hexdigest()

    return hashed_data

# Example Usage:
data_to_hash = "Hello, World!"

# Generate SHA-256 hash
sha256_result = generate_sha256_hash(data_to_hash)
print(f'SHA-256 Hash: {sha256_result}')

# Generate SHA-3 (Keccak) hash
sha3_result = generate_sha3_hash(data_to_hash)
print(f'SHA-3 Hash: {sha3_result}')
```

Message Padding:

SHA algorithms process data in fixed-size blocks. If the last block is not of the required size, padding is applied to meet the block size. The padding includes the original message length, ensuring a consistent block size for processing.

Initialization Vector (IV) Setup:

Each SHA algorithm uses a predefined initialization vector, also known as a chaining variable, to begin the hashing process. The IV is specified in the algorithm's design and plays a crucial role in generating a unique hash.

Breaking Input into Blocks:

The input message is divided into blocks of a fixed size. For instance, SHA-256 processes data in 512-bit blocks. Each block undergoes a series of operations in the compression function.

Compression Function:

The compression function is the core of SHA algorithms. It takes the current hash value (initially set as the IV) and the current block of data as inputs. The compression function applies a series of bitwise operations, logical functions, and modular addition to mix the inputs and produce a new hash value.

Iteration:

The process is iterated for each block of data, with the hash value updated at each step. The final hash value is the result of processing the entire input message.

Output Hash Value:

The resulting hash value is a fixed-size digest that is unique to the input data. It serves as a digital fingerprint, representing the integrity and authenticity of the original message.

In summary, the working principle of SHA algorithms involves dividing the input into blocks, applying a compression function iteratively, and producing a fixed-size hash value. The process is designed to be deterministic, providing a consistent and unique hash for a given input.

The implementation code of SHA shows how to use Python's hashlib library to generate SHA-256 and SHA-3 (Keccak) hash values. The code includes comments indicating where you can make configuration changes such as choosing a different SHA algorithm. You can customize the data_to_hash variable with your own data. Additionally, if you need a different SHA algorithm or digest size, you can modify the hashlib function calls accordingly. For example, you can use hashlib.sha3_512() for SHA-3 with a 512-bit digest size.

Vulnerabilities and Evaluation

The SHA family is considered secure for most cryptographic purposes. However, it's important to note that vulnerabilities can be discovered over time due to advancements in cryptanalysis and computing power. Here are some potential vulnerabilities and concerns related to SHA algorithms:

Length Extension Attacks:

Some SHA algorithms, especially the older ones such as SHA-1, are susceptible to length extension attacks. Attackers can extend a hash without knowing the secret key by exploiting the way these algorithms process input.

Collision Attacks:

While no practical collision has been found for SHA-2, theoretical vulnerabilities always exist in cryptographic algorithms. As computing power increases, the potential for collision attacks also rises.

Theoretical Concerns:

Cryptographers always look for potential weaknesses in algorithms, even if they are not currently exploitable. Researchers may discover new attack vectors or mathematical vulnerabilities in the future.

Quantum Computing:

The advent of quantum computers could potentially threaten the security of traditional cryptographic algorithms, including SHA. Shor's algorithm, for instance, could efficiently solve certain mathematical problems upon which many cryptographic protocols rely.

SHA-1 Deprecation:

SHA-1 is considered broken for cryptographic purposes due to practical collision attacks. It's deprecated in favor of stronger hash functions such as SHA-256. Organizations are encouraged to migrate to stronger algorithms.

Applications in Cryptography

Understanding the applications of hash algorithms in cryptography is crucial for building secure and reliable systems that can protect sensitive information and ensure the trustworthiness of data and communications. Here are some key points about the application of hash algorithms in cryptography:

Data Integrity

Hash algorithms are integral to ensuring the integrity of data by generating unique hash values or digests for each piece of information. These hash values serve as digital fingerprints, and any changes to the data result in a distinct hash value. This process creates a tamper detection mechanism, as even the slightest modification to the data will lead to a different hash value.

The computed hash values are commonly stored or transmitted alongside the corresponding data. Recipients can independently calculate the hash of received data and compare it to the originally provided hash value. A mismatch alerts the users to potential tampering or corruption, ensuring the detection of unauthorized alterations.

This approach is crucial in preventing undetected modifications to data. Even a minor change in the original data results in a substantially different hash value, making it highly effective in identifying tampering. Hash algorithms find applications in file verification, enabling users to verify the integrity of files by comparing hash values before and after transmission.

Moreover, in secure software distribution, developers often provide hash values for users to verify the integrity of downloaded files. This practice ensures that the software has not been compromised during the download process. Hash functions are also employed to generate checksums for data during transmission, enabling the prompt detection of errors or alterations in transmitted data.

Digital Signatures

Digital signatures, a crucial aspect of secure communication and digital transactions, heavily rely on hash algorithms to provide integrity, authenticity, and non-repudiation. Hash algorithms play a pivotal role in this process by condensing variable-length messages into fixed-size hash values, commonly referred to as message digests. The integration of hash functions in digital signatures enhances security and computational efficiency.

In the context of digital signatures, the process typically begins with the sender applying a hash function to the entire message. This produces a hash value or message digest that uniquely represents the content of the message. The fixed-size nature of the hash value simplifies the subsequent encryption process. The sender then encrypts this hash value using their private key, creating the digital signature.

The recipient, upon receiving the digitally signed message, uses the sender's public key to decrypt the signature. This decryption yields the original hash value. Simultaneously, the recipient independently calculates the hash value of the received message using the same hash function. A successful match between the decrypted hash and the independently calculated hash indicates that the message has not been tampered with during transmission.

The use of hash algorithms in digital signatures ensures the integrity of the message, as any alteration to the original content would result in a different hash value. This tamper-evident property is crucial for detecting and preventing unauthorized modifications to messages. Additionally, the public key infrastructure (PKI) ensures that only the sender's private key can generate a valid signature, establishing the authenticity of the sender and providing non-repudiation.

The efficiency of digital signatures is notable, thanks to the involvement of hash functions. Instead of encrypting the entire message, only the fixed-size hash value is encrypted, reducing computational overhead. This is particularly important in scenarios with limited computational resources or high-volume transaction environments.

In essence, the use of hash algorithms in digital signatures ensures a robust and reliable mechanism for securing digital communications. This cryptographic approach has found widespread application in fields such as financial transactions, legal documentation, and secure data exchanges, where the assurance of message integrity and the verification of sender authenticity are paramount. The integration of hash functions in digital signatures reflects a foundational element in modern cryptographic practices, contributing significantly to the establishment of trust and security in digital interactions.

Password Storage

Hash functions are commonly employed to store passwords securely in databases. Instead of storing plaintext passwords, systems store the hash values generated by applying a hash function to the passwords. This adds a layer of protection, as even if the database is compromised, attackers won't have direct access to the actual passwords. During the authentication process, when a user enters their password, the system hashes the entered password and compares it to the stored hash. This way, the system can verify the user's identity without exposing sensitive information. The use of hash functions for password storage enhances security by protecting user credentials and mitigating the impact of potential data breaches.

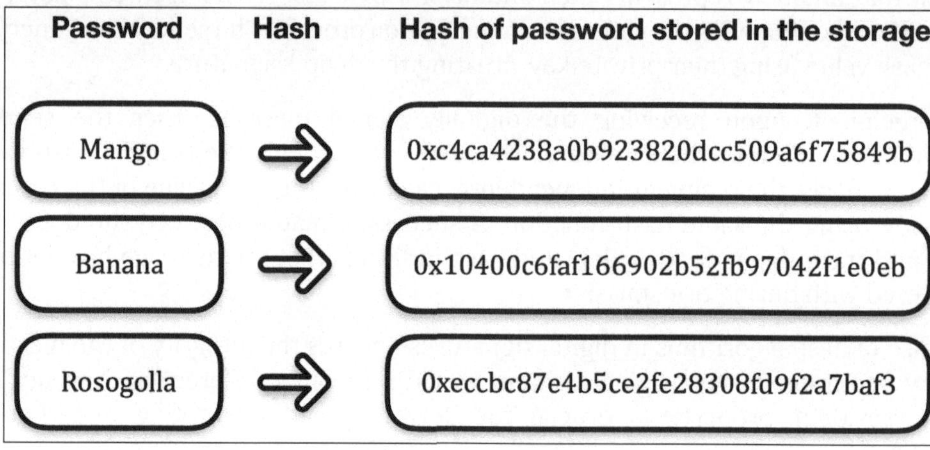

***Figure 5.3**: Password Storage using Hashing of the actual password*

Additionally, Salting- a technique involving adding a unique random value to each password before hashing–further strengthens the security of password storage systems by making it difficult for attackers to use precomputed hash tables (rainbow tables) to guess passwords. Salting is also valuable beyond password storage, as it can be applied to other sensitive data, such as unique identifiers, to prevent exposure of patterns in hashed outputs. This helps in protecting privacy and maintaining data security across various applications where hashing is used.

Blockchain Technology

Hash functions play a pivotal role in the fundamental mechanics and security of blockchain technology. At the heart of blockchain's structure is the use of cryptographic hash functions to create a secure and unalterable chain of blocks. Each block contains a hash of the previous block, forming a linked sequence. The irreversible nature of cryptographic hashes ensures that changing any block in the chain would require changing all subsequent blocks, providing a robust defense against tampering.

In addition to linking blocks, hash functions are employed in Merkle trees, a data structure that efficiently organizes transaction data within a block. The Merkle tree condenses individual transactions into a single hash at the top, known as the Merkle root. This enables nodes to verify the integrity of specific transactions without needing the entire block, enhancing the overall efficiency of blockchain networks.

Hash functions are also integral to the Proof of Work (PoW) consensus mechanism, a crucial component of many blockchain protocols. Miners engage in a computational race to find a nonce that, when hashed with the block data, produces a hash value below a predetermined target. This energy-intensive process adds new blocks to the blockchain, providing security against malicious actors and maintaining the integrity of the distributed ledger.

Overall, hash functions in blockchain technology ensure data integrity, immutability, and security. They play a vital role in creating a decentralized, transparent, and tamper-resistant system for recording and verifying transactions, forming the basis of trust in the digital realm.

Random Number and Key Derivation

Hash functions serve multiple critical roles in the realm of cryptography, extending their application beyond data integrity and blockchain technology. Two notable areas where hash functions play a significant role are in generating random numbers and key derivation.

Random Number Generation:

Hash functions are commonly employed in the generation of pseudo-random numbers. By taking an initial seed value and hashing it iteratively, a sequence of values is produced that appears random but is inherently deterministic. This means that the same seed will always generate the same sequence, making these numbers predictable in nature despite their seemingly random distribution. It is important to distinguish pseudo-random numbers from true random numbers: pseudo-random numbers are algorithmically generated and reproducible, whereas true random numbers are inherently unpredictable and cannot be reproduced. The pseudo-randomness provided by hash functions is particularly valuable in cryptographic applications, simulations, and scenarios requiring consistent yet non-reproducible sequences of numbers.

Key Derivation:

Hash functions play a crucial role in key derivation functions (KDFs), which are essential in securely deriving cryptographic keys from a given input. In scenarios like password-based key derivation, a user's password is hashed using a KDF to generate a strong cryptographic key. This process adds a layer of security by ensuring that even if the password is compromised, the derived key remains secure. Salting, a technique of adding a unique random value to each input before hashing, further enhances security, preventing precomputed attacks.

In both random number generation and key derivation, the properties of hash functions, such as determinism, irreversibility, and resistance to collisions, contribute to the security and reliability of these processes. The deterministic nature ensures consistency in random number generation, and the one-way function property of hash functions strengthens the security of key derivation. These applications demonstrate the versatility and significance of hash functions in various cryptographic contexts, enabling the creation of secure and unpredictable elements crucial for safeguarding sensitive information.

Message Authentication Codes (MACs)

Message Authentication Codes (MACs) represent a vital component of cryptographic protocols, ensuring both the authenticity and integrity of transmitted messages. Hash functions play a pivotal role within MACs, contributing to their robustness and reliability.

In the context of MACs, a secret key is employed to enhance the security of the authentication process. The sender combines this secret key with the message using a hash function. The resulting hash value, often referred to as the MAC, serves as a unique and cryptographic tag for the message. This MAC is then transmitted along with the original message to the recipient.

The recipient, possessing the shared secret key, repeats the process by combining the received message with the secret key and applying the same hash function. The generated MAC is compared with the transmitted MAC. If the two match, it verifies both the authenticity and integrity of the message. The use of the secret key ensures that only entities possessing the correct key can generate a valid MAC, thereby preventing unauthorized parties from tampering with the message.

One of the advantages of using hash functions in MACs is their one-way nature. Even if the MAC is intercepted, it should be computationally infeasible for an attacker to derive the original message or the secret key from the transmitted MAC. Additionally, the collision-resistant property of hash functions enhances the security of MACs, reducing the likelihood of different messages producing the same MAC.

This application of hash functions in MACs is widespread in secure communication protocols, such as in the generation of HMACs (Hash-based Message Authentication Codes). HMACs, a specific type of MAC, combine the characteristics of a hash function and a secret key to provide a robust mechanism for verifying the authenticity and integrity of messages. The utilization of hash functions in MACs stands as a testament to their versatility in cryptographic applications, contributing significantly to the establishment of secure and trustworthy communication channels.

Hash Collision Countermeasures

In our earlier discussions, we delved into the concept of hash collisions, where distinct inputs yield the same hash value, presenting a potential vulnerability in hash functions. As we've highlighted, collision attacks can undermine the integrity and security of cryptographic applications that rely on hash functions. Now, understanding and implementing effective countermeasures to mitigate the risks associated with hash collisions becomes paramount.

Countermeasures Against Hash Collisions:

Choose a Cryptographically Secure Hash Function

Selecting a cryptographically secure hash function is a pivotal countermeasure against hash collisions, a potential threat to the integrity and security of cryptographic applications. Cryptographically secure hash functions are characterized by several essential properties. First and foremost is collision resistance, where it should be computationally infeasible to find two distinct inputs that yield the same hash value. This property is critical in preventing attackers from deliberately crafting inputs that lead to collisions, safeguarding the reliability of the hash function.

In addition to collision resistance, a cryptographically secure hash function exhibits preimage resistance, making it challenging to reverse-engineer the input data from a given hash value. Second preimage resistance is also crucial, ensuring that finding a different input with the same hash as a known input is computationally infeasible. These properties collectively fortify the hash function against various cryptographic attacks, contributing to its overall strength.

The algorithmic strength of a hash function is a measure of its resilience against differential and linear cryptanalysis, two common types of cryptographic attacks. A cryptographically secure hash function is designed to withstand such attacks, reinforcing its reliability in real-world applications. Furthermore, adherence to industry standards and the use of widely recognized hash functions, such as SHA-256 and SHA-3, provide an additional layer of trust. These algorithms have undergone extensive scrutiny and analysis, earning their status as recommended choices for cryptographic applications.

In essence, the careful selection of a cryptographically secure hash function is foundational to the security of cryptographic systems. It ensures that the hash function meets the stringent requirements of data integrity, preventing malicious activities that could compromise the authenticity and trustworthiness of digital systems. As the cryptographic landscape evolves, the importance of choosing robust hash functions becomes increasingly significant in maintaining the resilience of digital infrastructure against potential collision-based attacks.

Use of Longer Hash Output

Increasing the length of the hash output is a strategic countermeasure aimed at enhancing the collision resistance of hash functions. The output length of a hash function determines the size of the hash value it produces. Commonly employed hash functions, such as SHA-256 (256-bit output), SHA-384, or even SHA-3 with varying output lengths, offer longer hash values compared to their predecessors.

The fundamental idea behind using longer hash output is to expand the output space, making it exponentially more challenging for attackers to find distinct inputs that yield the same hash value. In cryptographic terms, this is often referred to as increasing the entropy of the hash function. With a larger output space, the likelihood of a collision—two different inputs producing the same hash—decreases significantly.

The security strength of a hash function is intricately tied to the length of its output. As computational power increases over time, hash functions with longer output lengths provide a hedge against potential advancements in collision attacks. Shorter hash lengths, while still widely used for certain applications, may become more susceptible to brute-force or collision-based attacks as computational capabilities evolve.

The use of longer hash output is particularly relevant in scenarios where the impact of collisions could have severe consequences, such as in cryptographic protocols, digital signatures, or certificate authorities. By opting for hash functions with longer outputs, organizations and cryptographic practitioners contribute to a more robust defense against potential vulnerabilities and emerging threats, ensuring the sustained integrity and security of digital systems. This countermeasure aligns with the principle that a larger output space provides an additional layer of protection in the ever-evolving landscape of cryptographic security.

Salted Hashing

Salted hashing is a widely employed countermeasure to enhance the security of hash functions, particularly in the context of password storage. It involves adding a unique random value, known as a salt, to each input before hashing. The salt is a cryptographic technique used to thwart precomputed attacks, where attackers hash lists of common inputs (such as passwords) and compare the results against stored hashes.

Unique Salts for Each Input:

The essence of salted hashing lies in assigning a unique salt value to each input before hashing. This ensures that even if two users have the same password, their hashed values will differ due to the distinct salt values applied to each instance. This uniqueness disrupts the predictability that arises when multiple users share the same password.

Mitigation of Precomputed Attacks:

Precomputed attacks, also known as rainbow table attacks, involve attackers building tables of precomputed hash values for commonly used passwords. By introducing unique salts, the resulting hash values are specific to each user, rendering precomputed tables ineffective. Attackers would need to generate new tables for each salt, significantly increasing the computational effort required to crack passwords.

Enhanced Security for Common Passwords:

Salted hashing adds a layer of security, especially for users with common passwords. Without salts, attackers can quickly identify users with the same password by comparing hash values. Salting ensures that even if two users have identical passwords, their hashes will differ, thwarting the straightforward identification of common password use.

Individualized Security:

Each user's password is effectively treated as an individual case, with the introduction of salts preventing the aggregation of hash values that could lead to easier attacks. This individualization enhances the overall security of password storage systems, protecting against both targeted attacks and large-scale breaches.

Adaptability to System Changes:

The use of salts provides an adaptable security measure that can withstand changes in password policies or system configurations. As systems evolve, the addition of salts remains a reliable method to fortify the security of stored passwords without requiring alterations to the hashing algorithm itself.

In conclusion, salted hashing is a powerful countermeasure designed to mitigate the risks associated with precomputed attacks and enhance the security of password storage systems. Its effectiveness lies in introducing variability and uniqueness to hash values, making it a cornerstone practice in safeguarding sensitive user credentials in a variety of cryptographic applications.

Double Hashing (Hash-and-Hash)

Double hashing, also known as hash-and-hash, is a technique employed to mitigate the risk of hash collisions by applying a hash function twice to the input data. This strategy aims to strengthen collision resistance, particularly in scenarios where a primary hash function might exhibit vulnerabilities or encounters collisions.

Sequential Hashing:

The double hashing approach involves applying one hash function to the input data, producing an intermediate hash value. Subsequently, a second hash function is applied to this intermediate hash, yielding the final hash value. The process can be extended with more iterations for added security.

Collision Reduction:

The primary objective of double hashing is to reduce the likelihood of collisions, especially when an initial collision occurs in the first hash function. By subjecting the intermediate hash value to a second hashing operation, the chances of two different inputs producing the same final hash value decrease substantially. This provides an additional layer of security against intentional collisions.

Increased Computational Complexity:

Double hashing introduces increased computational complexity for potential attackers attempting to engineer collisions. The need to find two distinct inputs that not only collide in the first hash but also produce the same hash in the second iteration adds an additional hurdle, making the task computationally more challenging.

Adaptability to Hash Function Changes:

The double hashing technique is adaptable to changes in hash function configurations or replacements. If a vulnerability or collision risk is identified in the primary hash function, it is feasible to update the system by changing only the initial hashing algorithm while retaining the double hashing structure. This adaptability ensures ongoing security against evolving cryptographic threats.

Variability in Hash Output:

The sequential application of two hash functions introduces variability and unpredictability in the final hash output. Even if an attacker identifies a collision in the first hash, the second hash introduces an additional layer of complexity, making it computationally impractical to exploit the collision for malicious purposes.

Balancing Trade-Offs:

While double hashing enhances collision resistance, it also comes with increased computational overhead. The trade-off between security and performance needs to be considered in specific use cases. In applications where collision resistance is of utmost importance, such as in certain cryptographic protocols, the benefits of double hashing may outweigh the additional computational cost.

Security Considerations and Best Practices for Hash Algorithms

Ensuring the security of hash algorithms involves a multifaceted approach that encompasses several considerations and best practices. One fundamental aspect is selecting hash functions with proven cryptographic strength. This entails choosing algorithms that exhibit collision resistance, preimage resistance, and second preimage resistance. Regularly assessing hash functions for vulnerabilities and staying informed about cryptographic research are crucial to maintaining algorithmic resistance and addressing emerging risks.

Key management is another critical factor, especially when utilizing keyed hash functions such as HMAC. Implementing robust key management practices, such as regular updates and ensuring the randomness of key generation, enhances the overall security of hash-based applications. Additionally, when hashing passwords, salting is recommended to prevent precomputed attacks. Each user should have a unique salt, adding an extra layer of protection against attackers attempting to exploit common passwords.

Consideration of hash function output length is paramount. Longer hash outputs contribute to increased collision resistance by providing a larger output space, making it more challenging for attackers to find collisions. Regularly updating hash functions is essential to stay ahead of cryptographic threats, with careful migration planning ensuring compatibility and system stability during transitions.

Post-Quantum Considerations

As quantum computing advances, post-quantum considerations become increasingly vital. Exploring hash functions and cryptographic algorithms resistant to quantum attacks is imperative. Lattice-based cryptography is one such alternative, and its resistance to quantum attacks makes it a promising area of research. Staying informed about NIST's efforts in post-quantum cryptography standardization is essential, as NIST actively evaluates and standardizes post-quantum cryptographic algorithms, including hash functions.

Quantum-resistant hash functions and cryptographic schemes may become integral components of future cryptographic systems. Quantum Key Distribution (QKD) is another approach that leverages quantum principles to secure communication channels against quantum attacks. Hybrid cryptographic approaches, combining classical and post-quantum algorithms, provide transitional strategies to maintain security in the quantum era while ensuring compatibility with existing systems.

Periodic assessments of post-quantum security and collaboration with cryptography experts and organizations contributing to post-quantum research are recommended. As quantum computing technology evolves, ongoing reevaluation and adaptation of cryptographic strategies ensure robust and future-proof security measures. The dynamic landscape of cryptography necessitates a proactive and informed approach to address emerging threats and advancements.

Conclusion

In conclusion, the chapter on hashing has provided a comprehensive exploration of this fundamental concept in cryptography, covering various facets from its definition and introduction to the discussion of its properties. Beginning with understanding hashing as a process of mapping data of arbitrary size to fixed-size values, we delved into the foundational properties of hash functions–namely, determinism, efficiency, and the avalanche effect.

The chapter progressed to illuminate specific hashing algorithms, offering insights into widely used ones such as MD5 (Message Digest Algorithm 5) and the SHA (Secure Hash Algorithm) family. These algorithms, with their distinctive features, have found applications in diverse domains, from data integrity verification to digital signatures and password storage.

A significant portion of our exploration centered on the use cases of hashing in cryptography, showcasing its pivotal role in ensuring data integrity, authenticity, and confidentiality. From checksums to digital signatures, hashing emerged as a versatile tool with applications spanning a spectrum of security mechanisms.

The chapter also delved into a crucial consideration in the realm of hash functions–collisions. Hash collisions, the scenario where two distinct inputs yield the same hash value, were addressed, and countermeasure techniques were discussed. By employing strategies such as the use of cryptographically secure hash functions, salting, and double hashing, one can mitigate the risks associated with collisions, bolstering the reliability of hash-based systems.

The final segment of our exploration focused on security practices and best practices when working with hash algorithms in real-life implementations. By emphasizing factors such as cryptographic strength, key management, salting for passwords, and regular updates, we underscored the importance of maintaining robust security postures. Additionally, we touched upon post-quantum considerations, recognizing the evolving landscape of quantum computing and the necessity to align cryptographic practices with emerging standards.

Looking ahead, in subsequent chapters, we will delve deeper into specific applications of hashing, particularly its role in ensuring message integrity, a critical aspect of secure communication that further emphasizes the importance of robust hash functions in cryptographic protocols. As technology evolves, the insights and practices outlined here serve as a foundation for navigating the dynamic landscape of cryptographic systems, ensuring the continued integrity, security, and resilience of digital data in the face of emerging challenges.

CHAPTER 6
Message Integrity

Introduction

In the preceding chapter, our exploration delved into the intricate world of hashing, unraveling the properties and applications of various hash algorithms. As we transition into the current chapter, our focus turns to a fundamental aspect of secure communication: Message Integrity. Here, we embark on a journey to understand the critical role played by techniques ensuring the integrity of our messages, complementing the confidentiality conferred by encryption.

Message Integrity, distinguished from the realm of secrecy, aims to safeguard the integrity and authenticity of data during transmission. Unlike encryption, which conceals information, integrity mechanisms ensure that the received data remains unaltered and trustworthy. In this chapter, we will decipher the nuances of Message Authentication Code (MAC), a pivotal concept in ensuring message integrity. Our exploration begins with a thorough examination of MAC, elucidating its construction, components, and relevance in cryptographic schemes.

As we delve deeper, we will explore the construction of Message Authentication Codes, scrutinizing both symmetric key-based approaches and those employing hash functions. A special emphasis will be placed on HMAC (Hash-Based Message Authentication Code), shedding light on its significance and implementation nuances. Through this journey, we aim to provide a comprehensive understanding of the construction methodologies employed in MAC.

However, our narrative doesn't stop at the virtues of MAC. We will navigate through the limitations inherent in Message Authentication Codes, which exposes potential vulnerabilities and challenges in real-world applications. Furthermore, we will delve into the realm of Authenticated Encryption, a powerful paradigm that seamlessly combines confidentiality and integrity.

In conclusion, this chapter aspires to equip readers with a nuanced understanding of Message Integrity, building on the foundations laid in the preceding chapter on hashing. By exploring the intricacies of MAC, understanding its limitations, and unraveling the landscape of authenticated encryption, we aim to fortify your grasp on the multifaceted aspects of securing communication channels. Let's embark on this intellectual expedition into the realm of Message Integrity.

Structure

In this chapter, the following topics will be covered:

- Message Integrity
- Message Authentication Code (MAC)
- Limitations of Message Authentication Codes
- Authenticated Encryption

Message Integrity

In the realm of information security, two paramount objectives govern the safeguarding of data: secrecy and integrity. While secrecy ensures confidentiality by concealing information from unauthorized access, integrity focuses on maintaining the trustworthiness and accuracy of the data. Understanding the nuances of secrecy and integrity lays the foundation for robust security practices, guiding us through encryption, message authentication, and the intricate interplay between the two. Join us on this exploration as we navigate the intricate landscape of securing information in an interconnected world.

Importance of Data Trustworthiness

The importance of data trustworthiness, especially in the context of encryption using stream ciphers and block ciphers, extends beyond merely securing data from unauthorized access. While encryption is a fundamental aspect of information security, it primarily addresses the issue of confidentiality, ensuring that unauthorized parties cannot decipher the content of the communication. However, data trustworthiness involves additional considerations, making it crucial even when encryption is employed.

Here's a detailed explanation:

Integrity in Communication:

- **Encryption Focus**: Encryption is designed to prevent eavesdroppers from understanding the content of a message. It relies on algorithms that transform plaintext into ciphertext, with the goal of maintaining confidentiality during transmission.
- **Trustworthiness**: Trustworthy data encompasses not only confidentiality but also integrity. Ensuring that the transmitted data has not been tampered with during communication is a key aspect of trustworthiness. This includes detecting and preventing any unauthorized modifications or alterations.

Stream Cipher and Block Cipher Characteristics:

- **Stream Cipher**: In a stream cipher, data is encrypted one bit or byte at a time during transmission. It is well-suited for real-time communication but poses challenges for ensuring integrity. A slight alteration in the encrypted stream can result in significant changes in the decrypted message.
- **Block Cipher**: Block ciphers encrypt data in fixed-size blocks, providing a more structured approach. However, without integrity checks, modifications to individual blocks may go undetected.

Data Tampering Threats:

- **Tampering in Encrypted Data**: Without integrity mechanisms, encrypted data might be susceptible to tampering. An adversary could modify ciphertext, leading to unintended alterations in the decrypted content, potentially causing misinformation or system malfunctions.
- **Need for Verification**: Trustworthy data necessitates a way to verify that the received information has not been altered. Cryptographic hash functions, digital signatures, and message authentication codes play a role in ensuring data integrity.

Combined Approach for Trustworthy Communication:

- **Encryption Plus Integrity Measures**: To achieve comprehensive data trustworthiness, a combined approach involving encryption and integrity measures is essential. This ensures not only confidentiality but also the accuracy and reliability of the transmitted information.
- **Integrity Measures**: Employing cryptographic techniques such as Hash-based Message Authentication Codes alongside encryption helps in verifying the integrity of the data.

Real-World Implications:

- **Examples**: In scenarios where financial transactions, critical system commands, or sensitive information transfer occur, data integrity is paramount. A malicious alteration in financial transaction details or command instructions can lead to severe consequences.
- **Regulatory Compliance**: Many industries and sectors have regulatory requirements that mandate the assurance of data integrity in addition to confidentiality.

While encryption addresses the confidentiality aspect of secure communication, ensuring data trustworthiness demands additional measures to maintain integrity. Combining encryption with integrity verification mechanisms provides a robust foundation for secure and trustworthy data transmission.

Challenges in Ensuring Data Integrity

Ensuring the integrity of data has become a paramount concern in today's interconnected and data-driven world. The rapid evolution of communication technologies, coupled with the persistent threat of cyberattacks, presents a multifaceted challenge in safeguarding the trustworthiness of data. This chapter explores the key challenges in ensuring data integrity and discusses strategies to navigate this complex landscape.

One of the foremost challenges is the risk of data interception during transmission. Adversaries may exploit vulnerabilities in communication channels to intercept and tamper with data, compromising its integrity. Securing data against unauthorized access is crucial to maintaining its trustworthiness.

Man-in-the-middle attacks pose a significant threat to data integrity. In these scenarios, an attacker secretly intercepts and relays communication between two parties. This intermediary can modify the data during transit, leading to unauthorized alterations and potential integrity violations.

While encryption is a powerful tool for ensuring confidentiality, vulnerabilities in encryption algorithms or their implementation can undermine data integrity. Attackers exploiting these weaknesses may tamper with encrypted data, rendering integrity measures ineffective.

Insiders with privileged access pose a considerable risk to data integrity. Employees or individuals with internal access may intentionally or unintentionally manipulate data, leading to integrity compromises. Safeguarding against insider threats requires a combination of access controls and monitoring mechanisms.

Implementing rigorous integrity verification mechanisms can introduce computational overhead. Organizations may face challenges in striking a balance between robust integrity measures and the computational efficiency needed for real-time applications. Finding optimal solutions that ensure both security and performance is an ongoing challenge.

To navigate these challenges effectively, organizations can adopt a multifaceted approach. This includes exploring and implementing state-of-the-art encryption techniques, leveraging digital signatures and secure hash functions, and fostering a security-conscious culture to mitigate the risks associated with insider threats. By addressing these challenges, organizations can fortify their defenses against evolving threats and maintain the integrity of their valuable data.

Message Authentication Code (MAC)

In this section, we delve into the fundamental concept of Message Authentication Code and its pivotal role in guaranteeing the integrity of data. In the ever-evolving landscape of secure communication, the concept of MAC stands as a stalwart guardian, ensuring the sanctity of data integrity. A Message Authentication Code is a cryptographic construct that plays a pivotal role in verifying the authenticity and integrity of transmitted messages. Operating on the principles of hash functions and secret keys, a MAC generates a fixed-size code unique to a specific message, allowing recipients to independently verify the integrity of the received data. As we embark on this exploration, we unravel the construction, verification process, properties, and real-world applications of MACs, providing a holistic perspective on their significance in safeguarding the trustworthiness of digital communication.

Characteristics	Secrecy (Encryption)	Integrity
Objective	Conceals data, making it unreadable to unauthorized entities	Ensures data remains unaltered during transmission
Primary Mechanism	Encryption algorithms (for example, AES, DES)	Integrity mechanisms (for example, Hash functions, Message Authentication Codes)
Focus	Protects confidentiality	Guarantees data integrity
Outcome	Unreadable information to unauthorized parties	Assurance of unaltered and authentic data
Risk Addressed	Unauthorized access and information exposure	Tampering, alterations, and unauthorized modifications
Synthesis	Achieved through Authenticated Encryption combining encryption and integrity mechanisms	Formulates a holistic approach to secure communication by addressing both confidentiality and integrity

***Table 6.1**: Distinctions between secrecy (encryption) and integrity in the context of cryptography*

Definition and Purpose:

In cryptography, a Message Authentication Code is a short piece of information (often a fixed-size hash) that is generated using a secret key and appended to a message. The primary purpose of a MAC is to verify both the data integrity and the authenticity of a message. By using a MAC, the sender can ensure that the received message has not been altered or tampered with during transmission and that it indeed comes from a legitimate source with access to the secret key.

code = $M_k(m)$,

- **M** is the underline MAC algorithm,
- **k** is the secret key,
- **m** is the message.

Note that we do not assume that the message is secret; a MAC does not inherently provide confidentiality or secrecy to the message. The primary purpose of a MAC is to ensure the integrity and authenticity of a message, confirming that the message has not been altered and that it originates from a legitimate sender with access to the secret key.

The construction of a MAC involves combining the original message with a secret key through a specific algorithm, resulting in a unique code that is sent along with the message. The recipient, who shares the same secret key with the sender, can then independently compute the MAC for the received message using the same algorithm. If the computed MAC matches the one received with the message, it indicates that the message has not been modified and is indeed from the claimed sender.

$\mathbf{e_{k1}(m) \,||\, M_{k2}(e_{k1}(m))}$,

- **e** is the encryption algorithm in use,
- **M** is the underline MAC algorithm,
- **K1** is the encryption key and k2 is the MAC key,
- **m** is the message.

Confidentiality is a separate security requirement, typically addressed through encryption rather than MAC. Encryption ensures that the content of the message remains confidential by making it unreadable to unauthorized parties. In some cryptographic protocols, MAC and encryption may be combined to achieve both integrity/authenticity and confidentiality for the transmitted data. However, they serve distinct security goals, and it's essential to apply each mechanism appropriately based on the specific security requirements of a given scenario.

MACs play a crucial role in securing communication channels, preventing unauthorized alterations to data, and ensuring the overall trustworthiness of transmitted information. They find applications in various cryptographic protocols, digital signatures, and integrity verification mechanisms.

Construction of MAC

MACs can be constructed using various cryptographic techniques, including symmetric encryption algorithms. In this section, we explore how encryption algorithms are utilized to generate MACs, ensuring message integrity and authenticity.

Symmetric Encryption for MAC Construction:

Symmetric encryption algorithms, such as AES (Advanced Encryption Standard), provide a foundation for constructing MACs. The process involves using a secret key shared between the sender and receiver to compute a fixed-size authentication tag for a given message. This authentication tag serves as the MAC, providing a means to verify the integrity and authenticity of the message. The steps in symmetric encryption MAC construction are as follows:

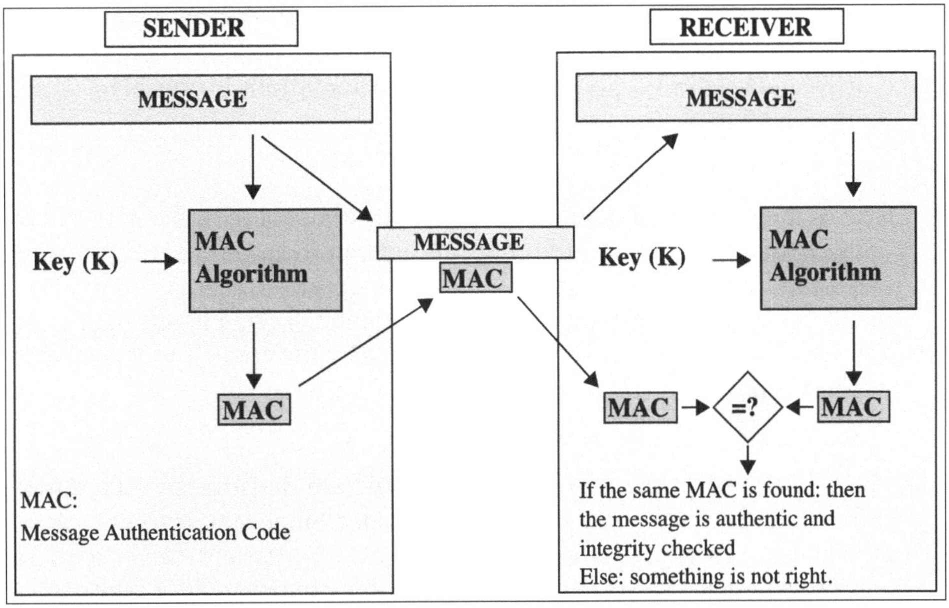

Figure 6.1: *Working Principle of MAC*

1. **Key Generation:** Both the sender and receiver agree on a secret key, which is securely shared between them.
2. **Message Padding (if necessary):** The message may need to be padded to a specific block size required by the encryption algorithm.
3. **Encryption:** The padded message is encrypted using the secret key and the chosen symmetric encryption algorithm (for example, AES).
4. **Authentication Tag Generation:** After encryption, a portion of the ciphertext (or the ciphertext itself) is used to compute the MAC. This can be achieved through various methods, such as encrypting a specific portion of the ciphertext again or applying a separate MAC algorithm such as HMAC to the ciphertext.
5. **Transmission:** The original message, along with the generated MAC, is transmitted to the receiver.
6. **Verification:** Upon receiving the message and MAC, the receiver recomputes the MAC using the received message and the shared secret key. If the computed MAC matches the received MAC, the message integrity and authenticity are confirmed.

Limitations of Using Only MAC

While Message Authentication Codes offer robust protection against message tampering and forgery, they have certain limitations that make them insufficient for comprehensive data security. Understanding these limitations is crucial for designing secure communication protocols and systems.

- **Lack of Confidentiality**

  One of the primary limitations of using only MACs is their inability to provide confidentiality for transmitted data. MACs solely focus on ensuring the integrity and authenticity of messages but do not encrypt the message contents. As a result, an adversary with access to the communication channel can intercept and view the plaintext messages, compromising the confidentiality of sensitive information.

- **Vulnerability to Replay Attacks**

  MACs are susceptible to replay attacks, where an adversary captures and retransmits previously authenticated messages. Since MACs do not incorporate mechanisms to prevent replayed messages, an attacker can resend validly authenticated messages multiple times, leading to potential security breaches or disruptions in communication.

- **Inflexibility in Key Management**

  Effective key management is essential for maintaining the security of MAC-based authentication systems. However, managing and distributing symmetric keys securely among communicating parties can be challenging, especially in large-scale networks or dynamic environments. The lack of flexibility in key management schemes may hinder the scalability and adaptability of MAC-based security solutions.

Transition to Authenticated Encryption

Given these limitations, relying solely on MACs may not suffice to ensure comprehensive data security in modern communication systems. To address the shortcomings of using only MACs, we will introduce authenticated encryption, a cryptographic technique that combines confidentiality, integrity, and authenticity in a single operation. By integrating encryption and authentication mechanisms, authenticated encryption provides a more robust and versatile approach to data security.

Authenticated Encryption

In the quest for robust data security, the cryptographic community has recognized the need for holistic solutions that address both confidentiality and integrity concerns in communication systems. Authenticated encryption emerges as a powerful cryptographic technique that seamlessly combines encryption and message authentication functionalities into a single operation.

Addressing Security Challenges:

Traditional encryption schemes, while effective in concealing the contents of transmitted data, lack mechanisms to verify the authenticity and integrity of messages. On the other hand, message authentication codes provide integrity protection but do not offer encryption, leaving data vulnerable to eavesdropping attacks. Recognizing these limitations, authenticated encryption aims to bridge the gap by offering a comprehensive approach to data security.

Simultaneous Confidentiality and Integrity:

At its essence, authenticated encryption offers the dual benefits of confidentiality and integrity assurance. By encrypting plaintext messages and generating authentication tags, authenticated encryption ensures that sensitive data remains confidential during transmission while also verifying its integrity upon receipt. This simultaneous protection against unauthorized access and tampering is essential for maintaining the trustworthiness of communication channels in an increasingly interconnected world. Whether it's safeguarding financial transactions, protecting sensitive personal information, or securing critical infrastructure, authenticated encryption plays a vital role in ensuring the integrity and privacy of data.

Streamlining Security Protocols:

In addition to enhancing data security, authenticated encryption also simplifies the design and implementation of secure communication protocols. By consolidating encryption and authentication mechanisms into a single cryptographic operation, authenticated encryption reduces the complexity and potential vulnerabilities associated with managing separate encryption and authentication layers. This streamlined approach not only improves the efficiency of security protocols but also enhances their resilience against various attack scenarios. From securing online transactions to safeguarding confidential communications, authenticated encryption offers a versatile and robust solution for modern cryptographic applications.

In the following sections, we will delve deeper into the principles and mechanisms of authenticated encryption, exploring different modes of operation and algorithms commonly used to achieve this security objective. Through comprehensive analysis and practical examples, we aim to elucidate the significance of authenticated encryption in modern cryptographic protocols and its pivotal role in safeguarding sensitive data against a myriad of threats.

Authenticated Encryption Modes

Authenticated encryption modes of operation provide a crucial mechanism for ensuring both the confidentiality and integrity of data in modern cryptographic systems. These modes combine encryption and authentication techniques to offer robust security guarantees against various threats, including eavesdropping, tampering, and forgery. Some common authenticated encryption modes include Galois/Counter Mode (GCM), Counter with CBC-MAC (CCM), Encrypt-then-MAC (EtM), and Encrypt-and-MAC (E&M). Each mode has its own characteristics, trade-offs, and suitability for different use cases. In the subsequent sections, we will delve deeper into the AES GCM and CCM modes of operation, exploring their design principles, security properties, and practical applications in ensuring the integrity and confidentiality of sensitive data.

CCM (Counter with CBC-MAC)

Counter with CBC-MAC is an authenticated encryption mode of operation that combines counter mode (CTR) encryption with Cipher Block Chaining Message Authentication Code authentication. It is commonly used in applications where both encryption and authentication are required, such as wireless networks, IoT devices, and secure communication protocols.

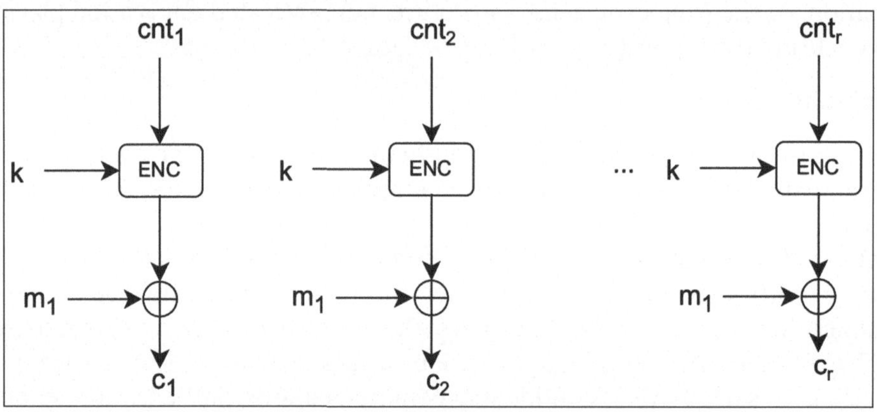

***Figure 6.2**: Counter Mode(CTR) Encryption Block of CCM*

Advantages of CCM:

- **Simplicity:** CCM provides simple and separate encryption and authentication generation blocks reducing implementation complexity.
- **Flexibility:** It supports variable length messages and allows for customization of security parameters such as the length of the authentication tag.
- **Lightweight:** CCM is suitable for resource-constrained environments due to its minimal memory and processing requirements.

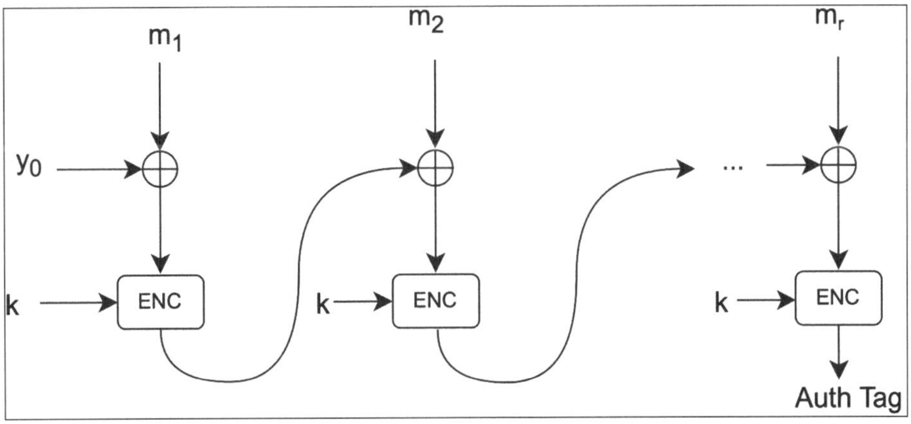

Figure 6.3: *CBC-MAC Block of CCM*

Limitations of CCM:

- **Nonce Requirements:** It requires a unique nonce for each message to prevent replay attacks, which can pose challenges in certain scenarios.
- **Complexity:** Implementing CCM correctly can be complex due to its reliance on both encryption and authentication mechanisms, requiring careful attention to security considerations.

Note: *In the AES CCM mode of operation, the length of the nonce (number used once) typically depends on the specific implementation and security requirements. However, in most cases, the recommended nonce length for AES CCM is 12 bytes (96 bits). This length is commonly used because it strikes a balance between security and efficiency. It provides a sufficiently large space for nonces, reducing the likelihood of collisions while keeping the overhead minimal for the authentication process. Using a shorter nonce length may compromise security, while using a longer nonce length may increase overhead and computational costs without significant security benefits. Therefore, 12 bytes is often considered a good compromise for most applications.*

Encryption and Decryption of CCM Mode with AES Algorithm in Python:

```
from Crypto.Cipher import AES
from Crypto.Random import get_random_bytes
from Crypto.Util.Padding import pad, unpad
from Crypto.Protocol.KDF import scrypt

def ccm_encrypt(message, key):
    nonce = get_random_bytes(12)
    aes_key = scrypt(key, salt=nonce, key_len=16, N=2**14, r=8, p=1)

    cipher = AES.new(aes_key, AES.MODE_CCM, nonce=nonce)
    ciphertext, tag = cipher.encrypt_and_digest(pad(message, AES.block_
size))
```

```
    return nonce + ciphertext + tag

def ccm_decrypt(ciphertext, key):
    nonce = ciphertext[:12]
    tag = ciphertext[-16:]
    ciphertext = ciphertext[12:-16]

    aes_key = scrypt(key, salt=nonce, key_len=16, N=2**14, r=8, p=1)

    cipher = AES.new(aes_key, AES.MODE_CCM, nonce=nonce)
    plaintext = unpad(cipher.decrypt_and_verify(ciphertext, tag), AES.
block_size)

    return plaintext

# Example usage
message = b"Hello, this is a secret message."
key = b"Th1sIsMyS3cr3tK3y"

encrypted_message = ccm_encrypt(message, key)
print("Encrypted message:", encrypted_message)

decrypted_message = ccm_decrypt(encrypted_message, key)
print("Decrypted message:", decrypted_message.decode('utf-8'))
```

Implementation Framework:

The CCM authenticated encryption mode is widely accepted and implemented in various cryptographic frameworks and standards, such as:

- **IEEE 802.15.4:** CCM is commonly used in the IEEE 802.15.4 standard for wireless personal area networks (WPANs).
- **TLS:** CCM is supported as a cipher suite in the Transport Layer Security (TLS) protocol for secure communication over the internet.
- **Zigbee:** Zigbee, a communication protocol for IoT devices, utilizes CCM to secure network traffic.

GCM (Galois/Counter Mode):

Introduction to GCM Authenticated Encryption Mode:

Galois/Counter Mode (GCM) stands as a cornerstone in modern cryptography, offering a robust solution for achieving both confidentiality and integrity in encrypted communications. GCM's widespread adoption stems from its ability to provide efficient and secure encryption while ensuring data integrity through authentication. Unlike traditional modes of operation, GCM combines encryption and authentication into a single algorithm, streamlining cryptographic protocols and reducing overhead.

GCM mode over CCM:

- One of the key advantages of GCM over other authenticated encryption modes, such as Counter with CBC-MAC, lies in its superior performance and efficiency. By leveraging the parallelizability of the Galois field multiplication and the counter mode encryption, GCM achieves high throughput and low latency, making it well-suited for applications requiring fast and secure data processing.
- In contrast to CCM, GCM offers enhanced flexibility in terms of nonce lengths, key sizes, and IV requirements, allowing for easier configuration and deployment in diverse environments. Additionally, GCM's ability to detect unauthorized modifications to encrypted data provides an added layer of security, making it suitable for safeguarding sensitive information in transit and at rest.
- Furthermore, GCM's adaptability across various cryptographic libraries and platforms makes it a preferred choice for implementing secure communication protocols. Its standardized design and widespread support in industry-standard cryptographic libraries ensure interoperability and compatibility across different systems and devices, facilitating seamless integration into modern security architectures.
- Overall, GCM represents a versatile and efficient solution for achieving authenticated encryption in cryptographic applications, offering a balance between performance, security, and ease of implementation. Its adoption in various cryptographic standards and protocols underscores its importance in modern cybersecurity practices, highlighting its significance as a foundational building block for secure communication channels and data storage systems.

How AAD is handled in GCM mode of operation:

In the GCM authenticated encryption mode of operation, Additional Authenticated Data is handled separately from the plaintext data during the encryption process. AAD consists of additional information that requires integrity protection but does not need to be encrypted. Examples of AAD include protocol headers, metadata, or any other data that should be authenticated but need not be kept confidential.

In GCM, AAD is included in the computation of the authentication tag (GMAC - Galois Message Authentication Code) but is not encrypted with the plaintext. Instead, the AAD is input directly into the authentication function along with the ciphertext. This allows the authentication tag to be computed over both the ciphertext and the AAD, providing integrity protection for both.

The AAD is typically provided to the encryption function separately from the plaintext data. It is concatenated with the ciphertext before the authentication tag is calculated. This ensures that any modifications to the AAD or the ciphertext will be detected during the authentication verification process.

By handling AAD separately from the plaintext, GCM provides a flexible and efficient mechanism for protecting additional data while ensuring the confidentiality and integrity of the encrypted communication.

Operating Steps of GCM Mode of Operation:

Let's delve into the components of the GCM mode of operation. Additionally, we'll utilize a figure titled "GCM Authenticated Encryption Operations" to provide a visual representation of these operations.

- **Initialization Vector:**
    - In the GCM mode of authenticated encryption, the initialization vector (IV) is used to initialize the counter (Counter i) for the counter mode encryption. The IV length in GCM mode is typically 96 bits (or 12 bytes). However, some implementations may support different IV lengths.
    - The IV is combined with a unique nonce (Number Used Once) to form the initial counter block. The nonce is usually provided by the sender and must be unique for each encryption operation with the same key. Concatenating the IV with the nonce ensures uniqueness, even if the same key is used for multiple encryption operations.
    - The IV and nonce combination is used to initialize the counter block, which is incremented for each block of plaintext during encryption. This ensures that the same plaintext encrypted with the same key produces different ciphertexts, enhancing security by preventing replay attacks and other vulnerabilities associated with key reuse.
- **Key Expansion:** The secret key undergoes key expansion to generate the necessary encryption keys. GCM typically uses a block cipher such as AES.
- **Encryption:** The plaintext is divided into blocks and encrypted using the counter mode along with the encryption keys derived from the secret key. The encryption process generates the ciphertext.
- **Authentication Tag Calculation:** Simultaneously with encryption, GCM computes an authentication tag (GMAC - Galois Message Authentication Code) over the ciphertext and any AAD. This tag provides integrity protection for both the ciphertext and AAD.
- **Output Generation:** The encrypted ciphertext and authentication tag are output as the final result of the encryption process.
- **Decryption (if needed):** In decryption, the received ciphertext, IV, secret key, and any AAD are provided as inputs. The decryption process reverses

the encryption steps to recover the original plaintext. The authentication tag calculated during encryption is also used to verify the integrity of the decrypted data.

- **Verification:** The received ciphertext, authentication tag, and any AAD are input into the verification process. The authentication tag is recalculated based on the received ciphertext and AAD, and compared to the received tag. If they match, the data integrity is verified.

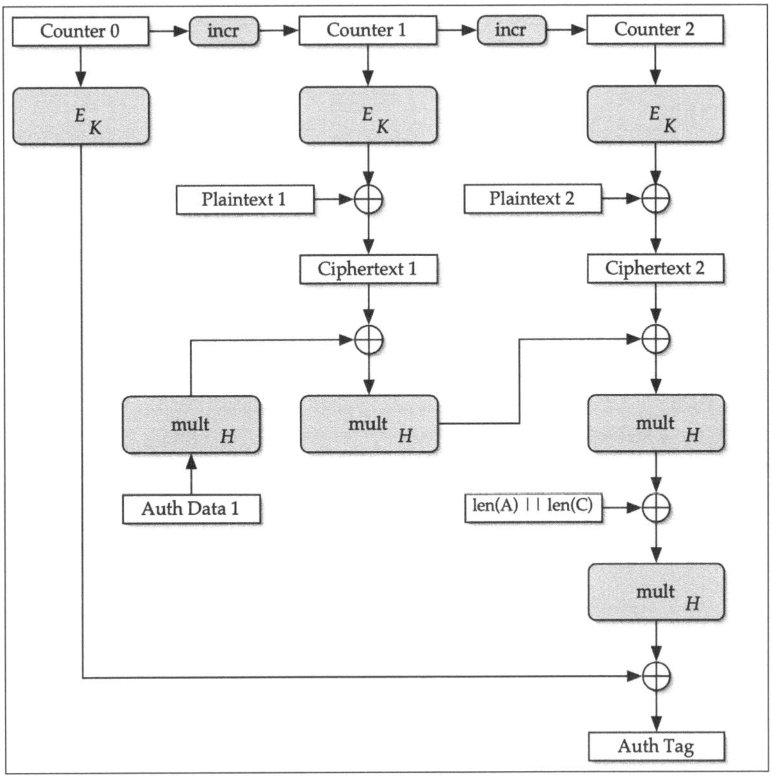

Figure 6.4: *GCM Authenticated Encryption Operations*

Differences between CCM and GCM Mode of Operation:

Aspect	CCM	GCM
Block Cipher Mode	Counter mode of encryption	Counter mode of encryption
Authentication Tag Generation	Achieved through CBC-MAC	Achieved through GMAC
Parallelization	Not inherently parallelizable	Highly parallelizable
Efficiency	Typically slower due to CBC-MAC overhead	Generally faster due to optimized parallel processing with GMAC

Pass through data	Require two passes through the; once during tag generation and once during encryption	A single pass through the data is enough for both encryption and tag generation
Adoption and Support	Widely adopted in standards such as IEEE 802.11i (Wi-Fi Protected Access 2)	Widely adopted in various standards and protocols, including TLS 1.2 and later

Table 6.2: *Differences between CCM and GCM Mode of Operation*

Encryption and Decryption of GCM Mode with AES Algorithm in Python:

```
from Crypto.Cipher import AES
from Crypto.Random import get_random_bytes

def aes_gcm_encrypt(key, plaintext, nonce):
    cipher = AES.new(key, AES.MODE_GCM, nonce=nonce)
    ciphertext, tag = cipher.encrypt_and_digest(plaintext)
    return ciphertext, tag

def aes_gcm_decrypt(key, ciphertext, nonce, tag):
    cipher = AES.new(key, AES.MODE_GCM, nonce=nonce)
    plaintext = cipher.decrypt_and_verify(ciphertext, tag)
    return plaintext

# Example usage:
key = get_random_bytes(16)  # 128-bit key
nonce = get_random_bytes(12)  # 96-bit nonce
plaintext = b'Sample plaintext for AES-GCM encryption'

ciphertext, tag = aes_gcm_encrypt(key, plaintext, nonce)
decrypted_plaintext = aes_gcm_decrypt(key, ciphertext, nonce, tag)

print("Plaintext:", plaintext)A
print("Ciphertext:", ciphertext)
print("Decrypted Plaintext:", decrypted_plaintext)
```

Implementation Framework:

The GCM mode of operation is widely adopted and standardized in various cryptographic frameworks and libraries. Some of the commonly used frameworks that support GCM include.

- **OpenSSL:** GCM is supported in the OpenSSL library, which is widely used for SSL/TLS protocols and cryptographic operations in various programming languages.
- **Java Cryptography Architecture (JCA):** Java provides native support for GCM through its cryptography APIs. Developers can use classes such as Cipher

and **`GCMParameterSpec`** to perform GCM encryption and decryption in Java applications.

- **Python Cryptography Toolkit (PyCryptodome): `PyCryptodome`** is a comprehensive cryptographic library for Python that includes support for GCM mode. Developers can use the **`Crypto.Cipher`** module to perform GCM encryption and decryption operations.
- **Microsoft .NET Framework:** GCM is also supported in the .NET Framework through classes such as **`AesGcm`** in the **`System.Security.Cryptography`** namespace.
- **Go (Golang) Cryptography Libraries:** Golang provides packages such as **`crypto/cipher`** and **`crypto/aes`** for implementing GCM mode encryption and decryption in Go applications.

Conclusion

In this chapter on cryptography integrity, we delved into the fundamental concepts of ensuring the integrity of digital data, emphasizing the importance of maintaining data trustworthiness in modern communication channels. We began by exploring the concept of message integrity, highlighting its role in detecting unauthorized modifications to data and ensuring data integrity during transmission. However, we also recognized the limitations of relying solely on message integrity schemes, as they do not provide confidentiality or protection against replay attacks.

To address these shortcomings, we introduced the concept of authenticated encryption, which combines encryption and message authentication to provide both confidentiality and integrity for transmitted data. We discussed two popular modes of authenticated encryption: CCM and GCM, exploring their respective advantages, disadvantages, and implementations. Through detailed explanations and code examples, we illustrated how these modes of operation enhance data security by offering robust protection against unauthorized modifications and tampering.

Looking ahead, our exploration of cryptography does not end here. In the next chapter, we will delve into a diverse array of cryptographic schemes beyond symmetric and asymmetric encryption, hashing, and message integrity. We will explore key exchange protocols, key derivation functions, password-based key derivation functions (PBKDFs), homomorphic encryption schemes, zero-knowledge proofs, and more. By expanding our understanding of these miscellaneous cryptographic schemes, we will further enrich our toolkit for building secure and privacy-preserving systems in the digital age.

CHAPTER 7
Miscellaneous Crypto Schemes

Introduction

In this chapter on miscellaneous crypto schemes, we embark on an exploration of diverse cryptographic techniques and protocols that extend beyond the realms of traditional encryption and integrity mechanisms. Building upon the foundational concepts covered in previous chapters, we delve into an array of advanced cryptographic tools designed to address various security challenges in digital communications.

Among the topics we will cover are digital signatures, which provide a robust means of verifying the authenticity and integrity of digital documents and messages. By employing cryptographic techniques, digital signatures ensure that a message has been signed by a specific sender and remains unaltered during transmission. We will delve into the inner workings of digital signature algorithms and their applications in securing electronic transactions, contracts, and communications.

Key exchange protocols form another critical aspect of secure communication, enabling parties to establish secure channels over potentially insecure networks. Through protocols such as Diffie-Hellman key exchange, parties can securely negotiate shared encryption keys without the risk of eavesdropping or interception. We will explore various key exchange algorithms and protocols, highlighting their mechanisms and security properties.

Key derivation functions (KDFs) play a vital role in deriving cryptographic keys from a given input, enhancing the security of cryptographic systems. These functions are crucial in scenarios where keys need to be derived from passwords or other low-entropy sources. We will discuss the purpose and applications of KDFs, examining their role in key generation and management.

Additionally, we will delve into the realm of homomorphic encryption, a revolutionary technique that enables computations to be performed on encrypted data without the need for decryption. Homomorphic encryption holds immense potential for privacy-preserving data analysis and secure outsourcing of computations. We will explore its principles, applications, and limitations in real-world scenarios.

Zero-knowledge proofs offer yet another fascinating avenue in cryptography, allowing one party to prove the validity of a statement to another party without revealing any additional information beyond the statement's truth. These proofs find applications in authentication, privacy-preserving protocols, and digital identity management. We will delve into the principles of zero-knowledge proofs and examine their practical implementations.

Finally, we will touch upon multiparty computation (MPC), a cryptographic protocol that enables multiple parties to jointly compute a function over their inputs while keeping those inputs private. MPC facilitates secure collaborative computations in scenarios where privacy is paramount, such as financial transactions and medical research. We will discuss the underlying principles of MPC and its applications in various domains.

Through this comprehensive exploration of miscellaneous crypto schemes, we aim to provide readers with a nuanced understanding of advanced cryptographic techniques and their applications in modern digital security.

Structure

In this chapter, the following topics will be covered:

- Digital Signature
- Key Exchange Protocol
- Key Derivation Functions
- Homomorphic Encryption
- Zero Knowledge Proofs
- Multiparty Computations

Digital Signature

Imagine you're sending a super important email, maybe it's a contract or some top-secret recipe for the world's best chocolate chip cookies. Now, you want to ensure that when you hit that "send" button, nobody can mess with your email along the way. That's where digital signatures come into play!

Digital signatures are like the electronic version of sealing an envelope with your signature. They're fancy cryptographic tools that let you sign digital documents or messages to prove that they came from you and haven't been tampered with. Akin to your sign on a piece of paper to show it's yours, digital signatures use math tricks to create a unique signature for each document or message.

But how do they work, you ask? Well, it's all about math magic! Digital signatures use something called public-key cryptography, which means there are two special keys involved: a public key and a private key. Think of the public key as your lock and the private key as your secret key that only you know. When you want to sign something, you use your private key to create a digital signature, which is basically a unique code that's added to the document or message.

Now, here's the cool part: anyone with your public key can check the digital signature to ensure it's legit. They can verify that the document really came from you and hasn't been altered since you signed it. It's like they're using your lock to open the envelope and check your signature inside.

Definition and Purpose

A digital signature is a cryptographic mechanism used to verify the authenticity, integrity, and non-repudiation of electronic documents, messages, or transactions. It involves the application of asymmetric encryption techniques, where a signer uses their private key to generate a unique digital signature for a given message or document. This signature, along with the original content, can be verified by anyone using the signer's corresponding public key, ensuring that the content has not been altered and that it was indeed signed by the claimed signer. Digital signatures play a crucial role in secure electronic communication, transaction authentication, and legal documentation, providing assurance of the origin and integrity of digital assets.

Generation and Verification

In mathematical terms, a digital signature σ for a message m is generated using a signer's private key *privKey* and a cryptographic hash function H typically following this formula:

$$\sigma = \text{Sign}(privKey, H(m))$$

To verify the signature, the recipient computes a hash of the received message m and then uses the corresponding public key *pubKey* to verify the signature:

$$\text{Verify}(pubKey, m, \sigma) = \text{True/ False}$$

where $\text{Verify}(pubKey, m, \sigma)$ returns true if the verification succeeds, indicating that the signature is valid for the message m, and false otherwise.

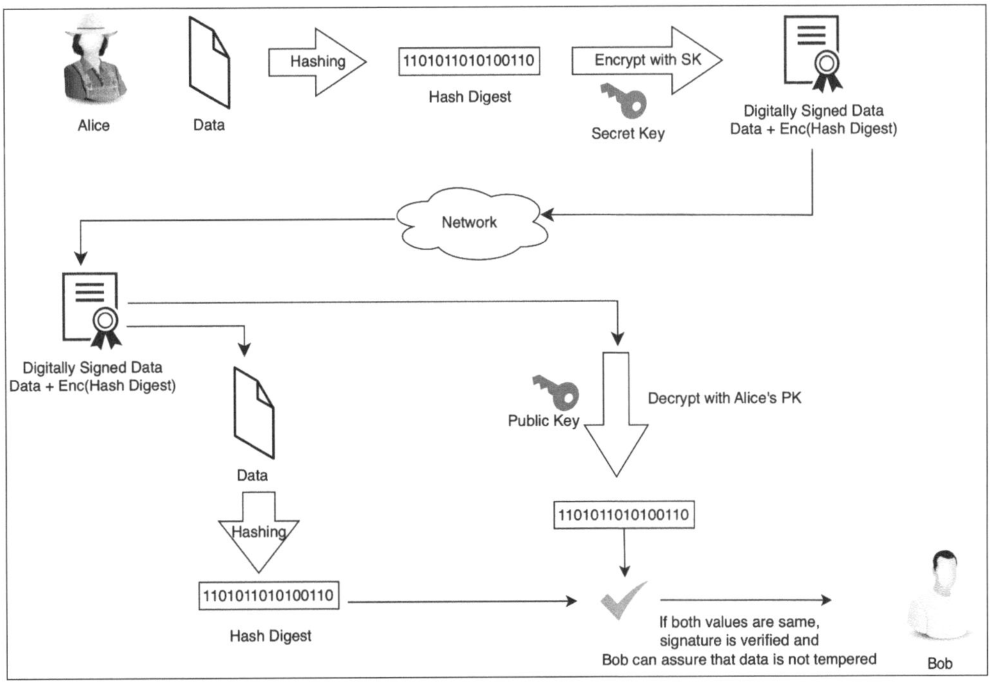

Figure 7.1: *Digital Signature E2E Flow*

Implementation Code

Here's a simple Python implementation of digital signatures using RSA without relying on any external library. This implementation includes key generation, message signing, and signature verification.

Note: *This implementation is purely educational and not suitable for real-world applications due to its lack of security optimizations and protections.*

```
import random
from hashlib import sha256

def gcd(a, b):
    while b != 0:
        a, b = b, a % b
    return a

def mod_inverse(e, phi):
    d = 0
    x1, x2, y1 = 0, 1, 1
    temp_phi = phi

    while e > 0:
```

```
        temp1 = temp_phi // e
        temp2 = temp_phi - temp1 * e
        temp_phi, e = e, temp2

        x = x2 - temp1 * x1
        y = d - temp1 * y1

        x2, x1 = x1, x
        d, y1 = y1, y

    if temp_phi == 1:
        return d + phi

def generate_key_pair(bits):
    p = get_prime(bits // 2)
    q = get_prime(bits // 2)
    n = p * q
    phi = (p - 1) * (q - 1)
    e = random.randrange(1, phi)
    g = gcd(e, phi)
    while g != 1:
        e = random.randrange(1, phi)
        g = gcd(e, phi)
    d = mod_inverse(e, phi)
    return ((e, n), (d, n))

def get_prime(bits):
    while True:
        num = random.getrandbits(bits)
        if is_prime(num):
            return num

def is_prime(num):
    if num < 2:
        return False
    for i in range(2, int(num**0.5) + 1):
        if num % i == 0:
            return False
    return True

def sign_message(private_key, message):
    hashed_message = int.from_bytes(sha256(message.encode('utf-8')).
digest(), byteorder='big') % private_key[1]
    d, n = private_key
    signature = pow(hashed_message, d, n)
    return signature
```

```
def verify_signature(public_key, message, signature):
    hashed_message = int.from_bytes(sha256(message.encode('utf-8')).
digest(), byteorder='big') % public_key[1]
    e, n = public_key
    hash_from_signature = pow(signature, e, n)
    return hashed_message == hash_from_signature
# Example usage:
message = "Hi"

# Generate key pairs
public_key, private_key = generate_key_pair(32)

print(f"Public Key: {public_key}")
print(f"Private Key: {private_key}")

# Sign the message
signature = sign_message(private_key, message)
print(f"Signature: {signature}")

# Verify the signature
is_valid = verify_signature(public_key, message, signature)
print("Signature verification successful!" if is_valid else "Signature
verification failed.")
```

Future Trends and Development

As quantum computing advances, the cryptographic landscape is poised for a significant shift. Traditional digital signature algorithms such as RSA and ECC are vulnerable to quantum attacks, specifically, Shor's algorithm, which can efficiently factor large integers and solve discrete logarithms. To counter this threat, researchers are developing post-quantum cryptographic algorithms designed to be secure against quantum adversaries. These include lattice-based, hash-based, code-based, and multivariate polynomial-based signatures. Organizations such as NIST (National Institute of Standards and Technology) are actively working on standardizing these algorithms to ensure a secure future in a post-quantum world. The transition to post-quantum cryptography will be a complex process, requiring updates to existing protocols and widespread adoption of new standards to maintain the security and integrity of digital signatures in the quantum era.

Digital signatures are integral to the functionality and security of blockchain technology. They are used to verify transactions and ensure the integrity of the blockchain ledger. As blockchain technology evolves, using digital signatures in smart contracts–self-executing contracts with the terms directly written into code–is becoming increasingly important. Smart contracts rely on robust digital signature schemes to automate and secure agreements between parties. Enhanced digital signature algorithms improve the security and efficiency of decentralized applications (dApps), making them more reliable and widely adopted. The immutable and transparent nature of blockchain, combined with the security of digital signatures, offers a powerful solution for various applications, from financial transactions to supply chain management.

The Internet of Things (IoT) is expanding rapidly, connecting billions of devices worldwide. Ensuring the security of these devices is a major challenge, given their limited computational resources and the diverse range of applications. Lightweight and efficient digital signature algorithms are crucial for IoT security, providing authentication and integrity without overwhelming device capabilities. Elliptic Curve Cryptography (ECC) is particularly suited for IoT environments due to its small key sizes and high security. Research is ongoing to develop even more compact and efficient signature schemes tailored for IoT devices. As IoT continues to integrate into critical infrastructure, healthcare, and everyday life, robust digital signature solutions will be essential to protect against cyber threats and ensure the integrity of data and communications.

Key Exchange Protocol

Key exchange protocols are fundamental components of secure communication systems, ensuring that parties can securely share cryptographic keys over an insecure channel. These protocols enable two or more parties to establish a shared secret, which can then be used to encrypt subsequent communications, ensuring confidentiality and data integrity. The primary purpose of key exchange protocols is to facilitate secure key distribution, a critical step in the establishment of secure communication channels.

The significance of key exchange protocols lies in their ability to mitigate the risk of eavesdropping and other forms of interception that can occur when transmitting keys over unprotected networks. By using cryptographic techniques, these protocols ensure that even if an adversary intercepts the communication, they cannot decipher the key being exchanged. This secure exchange is the cornerstone of many encryption systems, allowing parties to communicate securely without having to meet in person to exchange keys.

The concept of key exchange dates back to the late 1970s with the advent of public-key cryptography. Before this, secure key distribution was a significant challenge, often requiring the physical exchange of keys, which was impractical and insecure in many situations. The groundbreaking work of Whitfield Diffie and Martin Hellman in 1976 introduced the first practical key exchange protocol, now known as the Diffie-Hellman key exchange. This protocol allowed two parties to establish a shared secret over an insecure channel without requiring prior knowledge of each other's keys, revolutionizing the field of cryptography and laying the foundation for modern secure communications.

Following the introduction of the Diffie-Hellman protocol, the RSA algorithm, developed by Rivest, Shamir, and Adleman in 1977, provided another method for secure key exchange using the principles of public-key cryptography. These early innovations set the stage for a myriad of key exchange mechanisms developed over the ensuing decades, each with its unique advantages and applications.

In contemporary cryptographic systems, key exchange protocols continue to evolve, addressing emerging security threats and incorporating advances in mathematical research. Modern key exchange protocols, such as Elliptic Curve Diffie-Hellman (ECDH), offer enhanced security and efficiency, making them suitable for a wide range of applications, from securing internet communications to protecting data in mobile devices and IoT systems.

The historical evolution of key exchange protocols highlights their critical role in the development of secure communication technologies. From the pioneering work of Diffie, Hellman, and RSA, to the sophisticated algorithms in use today, key exchange protocols remain a dynamic and vital area of cryptographic research and application. As we continue to navigate an increasingly connected and digital world, the importance of secure key exchange protocols cannot be overstated, ensuring the confidentiality, integrity, and authenticity of our communications.

The Need for Key Exchange Protocol

In the digital age, ensuring secure communication is paramount. Key exchange protocols play a crucial role in safeguarding data by securely distributing encryption keys between parties. These protocols not only enable confidential and authenticated communication but also protect against various cyber threats. In this section, we will explore the fundamental reasons why key exchange protocols are essential for modern secure communication systems.

Secure Communication

Key exchange protocols ensure that the keys used for encrypting and decrypting messages are shared securely between parties. This ensures that only the intended recipients can read the encrypted messages, keys and messages have not been tampered with during transmission, and the communicating parties are authenticated and verified.

Symmetric Key Cryptography

Symmetric key algorithms are faster and more efficient than asymmetric algorithms for encrypting large amounts of data. Key exchange protocols are needed to securely share the symmetric keys used in these algorithms, solving the problem of distributing these keys securely over an insecure channel.

Asymmetric Key Cryptography

Asymmetric key exchange protocols, such as Diffie-Hellman, allow for secure communication without the need for a pre-shared secret. Each party generates a public-private key pair and exchanges public keys, making it scalable for large networks. Asymmetric key exchange is also used in digital signatures, which provide authentication, integrity, and non-repudiation for messages and documents.

Forward Secrecy

Key exchange protocols can provide forward secrecy, ensuring that the compromise of long-term keys does not compromise the security of past session keys. This is crucial for maintaining the security of communications over time.

Protection Against Eavesdropping and Man-in-the-Middle Attacks

Without a secure key exchange, any intercepted communication could be decrypted by an eavesdropper. Key exchange protocols ensure that even if the communication channel is compromised, the keys remain secure. They also include mechanisms to prevent attackers from intercepting and altering the key exchange process, ensuring that the keys exchanged are authentic and have not been tampered with.

Legal and Regulatory Compliance

Many industries are subject to regulations that require the use of secure communication methods to protect sensitive data. Key exchange protocols help organizations comply with these regulations by providing secure methods for key distribution. Additionally, key exchange protocols are often part of industry standards for secure communication, such as TLS/SSL for secure web traffic, ensuring interoperability and security in communication.

Applications in Real-World Scenarios

Applications such as instant messaging, email encryption, and secure file transfer rely on key exchange protocols to establish secure communication channels. Online transactions, such as those in banking and online shopping, use key exchange protocols to secure payment information and personal data. In IoT ecosystems, secure key exchange is essential for protecting data transmitted between devices and ensuring the integrity and authenticity of the communication.

Key exchange protocols are fundamental to the security of modern communication systems. They enable the secure distribution of encryption keys, protect against various attacks, and ensure compliance with legal and regulatory requirements. By providing confidentiality, integrity, authentication, and forward secrecy, key exchange protocols form the backbone of secure communication in a wide range of applications.

Classic Key Exchange Protocols

Here, we will discuss some of the classic key exchange protocols that have laid the groundwork for modern cryptographic practices.

Diffie-Hellman Key Exchange

Proposed by Whitfield Diffie and Martin Hellman in 1976, the Diffie-Hellman key exchange is one of the foundational and most influential protocols for key exchange. It enables two parties to securely establish a shared secret key, which can then be used to encrypt future communications.

How It Works:

1. Both parties agree on a large prime number p and a base g (which is a primitive root modulo p).
2. Each party generates a private key: a for Alice and b for Bob.
3. Alice computes $A = g^a \bmod p$ and Bob computes $B = g^b \bmod p$.
4. Alice sends A to Bob, and Bob sends B to Alice.
5. Alice computes the shared secret $s = B^a \bmod p$ and Bob computes the shared secret $s = A^b \bmod p$.
6. Both parties now have the same shared secrets, which can be used for secure communication.

Strengths:

- Secure against eavesdropping, as the shared secret is never transmitted.
- Provides a foundation for many other cryptographic protocols.

Weaknesses:

- Vulnerable to man-in-the-middle attacks if the identities of the communicating parties are not authenticated.

RSA Key Exchange

Named after its creators Rivest, Shamir, and Adleman, the RSA algorithm is extensively utilized for secure key exchange, digital signatures, and encryption. Unlike the Diffie-Hellman protocol, RSA relies on the computational challenge of factoring large composite numbers.

How It Works:

1. Each party generates a public-private key pair.
2. The sender encrypts the key with the recipient's public key.
3. The recipient decrypts the received key with their private key.

Steps:

1. Alice and Bob generate their RSA key pairs: (e_A, d_A, n_A) and (e_B, d_B, n_B).
2. Alice wants to send a key *k* to Bob. She encrypts *k* using Bob's public key e_B : C = k^{eB} mod n_B.
3. Alice sends c to Bob.
4. Bob decrypts c using his private key d_B: k = c^{dB} mod n_B.

Strengths:

- Provides both encryption and digital signatures
- Used for securely sharing symmetric keys

Weaknesses:

- Slower than symmetric key algorithms for large data
- Requires secure management of private keys

ElGamal Key Exchange

ElGamal encryption, developed by Taher ElGamal in 1985, is based on the Diffie-Hellman key exchange and offers both encryption and key exchange capabilities. It is used in various cryptographic systems, including PGP.

How It Works:

1. Both parties agree on a large prime number p and a base g.
2. Each party generates a private key and computes the corresponding public key.
3. The sender encrypts a message using the recipient's public key and a randomly generated ephemeral key.
4. The recipient decrypts the message using their private key and the ephemeral key.

Steps:

1. Alice and Bob agree on p and g.
2. Alice generates a private key a and public key A = g^a mod p.

3. Bob generates a private key b and public key B = g^b mod *p*.
4. Alice wants to send a key *k* to Bob. She generates a random ephemeral key *r* and computes c1 = gr mod p and c2 = k.Br mod p.
5. Alice sends (c1,c2) (c1 ,c2) to Bob.
6. Bob computes s = cb1 mod p and k = c2.s-1 mod p.

Strengths:

- Provides forward secrecy
- Flexible and can be adapted for various cryptographic tasks

Weaknesses:

- Larger ciphertext size compared to the original message
- Vulnerable to certain types of cryptographic attacks if not implemented correctly

Modern Key Exchange Protocols

Here, we will discuss some of the most prominent modern key exchange protocols.

Elliptic Curve Diffie-Hellman (ECDH)

Elliptic Curve Diffie-Hellman (ECDH) is an extension of the classic Diffie-Hellman key exchange protocol that uses elliptic curve cryptography (ECC) to provide the same level of security with smaller key sizes. This makes ECDH more efficient in terms of computational load, bandwidth, and storage requirements.

How It Works:

1. Both parties agree on an elliptic curve and a base point G on that curve.
2. Each party generates a private key and computes the corresponding public key by multiplying the base point by their private key.
3. The shared secret is derived by multiplying the public key of the other party by their own private key.

Steps:

1. Alice and Bob agree on an elliptic curve and base point G.
2. Alice generates a private key a and computes her public key A = *a*G.
3. Bob generates a private key b and computes his public key B = *b*G.
4. Alice computes the shared secret S = *a*B.
5. Bob computes the shared secret S = *b*A.

Strengths:

- More efficient than traditional Diffie-Hellman
- Smaller key sizes for equivalent security levels
- Suitable for resource-constrained environments such as IoT

Weaknesses:

- Requires careful implementation to avoid side-channel attacks

Post-Quantum Key Exchange Protocols

Post-quantum key exchange protocols are designed to be secure against attacks by quantum computers. These protocols use mathematical problems that are believed to be resistant to quantum attacks, such as lattice-based, code-based, and multivariate polynomial-based cryptography.

Examples:

1. **Lattice-Based Key Exchange (NewHope):**
    - Based on the hardness of the Learning with Errors (LWE) problem.
    - Offers strong security guarantees against quantum attacks.
2. **Code-Based Key Exchange:**
    - Uses problems related to error-correcting codes.
    - Example: McEliece cryptosystem.
3. **Supersingular Isogeny Diffie-Hellman (SIDH):**
    - Uses the properties of isogenies between supersingular elliptic curves.
    - Provides smaller key sizes compared to other post-quantum schemes.

Strengths:

- Designed to be secure against both classical and quantum attacks.
- A diverse range of mathematical foundations increases the resilience of cryptographic systems.

Weaknesses:

- Post-quantum protocols require more computational resources, leading to higher latency and energy consumption, which can be problematic for resource-constrained devices.
- Many post-quantum schemes have significantly larger key sizes, posing challenges for storage, transmission, and bandwidth in constrained systems.
- The relative immaturity of post-quantum protocols and the lack of

standardization introduce uncertainties about their practical security and long-term reliability.

- Implementing post-quantum protocols securely is complex and increases the risk of introducing vulnerabilities, especially from side-channel attacks.

Practical Implementations and Standards

The following example demonstrates the basic usage of key exchange protocols using Python libraries. The cryptography library is versatile and widely used for implementing cryptographic protocols, including key exchanges. The provided code snippets show how to perform the Elliptic Curve Diffie-Hellman (ECDH) key exchange, ensuring that both parties can securely compute a shared secret.

Key Derivation Functions

Key Derivation Functions (KDFs) play a fundamental role in the field of cryptography, serving as a critical bridge between raw cryptographic material and securely usable cryptographic keys. At their core, KDFs are designed to take an initial input–often a password, master key, or other secret–and transform it into one or more cryptographic keys suitable for specific uses. This transformation ensures that the resulting keys are both secure and tailored to the requirements of the cryptographic system in which they will be used.

The historical context of KDFs can be traced back to the early days of cryptography when simple password-hashing techniques were employed to safeguard user credentials. However, as computing power grew, and attacks became more sophisticated, it became clear that more robust methods were needed. Early KDFs such as PBKDF2 (Password-Based Key Derivation Function 2), which was introduced as part of the RSA PKCS #5 standard, marked a significant step forward by incorporating techniques such as salting and iteration to enhance security against brute-force and dictionary attacks. Over time, advancements in cryptography have led to the development of more sophisticated KDFs, each offering unique features to address emerging security challenges.

Example Code for Key Exchange Using Cryptography Library:

```
from cryptography.hazmat.primitives.asymmetric import ec
from cryptography.hazmat.primitives import serialization
from cryptography.hazmat.primitives.kdf.hkdf import HKDF
from cryptography.hazmat.primitives import hashes
from cryptography.hazmat.backends import default_backend

# Generate private keys for both parties
private_key_A = ec.generate_private_key(ec.SECP384R1(), default_back-
end())
```

```
private_key_B = ec.generate_private_key(ec.SECP384R1(), default_back-
end())

# Generate public keys
public_key_A = private_key_A.public_key()
public_key_B = private_key_B.public_key()

# Exchange public keys
# In a real scenario, this exchange would happen over a secure channel

# Compute shared secrets
shared_secret_A = private_key_A.exchange(ec.ECDH(), public_key_B)
shared_secret_B = private_key_B.exchange(ec.ECDH(), public_key_A)

# Both shared secrets should be the same
assert shared_secret_A == shared_secret_B

# Derive a key from the shared secret
derived_key = HKDF(
    algorithm=hashes.SHA256(),
    length=32,
    salt=None,
    info=b'handshake data',
    backend=default_backend()
).derive(shared_secret_A)

print(f"Derived Key: {derived_key.hex()}")
```

KDFs are crucial in cryptographic systems for several reasons. Firstly, they enhance security by ensuring that keys derived from potentially weak or low-entropy sources, such as user passwords, are strong and resistant to attacks. This is achieved through processes such as salting, which adds random data to the input to ensure that even identical inputs yield different outputs, and iteration, which repeatedly applies the KDF function to make brute-force attacks more computationally expensive. Secondly, KDFs enable the secure generation of multiple keys from a single master key, facilitating the secure management of cryptographic keys across different applications and services. This is particularly important in environments where different keys are required for encryption, authentication, and integrity checks, but a single master key must be protected.

Moreover, KDFs play a pivotal role in ensuring compliance with industry standards and regulations. Many cryptographic frameworks and protocols mandate the use of KDFs to meet security requirements, making them an integral part of secure communication protocols, secure storage systems, and various authentication mechanisms. For example, protocols such as TLS (Transport Layer Security) and secure file storage solutions rely on KDFs to derive session keys and encryption keys, respectively, from initial secrets shared between parties.

Trivially, Key Derivation Functions are indispensable tools in modern cryptography, providing the means to transform raw cryptographic material into secure, usable keys. Their evolution from simple password hashing methods to sophisticated algorithms reflects the ongoing advancements in cryptographic research and the ever-increasing need for robust security measures. As we delve deeper into the specifics of KDFs in this chapter, we will explore their types, properties, and applications, highlighting their significance in safeguarding digital communication and data.

Basic Concepts of KDFs

Key Derivation Functions (KDFs) require specific inputs to generate secure cryptographic keys. These inputs are carefully chosen to ensure the security and uniqueness of the derived keys. The primary inputs to a KDF include:

- **Master Key**: The primary secret input to the KDF, often a password, passphrase, or another form of initial keying material. The master key must be kept secure, as its compromise would jeopardize all derived keys.
- **Salt**: A random value added to the input of the KDF to ensure that identical inputs produce different outputs. Salting prevents precomputed attacks, such as rainbow table attacks, by making each key derivation unique.
- **Context**: Additional optional data used to differentiate key derivations for different purposes or applications. Contextual information helps ensure that keys derived for one purpose are not reused for another, enhancing security through domain separation.

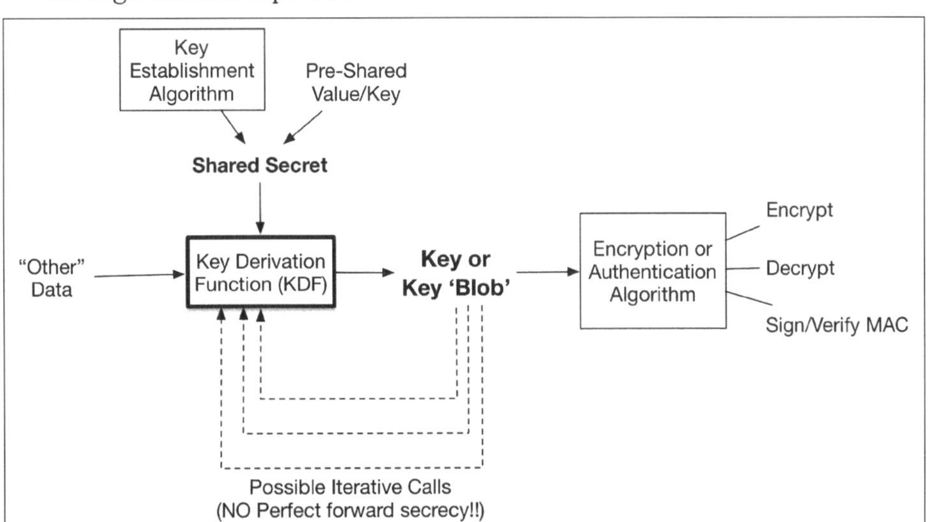

***Figure 7.2**: General Overview of Key Derivation Functions*

Desired Properties of a KDF

KDFs are designed with several essential properties to ensure they fulfill their role in cryptographic systems securely and efficiently:

- **Security**: The primary goal of a KDF is to generate strong, secure keys from potentially weak or low-entropy inputs. This involves resistance to brute-force attacks, dictionary attacks, and other forms of cryptanalysis. KDFs achieve security through techniques, such as salting and iteration.
- **Efficiency**: While ensuring security, a KDF must also be efficient in terms of computational resources and time. The balance between security and efficiency is crucial, as overly complex KDFs may be impractical for real-world use, while overly simple KDFs may be insecure.
- **Determinism**: A KDF must be deterministic, meaning that given the same inputs (master key, salt, and context), it will always produce the same output. Determinism ensures consistency and predictability in cryptographic key generation.
- **Scalability**: KDFs should support scalable parameters, allowing for adjustments in computational cost based on evolving security requirements. This typically includes configurable iteration counts and memory usage to adapt to advancements in computing power and attack techniques.

Common Use Cases for KDFs

KDFs are employed in a wide range of cryptographic applications, highlighting their versatility and importance:

- **Password Hashing**: KDFs are used to securely hash passwords for storage. Techniques such as PBKDF2, bcrypt, and Argon2 enhance security by incorporating salting and multiple iterations, making password cracking more challenging for attackers.
- **Key Management**: In key management systems, KDFs derive multiple cryptographic keys from a single master key. This approach ensures secure key separation for different cryptographic operations, such as encryption, decryption, and authentication.
- **Secure Communication Protocols**: KDFs are integral to secure communication protocols such as TLS and SSL. They derive session keys from shared secrets, enabling secure data transmission over potentially insecure networks.
- **Cryptographic Key Generation**: In various cryptographic systems, KDFs generate keys for encryption, digital signatures, and other cryptographic functions. This includes generating keys for symmetric encryption algorithms such as AES and for asymmetric schemes such as RSA or ECC.

- **File and Disk Encryption**: KDFs derive encryption keys for securing data at rest. Tools such as VeraCrypt and BitLocker use KDFs to generate strong encryption keys from user passwords, ensuring the confidentiality and integrity of stored data.

The basic concepts of Key Derivation Functions revolve around their inputs, desired properties, and diverse use cases. By transforming potentially weak or low-entropy inputs into strong, secure keys, KDFs play a pivotal role in ensuring the security and integrity of cryptographic systems. As we delve deeper into the specifics of different KDF algorithms and their applications, we will explore how these basic concepts are implemented and leveraged in various real-world scenarios.

Types of Key Derivation Functions

Key Derivation Functions (KDFs) come in various forms, each tailored for specific cryptographic needs. They can be broadly categorized into two main types: Password-based KDFs and Cryptographic KDFs.

Password-Based Key Derivation Functions

The Password-based Key Derivation Functions are designed specifically for generating cryptographic keys from passwords or passphrases. These KDFs are crucial for securely storing and using passwords in cryptographic applications.

PBKDF2 (Password-Based Key Derivation Function 2)

PBKDF2 is one of the most widely used Password-Based KDFs. It is defined in RFC 2898 and is part of the PKCS #5 standard. PBKDF2 operates by applying a pseudorandom function (typically HMAC-SHA-1 or HMAC-SHA-256) to the input password, combined with salt and iterates this process multiple times to produce a derived key.

Advantages of PBKDF2:

- **Security**: PBKDF2 is resistant to brute-force and dictionary attacks due to its use of multiple iterations and a salt value.
- **Standardization**: As part of the PKCS #5 standard, PBKDF2 is widely adopted and supported across various platforms and libraries.

Limitations of PBKDF2:

- **Efficiency**: While secure, PBKDF2 can be computationally intensive, which might be a disadvantage in resource-constrained environments.
- **Fixed Iteration Count**: Once the iteration count is set, it cannot adapt to increasing computational power over time.

Cryptographic Key Derivation Functions

Cryptographic KDFs are designed to derive cryptographic keys from more generalized secret inputs, such as shared secrets in key exchange protocols or master keys in key management systems. These KDFs are optimized for performance and security in cryptographic systems.

HKDF (HMAC-based Key Derivation Function)

HKDF, defined in RFC 5869, is a simple and robust KDF that is widely used in various cryptographic protocols, including TLS 1.3 and Signal. HKDF uses HMAC (Hash-based Message Authentication Code) as its core building block. It operates in two stages: an extraction stage and an expansion stage.

Advantages of HKDF:

- **Modularity**: The separation of extraction and expansion stages allows flexibility in different use cases.
- **Security**: HKDF inherits the security properties of the underlying HMAC function, providing strong cryptographic guarantees.
- **Simplicity**: HKDF is straightforward to implement and understand, making it a popular choice for cryptographic applications.

SP 800-108 KDFs

The NIST Special Publication 800-108 defines a family of KDFs based on HMAC, CMAC (Cipher-based Message Authentication Code), and KMAC (Keccak Message Authentication Code). These KDFs are designed to be versatile and secure for various cryptographic applications.

Types of SP 800-108 KDFs:

- **Counter Mode**: This KDF uses a counter and a pseudorandom function (PRF) to generate multiple keys from a single input key and context information.
- **Feedback Mode**: This KDF uses feedback from the output of the previous iteration to generate the next key, ensuring that each derived key is unique.
- **Double Pipeline Iteration Mode**: This KDF combines features of the counter and feedback modes to provide additional security and flexibility.

Advantages of SP 800-108 KDFs:

- **Flexibility**: The different modes provide options for various security and performance requirements.
- **Standardization**: As a NIST standard, SP 800-108 KDFs are widely recognized and trusted in the industry.

- **Adaptability**: These KDFs can be used with different PRFs, such as HMAC, CMAC, or KMAC, allowing for integration into diverse cryptographic systems.

The types of Key Derivation Functions encompass both Password-Based KDFs, like PBKDF2, and Cryptographic KDFs, such as HKDF and SP 800-108 KDFs. Each type serves distinct purposes and offers specific advantages tailored to the needs of secure key derivation in various cryptographic contexts. Understanding the differences and applications of these KDFs is crucial for implementing robust cryptographic systems.

Security Considerations

When implementing and using Key Derivation Functions (KDFs), it's essential to consider the various security threats they may face and employ strategies to mitigate these risks. This section discusses common threats to KDFs, strategies to enhance their security, and different KDFs in terms of security, cost, and performance.

Common Threats to KDFs

To better understand the security challenges associated with KDFs, it is crucial to examine the various threats they face. These vulnerabilities can undermine the effectiveness of KDFs and compromise the overall security of cryptographic systems. Here, we explore some of the most common threats to KDFs and their potential impacts.

Brute Force Attacks:

- **Definition**: Attackers attempt to guess the input to the KDF (for example, passwords) by trying all possible combinations.
- **Impact**: If a KDF is not designed to be computationally intensive, attackers can quickly try many possibilities and find the correct one.

Dictionary Attacks:

- **Definition**: Attackers use a pre-compiled list of commonly used passwords to guess the input to the KDF.
- **Impact**: Similar to brute force attacks, but potentially faster since it uses a list of likely passwords.

Side-Channel Attacks:

- **Definition**: Attackers exploit physical or implementation-specific characteristics (for example, timing information, power consumption) to infer the input to the KDF.
- **Impact**: Even strong cryptographic algorithms can be vulnerable if they leak information through side channels.

Collision Attacks:

- **Definition**: Attackers attempt to find two different inputs that produce the same derived key.
- **Impact**: Undermines the security of the system relying on the KDF if attackers can create malicious inputs that collide with legitimate ones.

Strategies to Enhance KDF Security

To strengthen the security of KDFs and mitigate potential threats, various strategies can be employed. These techniques enhance the resilience of KDFs against attacks and ensure the derived keys remain secure. Here, we outline key approaches to improving KDF security.

Salting:

- **Definition**: Adding a unique, random value (salt) to each input before processing it with the KDF.
- **Purpose**: Prevents precomputed attacks such as rainbow tables by ensuring that the same input always produces a different derived key.
- **Implementation**: Ensure that salts are unique and randomly generated for each input.

Iteration Count:

- **Definition**: Repeatedly applying the KDF to the input to increase computational cost.
- **Purpose**: Slows down brute force and dictionary attacks by making each guess more time-consuming.
- **Implementation**: Choose an iteration count that balances security and performance. Higher counts provide better security but require more processing time.

Memory-Hard Functions:

- **Definition**: KDFs that require significant memory resources to compute.
- **Purpose**: Mitigates attacks using specialized hardware (for example, GPUs, ASICs, and so on) by making the function expensive in terms of memory as well as computation.
- **Examples**: Argon2, scrypt, and so on.

Comparison of Different KDFs in Terms of Security and Performance

Selecting the appropriate KDF requires balancing security and performance to meet specific use case requirements. The following comparison highlights the strengths, weaknesses, and ideal applications of commonly used KDFs, helping in informed decision-making for secure cryptographic implementations.

PBKDF2:

- **Security**: Relies on salting and a high iteration count to deter brute force and dictionary attacks.
- **Performance**: Medium computational cost, widely supported but less efficient than modern alternatives.
- **Use Cases**: Commonly used for password hashing and encryption key derivation due to its balance of security and performance.

HKDF:

- **Security**: Utilizes HMAC for robust security, with salting and flexibility in input processing.
- **Performance**: Highly efficient and suitable for real-time applications.
- **Use Cases**: Preferred for key exchange protocols and secure session key derivation in protocols such as TLS.

scrypt:

- **Security**: Incorporates salting, high iteration count, and memory-hard functions to provide strong resistance against brute force attacks.
- **Performance**: High memory and CPU cost, making it secure but resource-intensive.
- **Use Cases**: Ideal for password hashing where maximum security is required.

Argon2:

- **Security**: Designed for high security with salting, iteration count, and memory-hard properties. Winner of the Password Hashing Competition (PHC).
- **Performance**: Adjustable cost parameters allow tuning for different security and performance needs.
- **Use Cases**: Password hashing and secure key derivation with customizable security parameters.

SP 800-108:

- **Security**: Offers flexibility with different modes (counter, feedback, double pipeline iteration) and can use various pseudorandom functions.
- **Performance**: Efficient and suitable for a wide range of cryptographic applications.
- **Use Cases**: General-purpose key derivation, adaptable to various security requirements.

KDFs are essential for securely deriving cryptographic keys from passwords and other secret inputs. Understanding the security threats they face and implementing appropriate strategies, such as salting, iteration count, and memory-hard functions, is crucial for maintaining their security. Different KDFs offer varying levels of security and performance, making it important to choose the right KDF based on the specific use case and security requirements.

Practical Applications of KDFs

Key Derivation Functions (KDFs) play a vital role in various practical applications within cryptographic systems. Their primary purpose is to derive secure keys from potentially weak inputs, such as passwords or other secrets, ensuring the robustness of the overall security architecture. Here, we explore three key applications of KDFs: secure password storage, key derivation for encryption keys, and deriving multiple keys from a single master key.

Secure Password Storage

One of the most common and crucial applications of KDFs is in the secure storage of passwords. Simply hashing passwords is insufficient due to the vulnerability to dictionary and brute-force attacks, especially when users often choose weak or common passwords. KDFs enhance the security of password storage by incorporating several mechanisms:

- **Salting**: A unique, random value (salt) is added to each password before applying the KDF. This ensures that even identical passwords will result in different derived values, thwarting precomputed attacks such as rainbow tables.
- **Iteration Count**: The KDF is applied repeatedly, making each guess computationally expensive and slowing down brute-force attacks.
- **Memory-Hard Functions**: Functions such as scrypt and Argon2 require significant memory resources, making attacks using specialized hardware less feasible.

For example, a system might use PBKDF2 with a high iteration count and a unique salt for each password, or Argon2, which adds a layer of memory hardness, to securely store user passwords. These techniques significantly enhance the security of stored passwords, protecting against common attack vectors.

Key Derivation for Encryption Keys

KDFs are essential for deriving strong encryption keys from potentially weak inputs, such as passwords or other secret values. This is critical in applications where users need to encrypt and decrypt sensitive data, ensuring that the derived keys are robust and resistant to attacks. Key derivation for encryption typically involves:

- **Deriving a Strong Key**: From a password or passphrase, a KDF generates a cryptographically strong key suitable for encryption algorithms.
- **Salting and Iterations**: Similar to password storage, salting and applying the KDF multiple times ensure that the derived keys are secure.

For instance, in file encryption applications, a user's password can be processed through a KDF such as PBKDF2 or HKDF to derive a strong encryption key, which is then used to encrypt the file. This ensures that even if the password is relatively weak, the derived key remains robust and secure.

Deriving Multiple Keys from a Single Master Key

In complex cryptographic systems, there is often a need to derive multiple keys from a single master key for different purposes, such as encrypting different data streams or securing multiple communication channels. KDFs provide a structured way to achieve this:

- **Hierarchical Key Derivation**: A master key is used as the input to a KDF, which then generates multiple subkeys, each used for a different purpose.
- **Context-Specific Information**: Additional context information can be included in the derivation process to ensure that each derived key is unique and contextually appropriate.

A common use case is in secure communication protocols such as TLS, where a master key derived from the initial key exchange is further processed to generate multiple session keys for encryption, integrity, and authentication purposes. HKDF is often used in these scenarios due to its flexibility and efficiency in deriving multiple keys from a single master key.

Implementation Examples

In this section, we will demonstrate the implementation of key derivation functions using Python. Key Derivation Functions (KDFs) are essential in cryptographic systems to derive secure keys from a master key or a password. We will see a few examples using popular KDFs, such as PBKDF2 and HKDF. These examples will illustrate how to securely derive keys suitable for various cryptographic purposes.

Example of PBKDF2 Implementation

PBKDF2 (Password-Based Key Derivation Function 2) is widely used for securely storing passwords and generating cryptographic keys. The following code snippet is a Python implementation using the **`hashlib`** library.

```
import hashlib
import os
```

```
def pbkdf2_key_derivation(password, salt=None, iterations=100000,
dklen=32):
    if salt is None:
        salt = os.urandom(16)  # Generate a random salt if not provided
    key = hashlib.pbkdf2_hmac('sha256', password.encode(), salt,
iterations, dklen)
    return key, salt

# Example usage
password = "securepassword"
key, salt = pbkdf2_key_derivation(password)
print(f"Derived key: {key.hex()}")
print(f"Salt: {salt.hex()}")
```

Example of HKDF Implementation

HKDF (HMAC-based Extract-and-Expand Key Derivation Function) is another widely used KDF suitable for deriving multiple keys from a single master key. The following code snippet is a Python implementation using the **`hashlib`** library.

Example Code for HKDF using `hashlib` library:

```
import hashlib
import hmac

def hkdf(key, salt, info, length=32, hash_func=hashlib.sha256):
    # Extract phase
    if salt is None:
        salt = bytes([0] * hash_func().digest_size)
    prk = hmac.new(salt, key, hash_func).digest()

    # Expand phase
    output_key = b""
    block = b""
    block_num = 0

    while len(output_key) < length:
        block_num += 1
        block = hmac.new(prk, block + info + bytes([block_num]), hash_
func).digest()
        output_key += block

    return output_key[:length]

# Example usage
master_key = b"masterkey"
salt = b"randomsalt"
```

```
info = b"application-specific info"
derived_key = hkdf(master_key, salt, info)
print(f"Derived key: {derived_key.hex()}")
```

In this section, we delved into the critical role that Key Derivation Functions (KDFs) play in modern cryptographic systems. Starting with an introduction to KDFs, we explored their historical context and the necessity of transforming weak keys, such as passwords, into strong cryptographic keys. This chapter emphasized the fundamental importance of KDFs in ensuring the security and integrity of various cryptographic operations.

We discussed the basic concepts underlying KDFs, including the essential inputs, such as master keys, salt, and context, as well as the desired properties such as security, efficiency, and determinism. Understanding these foundational aspects is crucial for selecting and implementing appropriate KDFs for different applications.

We then explored the different types of KDFs, specifically focusing on Password-Based KDFs such as PBKDF2 and Cryptographic KDFs such as HKDF and SP 800-108 KDFs. Each type of KDF was examined for its specific use cases, highlighting their respective strengths and applications in real-world scenarios.

Security considerations were a major focus, where we identified common threats to KDFs, including brute force attacks and side-channel attacks. Strategies to enhance KDF security were discussed, such as using salting, increasing iteration counts, and employing memory-hard functions. A comparison of various KDFs in terms of security and performance provided a practical guide for selecting the most suitable KDF for different requirements.

We also covered the practical applications of KDFs, demonstrating their use in secure password storage, key derivation for encryption keys, and deriving multiple keys from a single master key. These examples underscored the versatility and necessity of KDFs in maintaining the security of cryptographic systems.

Finally, we provided implementation examples of key derivation functions in Python, illustrating how to implement PBKDF2 and HKDF. These examples offered a hands-on approach to understanding the practical application of KDFs.

In summary, this chapter provided a comprehensive overview of Key Derivation Functions, highlighting their importance, functionality, and application in cryptographic systems. As we move forward, the knowledge gained here will be essential for understanding more advanced cryptographic schemes and protocols.

Homomorphic Encryption

In the ever-evolving landscape of cryptography, homomorphic encryption stands out as a groundbreaking advancement that addresses one of the most challenging aspects of data security: the ability to perform computations on encrypted data without revealing the underlying plaintext. This revolutionary technology opens up new possibilities for secure data processing, enabling privacy-preserving computations and enhancing the security of sensitive information across various domains.

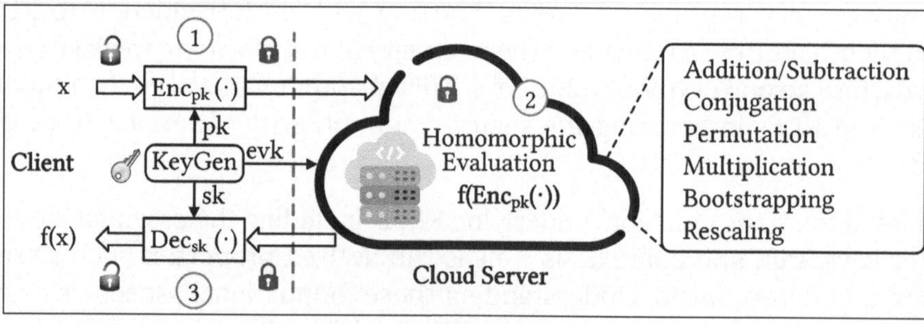

***Figure 7.3**: FHE-based crypto system*

The concept of homomorphic encryption dates back to the late 1970s, but it wasn't until Craig Gentry's seminal work in 2009 that a practical fully homomorphic encryption (FHE) scheme was realized. Gentry's scheme demonstrated that it is possible to perform arbitrary computations on encrypted data, producing encrypted results that, when decrypted, match the results of operations performed on the plaintext. This breakthrough paved the way for a myriad of applications, particularly in areas where data privacy and security are paramount.

Homomorphic encryption can be categorized into three main types: partially homomorphic encryption (PHE), somewhat homomorphic encryption (SHE), and fully homomorphic encryption (FHE). Each type offers varying degrees of functionality and complexity. PHE supports a limited number of operations on ciphertext, such as addition or multiplication. SHE extends this capability to a greater number of operations but still falls short of supporting arbitrary computations. FHE, the most powerful and versatile form, enables unlimited operations on encrypted data, making it a highly sought-after solution for secure computation. In the preceding figure, one pictorial functionality of an FHE crypto system is shown, where enumerated operations are (1) encryption, (2) homomorphic evaluation, and (3) decryption.

The importance of homomorphic encryption lies in its ability to transform how sensitive data is handled in various sectors. For instance, in healthcare, it allows medical researchers to analyze encrypted patient data without compromising privacy. In finance, it enables secure processing of encrypted financial transactions, reducing the risk of data breaches. In cloud computing, homomorphic encryption provides a robust method for ensuring data privacy while leveraging the computational power of cloud services.

Despite its immense potential, homomorphic encryption also faces significant challenges, particularly in terms of performance and efficiency. Fully homomorphic encryption schemes are computationally intensive and can be slower compared to traditional encryption methods. However, ongoing research and advancements in this field aim to address these limitations, making homomorphic encryption more practical for real-world applications.

Zero-Knowledge Proofs

Zero-Knowledge Proofs (ZKPs) represent a fascinating and pivotal concept in cryptography, where one party (the prover) can convince another party (the verifier) that they know a value or a statement is true without revealing any information about the value itself. This cryptographic method ensures that no knowledge beyond the validity of the statement is disclosed, hence the term "zero-knowledge."

Historical Context

The concept of Zero-Knowledge Proofs was first introduced in the 1980s by Shafi Goldwasser, Silvio Micali, and Charles Rackoff in their groundbreaking paper. They introduced the idea within the broader context of interactive proofs and complexity theory. This pioneering work laid the foundation for a whole new realm of cryptographic protocols that emphasize privacy and security.

Basic Concept

A Zero-Knowledge Proof typically involves three properties:

- **Completeness**: If the statement is true, an honest prover can convince an honest verifier of this fact.
- **Soundness**: If the statement is false, no dishonest prover can convince the honest verifier that it is true, except with some small probability.
- **Zero-Knowledge**: If the statement is true, no verifier learns anything other than the fact that the statement is true.

One of the classic examples of a Zero-Knowledge Proof is the "coloring problem," where a prover demonstrates they can color a graph according to specific rules without revealing the coloring itself. This example highlights how ZKPs can verify complex properties without disclosing the underlying information.

Use Cases

Zero-Knowledge Proofs have diverse applications across various fields, particularly in enhancing privacy and security in digital interactions:

- **Cryptocurrencies**: ZKPs are widely used in cryptocurrencies such as Zcash to provide anonymous transactions. They ensure the validity of transactions without revealing the sender, receiver, or amount.

- **Authentication**: ZKPs can enable secure authentication systems where users prove their identity without revealing passwords or other sensitive information.
- **Blockchain Technology**: ZKPs can enhance privacy in blockchain applications by enabling confidential transactions and smart contracts.
- **Regulatory Compliance**: They allow businesses to prove compliance with regulations without disclosing sensitive data, making them useful in financial audits and legal compliance.

Future Directions

The future of Zero-Knowledge Proofs looks promising, with ongoing research and development aimed at making ZKPs more efficient and applicable to a broader range of use cases:

- **Scalability**: Researchers are focused on improving the scalability of ZKPs, making them more practical for large-scale applications such as blockchain and secure multiparty computation.
- **Post-Quantum Security**: As the threat of quantum computing looms, ensuring that ZKPs remain secure against quantum attacks is a critical area of study.
- **Privacy-Enhancing Technologies**: ZKPs are expected to play a crucial role in the development of advanced privacy-preserving technologies, impacting fields, such as healthcare, finance, and data sharing.
- **Standardization**: Efforts are underway to standardize ZKP protocols, which will facilitate broader adoption and interoperability across different systems and platforms.

Zero-Knowledge Proofs are a cornerstone of modern cryptographic techniques, providing robust methods for proving statements without revealing any underlying information. Their applications are vast, spanning cryptocurrencies, authentication, and regulatory compliance, with significant potential for future advancements in scalability, quantum security, and privacy enhancement. As the digital world continues to evolve, ZKPs will undoubtedly remain integral to ensuring secure and private interactions across a myriad of platforms and applications.

Multi-Party Computation

Multi-Party Computation (MPC) is an advanced cryptographic technique that enables multiple parties to jointly compute a function over their inputs while keeping those inputs private. This means that no party learns anything about the other parties' inputs beyond what can be inferred from the output. The concept of MPC is rooted in the seminal works of Andrew Yao in the 1980s, particularly his famous "Yao's Millionaires' Problem," which introduced the notion of secure computation between two parties. Over the years, the field has evolved significantly, encompassing a wide range of protocols and techniques designed to achieve secure computation among multiple parties.

Basic Concepts

At its core, MPC allows parties to perform computations on their private data without revealing it to others. This is achieved through cryptographic protocols that ensure the privacy and correctness of the computation. The primary goal of MPC is to enable collaborative computation in a way that respects the confidentiality of each party's input. This is crucial in scenarios where data privacy is paramount, such as in financial transactions, medical data analysis, and collaborative data mining.

The basic operation of MPC involves:

- **Secret Sharing**: Each party's input is split into shares and distributed among all parties. This ensures that no single party has access to the complete input data of any other party.
- **Computation**: The parties jointly compute the function using the shares. Intermediate results are also kept in shares to maintain privacy throughout the computation.
- **Reconstructio**n: The final result is reconstructed from the shares, providing the output to all parties.

Use Cases

MPC has a wide range of applications across various domains:

- **Financial Services**: Banks and financial institutions can use MPC to perform joint risk analysis and fraud detection without revealing sensitive customer data.
- **Healthcare**: MPC enables collaborative research and analysis of medical data from different institutions while preserving patient privacy.
- **Supply Chain Management**: Companies can share and analyze supply chain data to optimize operations without disclosing proprietary information.
- **E-Voting**: MPC can ensure the privacy and integrity of votes in electronic voting systems, preventing vote manipulation and ensuring voter anonymity.

Future Directions

The future of MPC is promising, with ongoing research focusing on improving the efficiency and scalability of MPC protocols. Key areas of development include:

- **Performance Optimization**: Reducing the computational and communication overhead of MPC protocols to make them practical for large-scale applications.

- **Enhanced Security**: Developing protocols resistant to various types of attacks, including collusion among parties and side-channel attacks.
- **Integration with Other Technologies**: Combining MPC with other cryptographic techniques, such as homomorphic encryption and zero-knowledge proofs, to enhance its capabilities.
- **Standardization**: Establishing industry standards for MPC to facilitate its widespread adoption and interoperability among different systems.

Multi-Party Computation is a powerful tool in the cryptographic arsenal, offering a robust solution for secure collaborative computation. Its ability to protect data privacy while enabling joint computation makes it invaluable in numerous applications. As research progresses, MPC is expected to become more efficient and widely adopted, playing a crucial role in the future of secure data processing and analysis.

Conclusion

In this chapter, we embarked on a comprehensive exploration of various cryptographic schemes that form the bedrock of secure communications and data protection in the modern digital landscape. We delved into established techniques, such as digital signatures, key exchange protocols, and key derivation functions, each of which plays a critical role in ensuring the authenticity, confidentiality, and integrity of data. Key derivation functions (KDFs) were also thoroughly analyzed. We explained their purpose in deriving secure keys from a master key or password and ensuring the secure use of cryptographic systems, In addition to these well-established techniques, we ventured into emerging cryptographic schemes that are currently subjects of active research and development. Homomorphic encryption was discussed for its groundbreaking potential to perform computations on encrypted data without revealing the underlying information. Zero-knowledge proofs were examined for their ability to verify the truth of a statement without disclosing any additional information. Lastly, we explored multi-party computation (MPC), which enables collaborative computations while preserving the privacy of each party's input. In summary, this chapter has provided a holistic view of both foundational and innovative cryptographic systems. We have not only discussed the technical details and practical applications of these schemes but also highlighted their evolving nature and the ongoing research that seeks to enhance their security and efficiency. However, even the most sophisticated cryptographic techniques cannot safeguard a system in isolation. Weaknesses in implementation, integration, or complementary security measures can undermine their effectiveness.

In the next chapter, *Security is Only as Strong as the Weakest Link*, we will shift our focus to understanding how these vulnerabilities arise, the importance of holistic security practices, and strategies to fortify systems against potential exploitation.

CHAPTER 8
Security is Only as Strong as the Weakest Link

Introduction

In the rapidly evolving landscape of cybersecurity, organizations and individuals alike are constantly grappling with threats that can compromise sensitive data, disrupt operations, and undermine trust. While significant attention is often paid to high-profile technologies and sophisticated defense mechanisms, it is crucial to recognize that security is not determined solely by the most advanced elements of a system, but rather by the least secure component within it. This principle is encapsulated in the adage, "Security is only as strong as the weakest link," underscoring the idea that a single vulnerability, no matter how seemingly minor, can jeopardize the integrity of an entire security framework.

The concept of security as a chain–where each link represents a component or aspect of the system–provides a powerful analogy for understanding how interconnected and interdependent security measures truly are. Just as the strength of a physical chain is determined by its weakest link, the overall security of a system is dictated by its most vulnerable point. Whether it's a poorly configured firewall, outdated software, inadequate employee training, or a weak password, these weak links can serve as entry points for attackers, rendering even the most sophisticated security technologies ineffective.

This chapter aims to explore the broader implications of this security principle, emphasizing the need for a holistic approach that goes beyond simply bolstering strong points in the security chain. A well-rounded security strategy must account for every element of the system, ensuring that even the most minor components are robust and resilient against threats. This requires continuous vigilance, regular risk assessments, and a proactive stance toward identifying and fortifying potential weak spots. The importance of this comprehensive approach cannot be overstated, as attackers will invariably seek out and exploit the path of least resistance.

In the realm of cybersecurity, the weakest link could manifest in many forms. It could be technical, such as an unpatched software vulnerability; human, such as employees falling victim to phishing attacks; or procedural, such as inadequate security policies and controls. This chapter will delve into the various dimensions of the security chain, examining how these vulnerabilities emerge and what can be done to address them. By understanding the diverse nature of weak links, organizations can better equip themselves to strengthen their defenses and mitigate the risk of security breaches.

Moreover, this chapter will highlight the importance of risk management and the role it plays in identifying and prioritizing security efforts. Effective risk management involves not only recognizing existing weak links but also anticipating potential vulnerabilities that could arise as technologies and threats evolve. Through case studies, real-world examples, and expert insights, we will explore how organizations have navigated these challenges, learning valuable lessons from both successes and failures.

As we progress through this chapter, the goal is to impart a deeper appreciation for the intricacies of security management and the critical need to address vulnerabilities holistically. While no system can ever be completely invulnerable, by fortifying every link in the security chain, we can build resilient defenses that stand a much better chance against the myriad of threats in today's digital world. Ultimately, understanding that "security is only as strong as the weakest link" is not just a guiding principle: it is a call to action for everyone involved in safeguarding information and assets.

Structure

In this chapter, the following topics will be covered,

- Identifying Weak Links in Security Systems
- Case Studies of Security Breaches
- Human Factors in Security
- Technical Vulnerabilities
- Security Testing and Assessment

Identifying Weak Links in Security Systems

In any security system, the identification of weak links is a critical step toward ensuring a comprehensive and effective defense against potential threats. The maxim that "a chain is only as strong as its weakest link" holds true in cybersecurity, where a single vulnerability can lead to a cascading failure of security measures. This section delves into the importance of recognizing these weak points, exploring how they can compromise entire systems, and providing examples of common vulnerabilities that often go unnoticed until exploited by attackers.

The Domino Effect of a Single Weak Point

Security systems are designed to work as cohesive units, with multiple layers of defenses that protect against unauthorized access, data breaches, and other cyber threats. However, if one component within this system is compromised, it can create a domino effect, rendering other defenses ineffective. For instance, consider a scenario where an organization's software is up-to-date and its firewall robust, but its password policy is lax, allowing users to set easily guessable passwords. In such a case, attackers could bypass strong external defenses by exploiting this weak link, gaining access through simple password guessing or credential stuffing attacks.

A single weak point doesn't just increase the risk of a breach; it can also amplify the damage once an intrusion occurs. For example, inadequate access controls might allow an attacker to move laterally within a network, accessing sensitive information and escalating privileges without encountering further resistance. Similarly, poor network segmentation can allow malware or ransomware to spread rapidly across an organization, affecting all connected systems. This highlights the importance of a holistic approach to security: one that doesn't merely focus on reinforcing the strongest components but systematically identifies and mitigates weaknesses throughout the entire security infrastructure.

Common Weak Links in Security Systems

- **Human Error:** Human error is one of the most prevalent and often the most unpredictable weak links in any security system. Whether it's falling victim to phishing attacks, misconfiguration of security settings, or accidentally leaking sensitive information, human factors account for a significant portion of security incidents. Phishing, in particular, remains a leading cause of breaches, with attackers exploiting users' trust and lack of awareness to steal credentials or deliver malware. Mitigating human error involves comprehensive training, creating a culture of security awareness, and implementing user-friendly security protocols that reduce the likelihood of mistakes.
- **Outdated Software:** Software vulnerabilities are a prime target for cyber attackers, who exploit flaws in outdated software to gain unauthorized access or cause disruptions. Organizations often delay or neglect updating software due to operational constraints, compatibility issues, or oversight, creating windows of opportunity for attackers. Regular patch management, automated updates, and a clear policy for end-of-life software can significantly reduce the risks associated with outdated applications and systems.

- **Inadequate Access Controls:** Poorly managed access controls can lead to unauthorized users gaining entry to sensitive data or critical systems. Weaknesses such as excessive user permissions, lack of role-based access, and insufficient authentication measures such as the absence of multi-factor authentication (MFA) are common culprits. To strengthen access controls, organizations should adopt the principle of least privilege, ensuring that users have only the minimum level of access necessary for their roles, and implement robust authentication mechanisms to verify user identities.
- **Poor Network Configurations:** Network misconfigurations, such as open ports, lack of encryption, and improper firewall rules, can expose systems to external attacks. Attackers often scan networks for such vulnerabilities, looking for entry points that allow them to bypass defenses. Regular network audits, proper configuration management, and the use of advanced tools such as intrusion detection and prevention systems (IDPS) can help identify and correct these weaknesses before they are exploited.
- **Unsecured Third-Party Integrations:** Third-party vendors and service providers are often part of the extended security perimeter, and their vulnerabilities can become your vulnerabilities. If a third-party provider lacks robust security measures, it can serve as a backdoor into your systems. This was the case in several high-profile breaches where attackers compromised third-party providers to gain access to their target's network. To mitigate this risk, organizations should enforce strict security standards for third-party vendors, conduct regular security assessments, and establish clear protocols for managing third-party access to sensitive systems.
- **Lack of Incident Response Planning:** Even the most secure systems can fall victim to a breach, which makes a well-prepared incident response plan essential. Organizations without a clear response strategy can find themselves scrambling in the wake of an attack, leading to delayed response times, increased damage, and prolonged recovery. Developing and regularly testing incident response plans ensures that an organization can act swiftly and effectively when a security incident occurs, minimizing the impact and restoring operations as quickly as possible.

Importance of Proactive Identification

Identifying weak links in security systems is not a one-time task but an ongoing process that requires vigilance, regular assessments, and a proactive mindset. Organizations must employ tools, such as vulnerability scanners, conduct regular security audits, and keep abreast of the latest threat intelligence to stay ahead of potential weaknesses. By continuously monitoring and addressing weak links, organizations can create a resilient security posture that withstands both existing and emerging threats.

In summary, the identification of weak links in security systems is fundamental to building a robust defense against cyber threats. By understanding and addressing common vulnerabilities, such as human error, outdated software, inadequate access controls, and poor network configurations, organizations can significantly enhance their security posture. Proactive identification and remediation of these weak points ensure that the overall strength of the security chain is maintained, reducing the risk of compromise and bolstering the resilience of the entire system.

Case Studies of Security Breaches

One of the most powerful ways to understand the importance of addressing weak links in security systems is through real-world examples. Over the years, several high-profile security breaches have occurred due to vulnerabilities that were either overlooked or underestimated. In this section, we will examine case studies of notable breaches, analyzing the causes and consequences to highlight how a single weak point can lead to devastating outcomes. These examples will underscore the importance of proactive vulnerability management and the necessity of a comprehensive, multi-layered approach to security.

Target Data Breach (2013)

The Target data breach of 2013 remains one of the most significant and instructive examples of how a weak link in a supply chain can lead to a large-scale security failure. In this case, attackers gained access to Target's internal network through a third-party vendor, Fazio Mechanical Services, which provided HVAC systems to Target stores. The attackers exploited weak security practices at Fazio, which used default credentials and lacked multi-factor authentication (MFA) for remote access to Target's network. Once inside, the attackers were able to move laterally across Target's network, installing malware on point-of-sale (POS) systems and stealing the credit card information of 40 million customers.

Causes:

- **Weak Vendor Security**: The breach occurred because Fazio Mechanical Services had weak security practices. As a third-party vendor, Fazio was given access to Target's network, but the lack of robust security measures made it easy for attackers to gain entry.
- **Lack of Segmentation**: Target's network was not adequately segmented, which allowed the attackers to move from a vendor access point to critical areas of the network where payment data was stored.
- **Slow Detection**: Target's security team initially detected the malware but did not act quickly enough to stop the breach from spreading, highlighting a gap in incident response readiness.

Consequences:

- **Financial Losses**: Target faced costs of around $300 million, including fines, settlements, and expenses for upgrading its security systems.
- **Reputation Damage**: The breach caused significant damage to Target's reputation, leading to a loss of consumer trust and a decline in sales during the critical holiday season.
- **Industry-Wide Impact**: The breach also raised awareness across industries about the risks of third-party vendors and the importance of enforcing stringent security policies for supply chain partners.

This breach highlights how a seemingly peripheral weak link, such as a third-party vendor, can have catastrophic consequences if not adequately secured. It also underscores the importance of network segmentation, timely response to threats, and ensuring that vendors adhere to the same security standards as the organization.

Equifax Data Breach (2017)

The 2017 Equifax breach is a prime example of how failing to address known software vulnerabilities can lead to a major data breach. Equifax, one of the largest credit reporting agencies, suffered a breach that exposed the personal information of 147 million individuals, including Social Security numbers, birthdates, and addresses. The cause of the breach was a failure to patch a known vulnerability in the Apache Struts web application framework, despite the availability of a patch two months prior to the attack.

Causes:

- **Failure to Patch Vulnerabilities**: The vulnerability in Apache Struts had been publicly disclosed, and a patch was available. However, Equifax's security team failed to apply the patch promptly, allowing attackers to exploit the flaw and gain access to sensitive data.
- **Inadequate Internal Controls**: Equifax lacked robust internal controls to ensure that critical patches were applied quickly across their systems. The lack of oversight and accountability allowed the vulnerability to remain unaddressed.
- Weak Network Segmentation: Once inside the network, the attackers were able to access multiple databases due to poor network segmentation, gaining access to sensitive data that should have been better protected.

Consequences:

- **Massive Data Exposure**: The breach exposed the highly sensitive personal information of nearly half the U.S. population, making this one of the largest and most damaging breaches in history.

- **Financial and Legal Fallout**: Equifax faced over $700 million in settlements and fines, in addition to the costs associated with legal fees, security improvements, and consumer credit monitoring services.
- **Erosion of Trust**: As a company responsible for safeguarding personal financial data, Equifax's reputation suffered irreparable damage. The breach also led to increased scrutiny of how organizations handle and protect consumer data.

The Equifax breach demonstrates the risks associated with unpatched vulnerabilities and the importance of maintaining a robust patch management process. It also highlights the need for proper internal oversight and network segmentation to prevent attackers from gaining unrestricted access to sensitive data.

Capital One Data Breach (2019)

The Capital One data breach of 2019 affected 106 million individuals and was caused by a misconfigured firewall in an Amazon Web Services (AWS) cloud server. A former AWS employee exploited the misconfiguration to gain access to Capital One's customer data, including Social Security numbers, bank account details, and credit card application information.

Causes:

- **Cloud Misconfiguration**: Thc brcach was madc possiblc by a misconfigured firewall in Capital One's AWS cloud environment. This allowed the attacker to access data that should have been protected by more stringent security controls.
- **Overprivileged Roles**: The attacker exploited overly permissive IAM (Identity and Access Management) roles, allowing them to perform actions beyond what was necessary, thus escalating the impact of the breach.
- **Slow Detection**: Although AWS offers several security monitoring tools, Capital One was slow to detect the breach, which gave the attacker time to access and exfiltrate large amounts of data.

Consequences:

- **Data Exposure**: The personal data of 106 million people, including sensitive financial information, was exposed. This data could be used for identity theft and other malicious activities.
- **Financial Penalties**: Capital One agreed to pay $80 million in fines, as well as the costs of lawsuits and consumer protections. The company also had to invest in upgrading its cloud security posture.
- **Increased Cloud Security Awareness**: This breach raised awareness across industries about the risks of cloud misconfigurations and the need for strong cloud security policies and practices.

This case highlights the risks associated with cloud environments, particularly when security misconfigurations go unnoticed. It also emphasizes the importance of properly configuring access controls and roles in cloud infrastructure, as well as the need for continuous monitoring and incident detection in cloud-based systems.

Lessons Learned from These Case Studies

These examples illustrate that security breaches often arise from overlooked or poorly managed weak links in security systems. Whether it's human error, unpatched software, misconfigurations, or poor access controls, these vulnerabilities can lead to catastrophic consequences if not addressed. The case studies emphasize the following key takeaways:

- **Proactive Vulnerability Management**: Organizations must adopt a proactive approach to identifying and addressing vulnerabilities before attackers can exploit them. This includes regular patching, continuous monitoring, and frequent security audits.
- **Supply Chain Security**: Third-party vendors and service providers often introduce additional risks. Organizations must enforce strict security standards for third-party integrations and ensure that vendors comply with these requirements.
- **Incident Response and Detection**: The ability to detect and respond to security incidents in real-time is crucial. Slow detection and response can significantly amplify the damage caused by a breach, making it essential to have robust incident response plans and security monitoring tools in place.
- **Cloud Security**: As organizations increasingly move to cloud environments, the importance of proper cloud security practices cannot be overstated. Misconfigurations and over-privileged roles are common issues that must be addressed to ensure cloud data remains secure.

These breaches underscore the importance of viewing security holistically, addressing every potential weak link in the security chain to build a strong, resilient system that can withstand both internal and external threats.

Human Factors in Security

When it comes to securing an organization, the human element is often one of the most unpredictable and challenging factors to manage. Even the most sophisticated technology solutions and well-designed security architectures can be rendered ineffective by human errors or intentional malicious actions. Human behavior plays a pivotal role in the strength or vulnerability of a security system, and attackers frequently exploit this weakest link to bypass even the most secure infrastructures. In this section, we will explore how human factors, including social engineering attacks, insider threats, and lack of security awareness, can introduce vulnerabilities into an organization, and how proper training and awareness programs can mitigate these risks.

Social Engineering Attacks

One of the most common ways attackers exploit human behavior is through social engineering, a tactic that manipulates individuals into divulging sensitive information or performing actions that compromise security. Unlike traditional hacking, which focuses on exploiting technical vulnerabilities, social engineering relies on psychological manipulation to deceive individuals into bypassing security protocols.

- **Phishing Attacks:** One of the most widespread forms of social engineering is phishing, where attackers impersonate legitimate entities, such as a trusted company or colleague, to trick users into providing login credentials, credit card numbers, or other sensitive data. Phishing attacks often take the form of emails, phone calls, or text messages that appear genuine, prompting the recipient to click malicious links or open infected attachments.
- **Spear Phishing:** More targeted than general phishing, spear phishing involves personalized attacks directed at specific individuals or organizations. Attackers research their targets extensively, crafting messages that seem highly credible, which significantly increases the likelihood of success. High-ranking executives, known as "whales," are often the targets of these attacks due to their access to critical systems and data.
- **Baiting and Pretexting:** In baiting attacks, attackers leave physical media, such as USB drives, in places where employees will find them, hoping they will insert them into company computers. Pretexting involves attackers creating a fabricated scenario to gain trust and extract information, such as pretending to be from the IT department and asking for credentials to "fix" a problem.

The danger of social engineering lies in its ability to bypass technical security measures by exploiting human psychology. The most secure systems can be compromised if employees are tricked into handing over the keys, which is why education and awareness are crucial.

Insider Threats

While external attackers pose a significant risk, internal threats are equally, if not more, dangerous. Insider threats arise from individuals within the organization who have legitimate access to systems and data but use that access maliciously or negligently. These threats can come from employees, contractors, or business partners and are often harder to detect because the individual already has authorized access to sensitive areas of the system.

- **Malicious Insiders:** These are individuals who intentionally seek to harm the organization, often for financial gain, revenge, or ideological reasons. Malicious insiders may steal sensitive data, sabotage systems, or sell confidential information to competitors or criminal organizations. Edward Snowden's disclosure of classified NSA documents is a notable example of an insider threat causing global consequences.
- **Negligent Insiders:** Not all insider threats are intentional. Negligent insiders unintentionally create security vulnerabilities through careless actions, such as weak password practices, sharing sensitive information in insecure environments, or failing to follow established security protocols. For example, an employee who stores unencrypted data on a personal device or uses the same password across multiple systems can expose the organization to attacks.
- **Compromised Insiders:** These individuals are legitimate employees or users whose accounts have been compromised by external attackers. Once attackers gain control of an insider's credentials, they can operate within the system undetected, often causing extensive damage before the breach is discovered.

Organizations must implement robust monitoring systems to detect unusual activities, educate employees about security best practices, and establish strong access control policies limiting the scope of what any individual can access.

Importance of Security Awareness Training

Given the susceptibility of humans to social engineering and the risks posed by insider threats, one of the most effective ways to mitigate these vulnerabilities is through comprehensive security awareness training. Employees should be seen not as potential weak links but as the first line of defense against attacks, provided they are equipped with the right knowledge and tools.

- **Understanding Threats:** Security awareness training helps employees recognize various forms of attacks, such as phishing emails, phone-based scams, and baiting tactics. By teaching employees how to identify suspicious activities, organizations can reduce the chances of a successful social engineering attack.
- **Security Best Practices:** Training should emphasize the importance of following security protocols, such as creating strong passwords, enabling multi-factor authentication (MFA), encrypting sensitive data, and using secure networks. Employees should be reminded of the dangers of clicking unknown links, opening unsolicited attachments, and sharing sensitive information via insecure communication channels.
- **Incident Reporting:** Employees should be trained not only to recognize potential security threats but also to respond appropriately when they

encounter suspicious activities. Reporting incidents promptly allows the security team to take immediate action, minimizing damage from attacks. Regular simulations of phishing attacks and other scenarios can reinforce this behavior.

- **Culture of Security:** Security awareness training should not be treated as a one-time exercise but as an ongoing process that fosters a culture of security within the organization. When security becomes ingrained in the daily habits of employees, it strengthens the organization's overall security posture.

User Behavior as a Weak Link

Even with training, user behavior can still introduce vulnerabilities into a system. Bad habits, such as using weak passwords, sharing credentials, or bypassing security protocols for convenience, are common examples of how users can create weak links in an otherwise secure system.

- **Password Practices:** Weak passwords and password reuse across multiple systems remain significant security risks. Despite recommendations for using strong, unique passwords and password managers, many users continue to prioritize convenience over security. The use of weak or reused passwords makes it easier for attackers to gain unauthorized access through brute-force attacks or credential stuffing.
- **Insecure Personal Devices:** The rise of remote work and the use of personal devices for work purposes (BYOD - Bring Your Own Device) have increased the risk of insecure devices accessing corporate networks. Personal devices may lack the same level of security controls as company-issued devices, making them easier targets for malware or data theft.
- **Shadow IT:** Shadow IT refers to employees using unauthorized software or services to complete their tasks. This often happens when IT-approved solutions are seen as too slow or cumbersome. While it may improve productivity in the short term, shadow IT introduces significant security risks, as these tools are often not vetted or monitored by the organization's security team.

Human factors in security, including social engineering, insider threats, and insecure user behavior, can significantly weaken an organization's security posture. While technology plays a vital role in defending against external threats, humans remain the first and often weakest line of defense. Comprehensive security awareness training, a strong culture of security, and vigilant monitoring of insider activities are essential to mitigating the risks posed by human behavior. Addressing these human-related vulnerabilities is critical to ensuring the overall security chain remains intact, with no weak links for attackers to exploit.

Technical Vulnerabilities

Technical vulnerabilities represent one of the most critical areas of weakness in any security system. These vulnerabilities arise from flaws in the design, implementation, or configuration of hardware, software, and network components. While human factors can introduce vulnerabilities through behavior, technical vulnerabilities are often exploited through automation and can affect systems at scale, making them a prime target for cybercriminals. In this section, we will explore common types of technical weaknesses, including software bugs, unpatched systems, and misconfigured devices, along with strategies for identifying and mitigating these vulnerabilities.

Software Bugs and Coding Flaws

Software bugs are inevitable in complex systems, often arising from mistakes in the development process. These flaws can manifest in various forms, from memory corruption and buffer overflows to logic errors and race conditions. Once discovered, software bugs provide attackers with a potential entry point into a system, allowing them to compromise functionality or gain unauthorized access.

One of the most dangerous types of bugs is buffer overflow, which occurs when a program writes more data to a buffer than it can hold, causing adjacent memory locations to be overwritten. This can lead to arbitrary code execution, where attackers gain control of the system by inserting and executing malicious code. Another critical issue is SQL injection, where improper handling of user input in web applications allows attackers to execute malicious SQL queries on the backend database, leading to data leaks or unauthorized modifications.

To mitigate the risk posed by software bugs, secure coding practices must be adopted throughout the development lifecycle. This includes performing thorough code reviews, conducting static and dynamic analysis, and utilizing fuzzing techniques to test the software's response to unexpected inputs. Additionally, automated vulnerability scanning tools can be deployed to detect common security weaknesses in the code, such as those listed in the OWASP Top 10 vulnerabilities. Secure development frameworks and guidelines, such as DevSecOps, emphasize integrating security measures early in the development process to minimize these risks.

Unpatched Systems

Even well-designed systems are susceptible to vulnerabilities if they are not updated. Cybercriminals are constantly searching for weaknesses in widely-used software, and when they discover vulnerabilities, they may create exploits to target systems that have not yet been patched. Failing to apply software patches and updates promptly leaves organizations vulnerable to attacks that could have easily been prevented.

A prime example of the damage caused by unpatched systems is the WannaCry ransomware attack in 2017, which exploited a vulnerability in Windows operating systems. Despite Microsoft having released a patch for the vulnerability two months prior, many organizations failed to update their systems, resulting in widespread infections and disruptions to critical infrastructure worldwide.

To address this issue, organizations must establish a robust patch management strategy. This includes regularly monitoring software vendors for security updates, prioritizing critical patches, and applying them promptly. Automated patch management solutions can streamline this process by scanning systems for outdated software and deploying patches across the network. For particularly sensitive or critical systems, vulnerability assessments should be performed to determine whether additional security controls are necessary until patches can be applied.

Misconfigured Devices

Misconfiguration of devices and systems is another significant source of security vulnerability. Whether a firewall left with default settings, a database exposed to the Internet without proper authentication, or an IoT device with insecure settings, misconfigurations cause serious security gaps that attackers can exploit.

A notorious example is the Equifax data breach, where attackers exploited a vulnerability in a web application framework that was not properly configured and patched. This allowed attackers to steal sensitive personal data from over hundreds of millions of individuals. Another common issue is misconfigured cloud services, where organizations inadvertently leave cloud storage buckets or virtual machines accessible to the public, leading to data leaks.

To mitigate the risks posed by misconfigured devices, organizations must implement strong configuration management practices. This involves setting secure defaults for all systems, removing unnecessary services, and hardening configurations to reduce the attack surface. Regular audits and penetration testing are essential for identifying misconfigurations that may have been overlooked or introduced after deployment. Tools such as Security Configuration Management (SCM) solutions can automate the process of checking systems for common configuration errors and enforcing security policies.

Technical vulnerabilities are an inherent part of any security system, arising from software bugs, unpatched systems, and misconfigured devices. Each of these weaknesses provides a potential entry point for attackers, and if left unaddressed, can lead to devastating breaches. However, organizations can significantly reduce the likelihood of exploitation by adopting proactive strategies, such as secure coding practices, patch management, and regular vulnerability assessments. The identification and mitigation of technical vulnerabilities require a continuous and dynamic approach, as attackers constantly evolve their tactics. Therefore, staying vigilant, informed, and responsive to emerging threats is crucial for maintaining a strong security posture in today's ever-changing landscape.

Security Testing and Assessment

Security testing and assessment are essential processes for evaluating the effectiveness of a system's security controls and identifying any weaknesses or vulnerabilities before they can be exploited. In a rapidly evolving threat landscape, where new attack vectors emerge frequently, regular testing provides organizations with critical insights into their security posture. The goal of these assessments is to uncover weak links–whether they are technical vulnerabilities, configuration issues, or human errors–and address them to reduce the overall risk.

In this section, we will explore various methods of security testing and assessment, such as penetration testing, vulnerability scanning, and risk assessments, and explain how these practices help maintain the integrity of a system.

Penetration Testing

Penetration testing, often referred to as ethical hacking, is a process where security professionals simulate real-world cyberattacks to evaluate the security of a system. The goal is to identify vulnerabilities that attackers could exploit, helping organizations understand and remediate weaknesses before they lead to breaches. Unlike other forms of security testing, penetration testing is active and intrusive, meaning it tries to exploit vulnerabilities rather than just identify them.

Penetration testing can be categorized into three types, each offering different levels of insight into the system being tested:

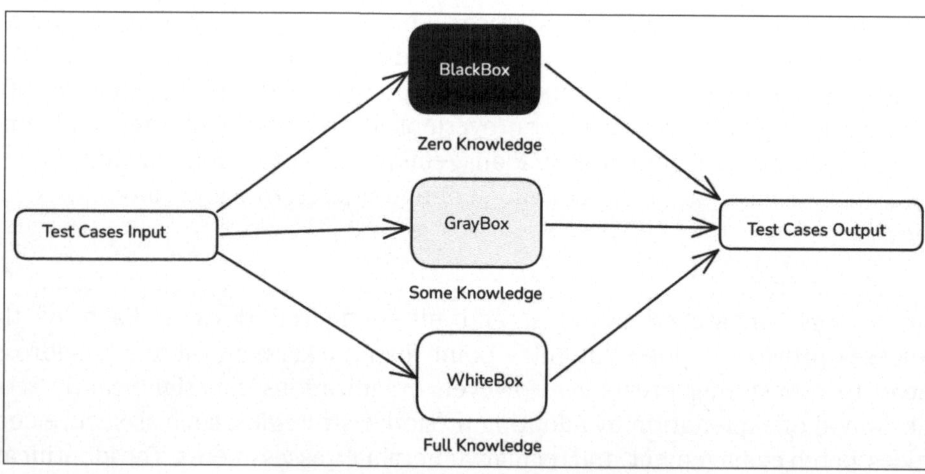

***Figure 8.1**: Penetration Testing Types*

1. Black-Box Testing

In black-box testing, the penetration testers have no prior knowledge of the system or network architecture. They approach the test from an external attacker's perspective, trying to breach the defenses using publicly available information or exploiting weaknesses in the system. This type of test mimics the actions of an outsider who does not have privileged access, making it useful for testing perimeter defenses, such as firewalls, web applications, and external servers.

Black-box testing is particularly valuable because it provides insight into how an external attacker might exploit publicly accessible systems. However, its drawback is that it may not uncover deep, internal vulnerabilities since the testers don't have insider knowledge.

2. White-Box Testing

White-box testing is the opposite of black-box testing, where testers are given complete knowledge of the system, including network architecture, source code, configurations, and other internal details. This allows testers to thoroughly analyze the system from an internal perspective, looking for vulnerabilities hidden deep within the code or configurations.

White-box testing is useful for identifying subtle vulnerabilities that an external attacker might not easily find, such as insecure coding practices, misconfigurations, or logical errors in the system. This approach is especially effective for code reviews, database analysis, and evaluating complex internal systems. However, it requires a deep understanding of the system and may not simulate an external attacker's approach effectively.

3. Gray-Box Testing

Gray-box testing is a hybrid approach that falls between black-box and white-box testing. Testers are given partial knowledge of the system, such as access credentials, system architecture, or some source code. This simulates the perspective of an insider or someone with limited access trying to escalate their privileges or exploit the system from within.

Gray-box testing allows testers to explore both external and internal vulnerabilities, making it a balanced approach. It helps identify weaknesses such as privilege escalation, session management flaws, or other issues that might arise when an attacker has limited insider knowledge. This type of test is useful for scenarios, such as evaluating internal security policies or testing the resilience of user accounts with varying access levels.

Penetration Testing Process

Regardless of the type, penetration testing typically follows a structured process that includes the following phases:

1. **Planning and Reconnaissance:** The testers gather information about the target system, including details on network architecture, servers, and applications. In black-box testing, this phase relies heavily on publicly available information, while in white-box and gray-box testing, the organization may provide internal documentation.
2. **Scanning:** The testers use tools to analyze the target system and identify potential entry points. This involves network mapping, port scanning, and vulnerability assessment tools to discover weaknesses, such as open ports, outdated software, or exposed services.
3. **Gaining Access:** Once vulnerabilities are identified, the testers attempt to exploit them to gain access to the system. They may use techniques, such as SQL injection, cross-site scripting (XSS), or phishing attacks. The goal is to penetrate the system's defenses to access sensitive data or escalate privileges.
4. **Maintaining Access:** In this phase, testers try to maintain their access to the system, simulating how an attacker might establish persistence in the network. They could create backdoors, escalate privileges, or plant malicious software to keep control of the system even after initial detection.
5. **Analysis and Reporting:** After the testing is complete, the testers compile a detailed report outlining the vulnerabilities they discovered, how they exploited them, and the potential impact of these vulnerabilities. The report also provides recommendations for remediation, helping the organization strengthen its security defenses.

Benefits and Challenges of Penetration Testing

Penetration testing provides organizations with valuable insight into their security posture. By simulating real-world attacks, it helps identify critical vulnerabilities that could otherwise go unnoticed. Here are some key benefits and challenges:

- **Identifying Unknown Weaknesses:** Penetration testing can reveal vulnerabilities that might not be detected through automated scans or audits. For instance, human errors in configuration or subtle logic flaws in code may only become evident during a real-world attack simulation.
- **Validating Security Controls:** Penetration testing ensures that security controls, such as firewalls, intrusion detection systems, and access control mechanisms, are functioning as intended. It can uncover misconfigurations or gaps in these defenses.

- **Simulating Real-World Attacks:** By simulating an actual attacker's approach, penetration testing provides a more realistic assessment of an organization's vulnerabilities. This is crucial for understanding how well the system would hold up under actual threat conditions.
- **Enhancing Incident Response:** Penetration testing helps organizations refine their incident response processes by simulating attack scenarios. Organizations can evaluate how quickly they detect and respond to intrusions, helping improve their overall resilience.
- **Scope Limitations:** Penetration tests typically have a defined scope, and testers are often limited in what they can target. This means that certain vulnerabilities, especially in areas outside the test scope, might not be identified.
- **False Sense of Security:** A successful penetration test does not mean the system is entirely secure. New vulnerabilities may arise after the test, or hidden flaws might have been missed. Regular, ongoing testing is required to maintain security.
- **Cost and Complexity:** Penetration testing can be expensive and complex, especially for large organizations with sprawling infrastructure. Hiring skilled professionals to conduct thorough testing is a necessary investment, but it may strain smaller businesses.

Penetration testing plays a vital role in identifying weaknesses in security systems before malicious actors can exploit them. Whether conducted as a black-box, white-box, or gray-box test, penetration testing allows organizations to gain a deeper understanding of their security posture and uncover hidden vulnerabilities. By incorporating penetration testing into regular security assessments, businesses can proactively strengthen their defenses, validate their security controls, and mitigate the risk of breaches. Despite its challenges, penetration testing remains a critical tool for staying ahead in the ever-evolving cybersecurity landscape.

Vulnerability Scanning

While penetration testing simulates real-world attacks by actively exploiting system vulnerabilities, vulnerability scanning focuses on identifying and cataloging weaknesses in systems, software, and networks without necessarily attempting to exploit them. These methods offer a more automated, continuous approach to assessing security and are often used to maintain ongoing awareness of a system's security posture. The primary goal of a vulnerability scan is to identify potential security risks, such as outdated software, missing patches, open ports, or weak configurations, without actively exploiting those vulnerabilities.

Vulnerability scanners use databases of known vulnerabilities, such as the Common Vulnerabilities and Exposures (CVE) database, to match system weaknesses against publicly available information. These tools are widely used in both enterprise environments and smaller organizations because they are relatively easy to deploy and can provide a quick, high-level overview of the system's security health.

Key Steps in Vulnerability Scanning:

1. **Discovery:** The scanner first identifies all devices, services, and systems within the target environment. This may involve mapping the network, identifying open ports, and detecting running services. In this step, the tool gathers a detailed inventory of the infrastructure.
2. **Assessment:** Once the assets are identified, the vulnerability scanner compares the configuration of each device, application, or system against a known set of vulnerabilities. This includes checking for unpatched software, misconfigurations, or outdated versions of applications.
3. **Analysis and Reporting:** After scanning, the tool generates a report detailing the vulnerabilities found, ranked by severity. Each vulnerability is typically accompanied by information about the potential risk, the affected system, and remediation recommendations.
4. **Remediation:** Once the report is reviewed, IT teams can prioritize and address the vulnerabilities by applying patches, reconfiguring systems, or updating software versions.

Types of Vulnerability Scanning:

- **Network-Based Scanning:** Focuses on discovering vulnerabilities in network devices, such as routers, switches, firewalls, and servers. This type of scanning looks for open ports, unsecured protocols, and other network-level issues that may expose the system to attacks.
- **Host-Based Scanning:** Involves scanning individual systems (hosts), such as servers, workstations, and devices for vulnerabilities. This scan identifies misconfigurations, unpatched software, and weak security settings specific to each host.
- **Application Scanning:** Focuses on web applications, mobile apps, or cloud services to detect vulnerabilities, such as cross-site scripting (XSS), SQL injection, and insecure APIs. Application vulnerability scans ensure that critical flaws within software components are addressed.
- **Database Scanning:** Looks specifically at database systems to find vulnerabilities related to database configurations, stored procedures, and other database-specific issues.

Advantages of Vulnerability Scanning:

- **Automation:** Vulnerability scanning tools are highly automated and can perform continuous, routine assessments of large-scale networks and systems without human intervention. This ensures that organizations maintain a regular view of their security posture.

- **Quick Feedback:** Vulnerability scanning is typically faster than penetration testing and provides quick insights into security weaknesses. This allows organizations to respond promptly to vulnerabilities before they are exploited.
- **Cost-Effective:** Vulnerability scans are generally less expensive than penetration testing or other manual testing methods, making them accessible for organizations of all sizes.

Static Analysis

Static analysis, also known as Static Application Security Testing (SAST), is a method of analyzing the source code or binary of a software application without executing it. Unlike dynamic testing methods that test an application while running, static analysis examines the structure, logic, and syntax of code to detect vulnerabilities. Static analysis is primarily used during the Software Development Life Cycle (SDLC) to catch security flaws before the software is deployed.

Working of Static Analysis

In static analysis, specialized tools automatically scan the source code or compiled binary of an application to identify common security flaws. The analysis doesn't require the program to be running and doesn't interact with the network, making it ideal for identifying vulnerabilities that arise from insecure coding practices. The scanner looks for patterns or signatures that are indicative of security risks, such as:

- Buffer overflows
- SQL injections
- Cross-site scripting (XSS) vulnerabilities
- Hard-coded credentials
- Improper input validation

Static analysis tools can analyze both proprietary and open-source software, offering comprehensive code coverage without the need to run the application.

Advantages of Static Analysis:

- **Early Detection:** One of the biggest advantages of static analysis is its ability to detect vulnerabilities early in the development process. By scanning source code before deployment, developers can fix issues before they become real-world security problems.
- **Comprehensive Code Review:** Static analysis covers a wide array of security vulnerabilities and best practices. It analyzes the complete codebase, including all paths of execution, ensuring comprehensive coverage.

- **Developer-Friendly:** By integrating static analysis tools into the development pipeline, developers can get real-time feedback on the security of their code. This allows teams to implement security fixes during the development process rather than in post-production.

Strategies for Enhancing Vulnerability Scanning and Static Analysis

To improve the effectiveness of vulnerability scanning and static analysis, organizations can adopt the following practices:

- **Integrate into Continuous Development:** By integrating vulnerability scanning and static analysis tools into the CI/CD (Continuous Integration/Continuous Deployment) pipeline, organizations can ensure that security assessments are part of the regular software development process.
- **Validate with Penetration Testing:** To reduce false positives and ensure a more comprehensive security posture, vulnerability scanning and static analysis should be complemented with penetration testing. This combination provides both automated detection of known issues and in-depth testing for complex, real-world vulnerabilities.
- **Regular Updates:** Ensure that vulnerability scanners and static analysis tools are regularly updated to incorporate the latest vulnerability databases, code signatures, and detection algorithms. Keeping tools up to date is essential for detecting new and emerging threats.
- **Prioritize Remediation:** Not all vulnerabilities identified by scans or static analysis are critical. Organizations should establish a risk-based approach to prioritize remediation efforts, focusing on high-impact vulnerabilities first.

Vulnerability scanning and static analysis are invaluable tools in an organization's security arsenal. While they offer automation and scalability in detecting known security weaknesses, they should be used in conjunction with other security measures, such as penetration testing and manual code reviews to ensure a thorough defense. When used effectively, these tools help developers and security teams identify and address vulnerabilities early and often, enhancing the overall security posture of the system.

Risk Assessment

Risk assessment is a critical component of the security process, as it provides a structured way to identify, analyze, and prioritize the potential risks that could affect a system's security. Rather than merely focusing on individual vulnerabilities or weaknesses, a risk assessment takes a holistic view of the entire system, its assets, potential threats, and the likelihood of those threats being realized. This comprehensive approach helps organizations focus their resources on the most critical risks to ensure that security measures are applied where they will have the greatest impact.

Key Steps in Risk Assessment:

1. **Asset Identification**: The first step in risk assessment is to identify the valuable assets within the organization. These assets may include sensitive data (such as personal, financial, or intellectual property), hardware, software, infrastructure, or human resources. It's essential to categorize and prioritize these assets based on their importance to the organization's operations and their sensitivity.
2. **Threat Identification**: Threats refer to any potential event or actor that could exploit vulnerabilities in the system and cause harm. These can include natural disasters (floods, fires), cyber threats (hackers, malware, ransomware), human error (accidental data breaches, misconfigurations), and insider threats (disgruntled employees, espionage). Identifying relevant threats helps organizations understand the different ways in which their assets might be at risk.
3. **Vulnerability Assessment**: Once potential threats are identified, it's important to identify the vulnerabilities in the system that those threats could exploit. Vulnerabilities could be technical (such as unpatched software and weak encryption), physical (such as unlocked server rooms), or organizational (such as poor access controls or lack of security training). This step usually involves techniques, such as vulnerability scanning, code reviews, and system audits.

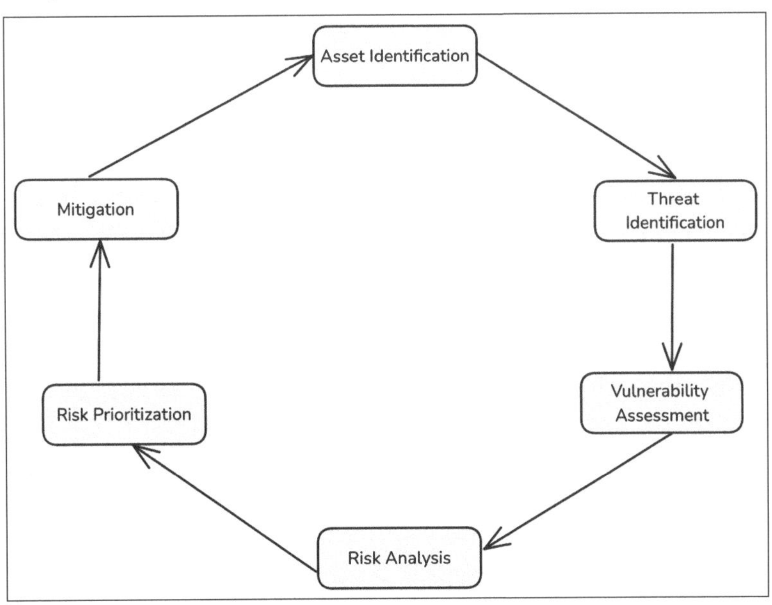

***Figure 8.2**: Steps in Risk Assessment*

4. **Risk Analysis**: Risk analysis involves combining the information gathered in the previous steps to assess the likelihood and potential impact of each identified threat exploiting a vulnerability. This is typically done using a combination of qualitative and quantitative methods:
    a. **Qualitative Risk Analysis**: This method involves categorizing risks into levels, such as high, medium, or low based on their potential impact and likelihood. It relies on the judgment and expertise of security professionals and stakeholders.
    b. **Quantitative Risk Analysis**: This method involves assigning numerical values to the probability of a threat occurring and its potential financial or operational impact. For example, organizations might estimate the cost of a data breach in terms of lost revenue, legal penalties, and reputational damage.
5. **Risk Prioritization**: Not all risks carry the same weight, so risk prioritization is crucial. The goal is to focus on the risks that pose the greatest potential harm. High-impact, high-likelihood risks should be addressed first, while low-impact, low-likelihood risks may be mitigated later. Risk prioritization helps organizations allocate resources efficiently to the most pressing security concerns.
6. **Mitigation and Control Measures**: Once risks are prioritized, the organization must determine how to mitigate them. Mitigation strategies can include:
    a. **Preventive Measures**: Implementing controls that reduce the likelihood of a threat exploiting a vulnerability (for example, patch management, firewalls, access controls).
    b. **Detective Measures**: Installing systems that detect threats when they occur (for example, intrusion detection systems, monitoring tools).
    c. **Corrective Measures**: Preparing for effective incident response and recovery if a threat is realized (for example, backup systems, disaster recovery plans).
7. **Residual Risk Evaluation**: After mitigation strategies are applied, some risks may still remain. Residual risks are those that cannot be fully eliminated but must be accepted by the organization. Evaluating these risks helps organizations determine whether additional measures are required or whether they are willing to accept a certain level of risk.

Types of Risk Assessments

There are different types of risk assessments based on the depth of the evaluation and the scope of the system being assessed. These include:

1. **Qualitative Risk Assessment**: This method uses subjective measures (such as expert judgment and experience) to categorize risks. It is useful when numerical data is scarce or when a quick, high-level overview is needed.
2. **Quantitative Risk Assessment**: This approach uses numerical data and statistical models to calculate risk, making it more precise. It requires extensive data collection and analysis and is often used in conjunction with a cost-benefit analysis to weigh the costs of mitigation against the benefits.
3. **Dynamic Risk Assessment**: This type of assessment is ongoing and adapts to changes in the environment, such as new threats, evolving business processes, or technological changes. It's often employed in high-risk industries where continuous monitoring is required.
4. **Compliance-Based Risk Assessment**: Focuses on aligning with legal and regulatory frameworks. This is often used in industries such as healthcare or finance, where non-compliance can lead to severe penalties.

Risk Assessment in Cybersecurity

In cybersecurity, risk assessment plays a crucial role in safeguarding digital assets and infrastructure. Given the complexity of modern networks, organizations must assess the risks that stem from various sources such as:

- **Cyber Threats**: These include malicious actors, such as hackers, organized crime, nation-state actors, and insider threats. Their techniques range from phishing attacks to advanced persistent threats (APTs) and ransomware.
- **System Vulnerabilities**: These can result from outdated software, unpatched systems, weak encryption, or insecure configurations.
- **Regulatory Compliance Risks**: In highly regulated industries (for example, healthcare, finance), failure to comply with cybersecurity regulations can result in penalties and legal consequences. Therefore, compliance risks are also factored into the assessment.
- **Third-Party Risks**: Organizations often rely on third-party vendors or partners. Any vulnerability in these external systems can be exploited to attack the primary organization.

Strategies for Effective Risk Management

- **Regular Risk Assessments**: Security environments are dynamic, and new risks can emerge as technology evolves. Conducting regular risk assessments ensures that organizations stay aware of evolving threats and vulnerabilities.
- **Comprehensive Asset Inventory**: Understanding what needs protection is fundamental to any risk assessment. Without a comprehensive asset inventory, it's difficult to prioritize and protect critical resources effectively.

- **Incorporating Threat Intelligence**: By integrating threat intelligence into the risk assessment process, organizations can stay informed about emerging risks and vulnerabilities, enabling them to proactively address potential threats.
- **Risk Acceptance and Transfer**: Some risks cannot be fully eliminated, and organizations must decide how to handle them. Options include accepting the risk, transferring the risk (for example, through cyber insurance), or mitigating it as much as possible.
- **Continuous Monitoring**: Post-assessment, continuous monitoring systems help detect and respond to new risks in real-time, ensuring that any emerging threats are promptly addressed.

Risk assessment is an ongoing process that helps organizations stay ahead of potential threats by continuously evaluating and addressing security risks. By identifying and analyzing vulnerabilities, prioritizing risks, and implementing appropriate mitigation strategies, organizations can significantly strengthen their security posture. However, it's important to recognize that risk assessment isn't a one-time task: it requires continuous updates and monitoring to keep pace with the rapidly evolving threat landscape. Ultimately, effective risk management enables organizations to focus resources on the most critical security concerns and make informed decisions about how to protect their most valuable assets.

Conclusion

In this chapter, we explored the fundamental truth that security systems are only as strong as their weakest link. By understanding this principle, we highlighted how even a single vulnerability, whether technical or human, can cause a domino effect, leading to a complete security breakdown. Our journey began with identifying weak points in security chains, demonstrating how seemingly minor flaws can unravel even the most sophisticated security infrastructures. Through real-world case studies, we saw the devastating consequences of exploiting weak links, from high-profile breaches to data thefts, all of which underscore the importance of constantly assessing and fortifying vulnerabilities. We learned that often, it is not the complex technological defenses but rather human error, such as poor password management or falling for social engineering tactics, that contributes most frequently to security compromises. In this light, we discussed the critical role of the human factor in security, emphasizing that awareness, training, and behavioral change are as vital as any technical defense. On the technical side, we delved into common vulnerabilities, such as software bugs, misconfigured systems, and outdated patches, which serve as gateways for attackers. We examined strategies for identifying these technical weaknesses and mitigating them, whether through regular updates, access controls, or careful system configuration. We then moved into the realm of Security Testing and Assessment, focusing on methods that help identify and address these weak links before attackers can exploit them. We discussed the importance of penetration testing, where ethical hackers simulate attacks to uncover potential flaws, and vulnerability scanning, which detects known weaknesses in systems and applications. Static analysis, particularly useful in early development stages, was also covered as a technique for identifying vulnerabilities in source code. Following this, we looked at risk assessment, a broader approach that evaluates the likelihood and potential impact of various security threats, helping organizations prioritize their defenses.

As we conclude this chapter, it becomes clear that security is a multi-layered and continuous effort, combining both human vigilance and technical precision. The lessons we've covered–from identifying weak points and understanding human behavior to applying rigorous technical safeguards and performing thorough assessments–form the backbone of resilient security strategies. In the next chapter, we will explore Transport Layer Security (TLS) Communication, a practical use case that brings together many of the security principles we discussed throughout this book. By examining how TLS secures online communication, we'll see how encryption, key exchange, and authentication come together in real-world applications, further cementing the importance of a holistic, layered approach to cybersecurity.

Chapter 9
TLS Communication

Introduction

In our previous chapter, we delved into the fundamental principle of security: "We are only as secure as the weakest link." Through case studies, technical vulnerabilities, and human factors, we explored how security systems can fail when their weakest elements are exposed. Now, we shift our focus to a critical real-world implementation of cryptographic principles: Transport Layer Security (TLS).

TLS is the backbone of secure communication over the internet, ensuring the confidentiality, integrity, and authenticity of data transmitted between parties. In this chapter, we will explore the inner workings of TLS, discussing how it enables secure communication in a variety of applications, from web browsing to email and secure file transfer. This chapter will provide a deep dive into every aspect of TLS, beginning with its handshake process and protocol structure and examining the cryptographic algorithms it uses.

We will also analyze TLS 1.2 and TLS 1.3, comparing their features and improvements, especially in light of emerging security threats. The chapter will further explore TLS certificates and the role of Certificate Authorities (CAs) in validating the authenticity of communication parties. As we progress, we'll discuss the security considerations involved in TLS implementation, best practices for using TLS effectively, and emerging trends shaping the future of TLS.

By building on the foundational concepts of security covered earlier, this chapter will emphasize how TLS addresses key vulnerabilities and serves as an essential layer of defense. Let's now explore TLS communication in detail, highlighting the importance of each component and ensuring a comprehensive understanding of its role in maintaining secure digital interactions.

Structure

In this chapter, the following topics will be covered:

- Introduction to TLS
- TLS Handshake Process

- Cryptographic Algorithm Used in TLS
- Practical Example
- TLS Certificates and Certificate Authority (CAs)
- Applications of TLS
- Future Directions for TLS

Introduction to TLS

Transport Layer Security (TLS) is a vital protocol that ensures secure communication over the internet. Its primary goal is to protect data transmitted between users and servers, making it critical for the vast range of online activities we engage in today: browsing websites, sending emails, or conducting financial transactions. TLS provides a robust defense against eavesdropping, tampering, and forgery by encrypting data, maintaining its integrity, and verifying the authenticity of both parties involved in the communication. Without TLS, our online interactions would be highly susceptible to cyber-attacks, including data theft and Man-In-The-Middle (MITM) attacks.

TLS evolved from its predecessor, Secure Sockets Layer (SSL), to address critical vulnerabilities that had been discovered in earlier internet protocols. As the web has grown into a more complex and essential part of modern life, the need for secure, reliable communication channels has become paramount. This transition from SSL to TLS, particularly with the advancement from TLS 1.2 to TLS 1.3, reflects an ongoing effort to adapt security protocols to an ever-changing threat landscape.

Historical Context: From SSL to TLS

The origins of TLS date back to the early development of the internet in the 1990s. The first major step toward secure online communication was SSL, initially developed by Netscape in 1995. SSL 2.0, and later SSL 3.0, provided encryption and basic security for websites, but both versions were quickly found to have significant weaknesses. These flaws included vulnerabilities to MITM attacks, protocol downgrade attacks, and weak cryptographic algorithms that no longer met the security needs of modern internet communications.

Recognizing the limitations of SSL, the Internet Engineering Task Force (IETF) developed TLS as a more secure replacement. The first version of TLS, TLS 1.0, was released in 1999. Over time, new versions emerged–TLS 1.1 and TLS 1.2–which offered stronger encryption standards, improved integrity checks, and better protection against emerging security threats. The latest version, TLS 1.3, released in 2018, introduced significant improvements, such as reducing handshake times for faster connections and eliminating outdated cryptographic algorithms vulnerable to attacks. These enhancements have made TLS 1.3 the most secure and efficient protocol for encrypted communication to date, addressing the vulnerabilities that plagued SSL.

The transition from SSL to TLS was essential not just to patch vulnerabilities but also to accommodate the growing scale and complexity of the internet. TLS's ongoing evolution reflects a proactive approach to addressing security risks as they arise, ensuring that internet communications remain confidential and secure.

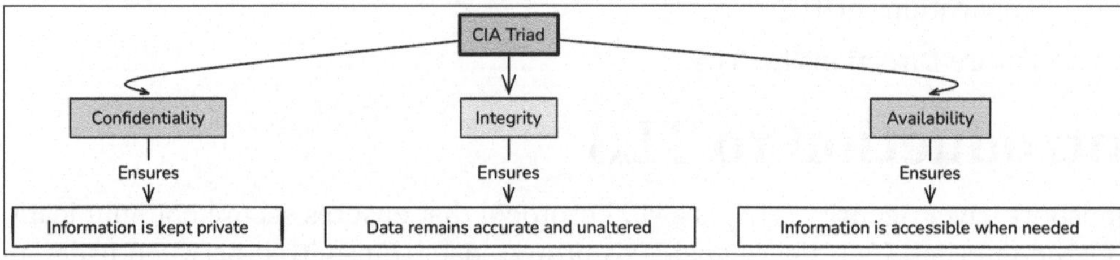

Figure 9.1: CIA *Triad*

Basic Concept: Securing Communication Through TLS

At its core, TLS is a cryptographic protocol that provides three essential security features for Internet communication: confidentiality, integrity, and authentication.

- **Confidentiality:** TLS ensures that the data exchanged between a client (for example, a web browser) and a server is encrypted, preventing unauthorized parties from reading or intercepting it. Even if attackers manage to capture the data during transmission, they would be unable to decipher the content without the appropriate decryption keys.
- **Data Integrity:** TLS guarantees that the data exchanged remains unaltered during transmission. It uses cryptographic hash functions to verify that the data has not been tampered with, assuring that the message received is exactly what was sent.
- **Authentication:** TLS provides mechanisms to authenticate both the server and, optionally, the client. Typically, this is done using digital certificates, which confirm the identity of the server (and sometimes the client) involved in the communication. This authentication prevents malicious entities from impersonating legitimate services, mitigating risks such as MITM attacks.

The TLS handshake is an integral part of the protocol, where both parties agree on encryption methods and exchange keys before starting the secure session. The handshake ensures that all necessary cryptographic parameters are in place, allowing the secure exchange of data to proceed with confidence. As internet security needs have evolved, so too has the TLS handshake process, modern iterations of TLS, such as TLS 1.3, have significantly streamlined the handshake process to improve both security and speed.

TLS Handshake Process

The TLS handshake is a critical component of the TLS protocol, laying the groundwork for a secure communication session between a client (such as a web browser) and a server. The handshake occurs at the beginning of a TLS session and negotiates all the necessary cryptographic parameters to ensure that any subsequent communication is confidential, authenticated, and has integrity. During the handshake, both parties agree on a shared key that will be used for symmetric encryption, authenticate each other's identities (mainly using digital certificates), and establish the cryptographic algorithms they will use.

Here's a simplified breakdown of the steps involved in a typical TLS handshake:

1. **Client Hello:** The client initiates the handshake by sending a message to the server. This message includes information such as the version of TLS it supports, a randomly generated number (used later in key generation), and a list of supported cipher suites and compression methods.

2. **Server Hello:** The server responds with a message that contains its chosen cipher suite and TLS version (based on what the client offered). It also includes a random number and its digital certificate, which contains its public key.

3. **Server Authentication and Key Exchange:** The server sends its certificate to the client, allowing the client to verify its identity. In some cases, the server might also send its key exchange parameters (for methods such as Diffie-Hellman or Elliptic Curve Diffie-Hellman).

4. **Client Key Exchange:** The client verifies the server's certificate and generates a pre-master secret, which is encrypted with the server's public key and sent to the server. Both the client and server then use this pre-master secret, along with the random values exchanged earlier, to generate the session keys used for symmetric encryption.

5. **Session Key Generation:** Both parties use the pre-master secret and their random numbers to generate identical session keys. These keys will be used for symmetric encryption and decryption during the data transfer phase of communication.

6. **Finished Messages:** After generating the session keys, both the client and server send a "Finished" message to confirm that the handshake has been successful and that they can start securely exchanging data.

At the end of this process, the TLS handshake is complete, and both parties can now use symmetric encryption to securely transfer data.

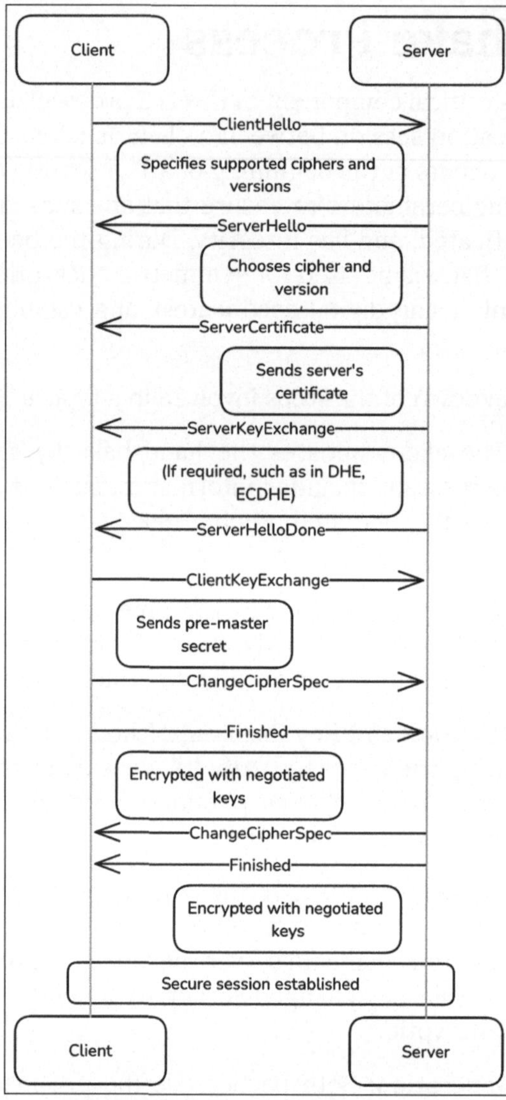

***Figure 9.2**: TLS Handshake Process*

Symmetric and Asymmetric Cryptography in TLS

TLS relies on both symmetric and asymmetric cryptography to ensure secure communication. The TLS handshake uses asymmetric cryptography during the initial stages, particularly for server authentication and key exchange, but switches to symmetric cryptography for encrypting the actual data transferred during the session.

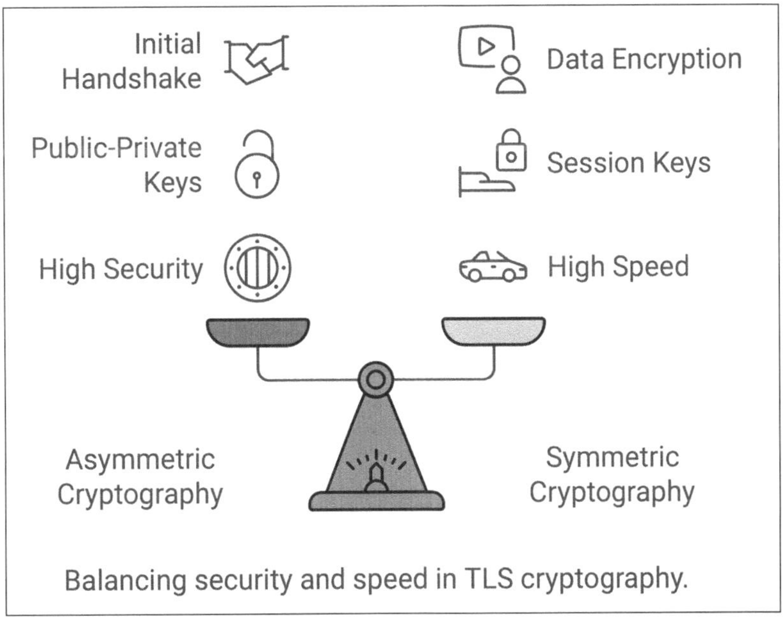

Figure 9.3: *Balancing security and speed in TLS cryptography*

- Asymmetric cryptography involves the use of a public-private key pair. The server typically uses its private key to sign messages or decrypt the pre-master secret sent by the client. The public key, contained in the server's certificate, is used by the client to verify the server's identity and to encrypt the pre-master secret.
- Symmetric cryptography is employed once the session keys have been exchanged. Symmetric cryptography is faster and more efficient for bulk data encryption compared to asymmetric cryptography. TLS uses symmetric encryption algorithms such as AES to encrypt the data, ensuring confidentiality during the session.

This hybrid approach leverages the security of asymmetric cryptography for the key exchange and authentication phases while benefiting from the speed of symmetric cryptography for actual data encryption.

Cryptographic Algorithms Supported in TLS

The Transport Layer Security (TLS) protocol relies on various cryptographic algorithms to provide confidentiality, integrity, and authentication for secure communication. These algorithms are used for different purposes during a TLS session, such as encrypting data, verifying authenticity, and ensuring data integrity. TLS employs a combination of symmetric and asymmetric cryptography, hash functions, and key exchange methods to achieve robust security. Here's an in-depth look at the cryptographic algorithms used in TLS:

- Symmetric Encryption Algorithms
- Asymmetric (Public Key) Encryption Algorithms
- Hash Functions
- Key Exchange Algorithms
- Cipher Suites

Let's dive deeper into each category:

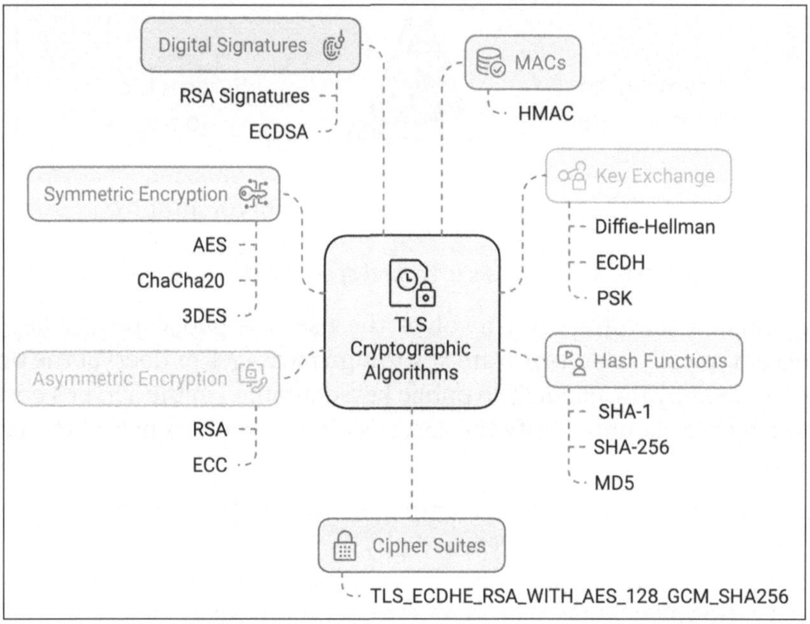

Figure 9.4: *Algorithms Supported by TLS*

Symmetric Encryption Algorithms

Symmetric encryption algorithms use a single shared secret key for both encryption and decryption. These algorithms provide confidentiality for data transmitted over the network. In TLS, symmetric encryption is used to encrypt the actual communication after the initial handshake.

Common symmetric encryption algorithms supported in TLS include:

- **AES (Advanced Encryption Standard):** AES is the most widely used symmetric encryption algorithm in TLS. It supports various key sizes, such as 128-bit, 192-bit, and 256-bit keys. AES is considered highly secure and efficient, and it can operate in different modes, including:

  - **GCM (Galois/Counter Mode):** A mode of operation that provides both encryption and authentication, ensuring data integrity. It is widely used in TLS 1.2 and 1.3 due to its efficiency and security.
  - **CBC (Cipher Block Chaining):** An older mode of operation where each block of plaintext is XORed with the previous ciphertext block before being encrypted. While it was used in earlier versions of TLS, vulnerabilities such as BEAST and Lucky13 have made CBC less popular.
- **ChaCha20:** A modern stream cipher that is used in combination with the Poly1305 message authentication code. ChaCha20 is particularly useful in environments where hardware acceleration for AES is not available, such as mobile devices. It provides strong encryption while being efficient on low-power devices.

Symmetric encryption algorithms in TLS ensure that data remains confidential during transmission, making it unreadable to eavesdroppers.

Asymmetric (Public Key) Encryption Algorithms

Asymmetric encryption algorithms use a pair of keys: a public key for encryption and a private key for decryption. These algorithms are used in the TLS handshake process for secure key exchange and server authentication.

Common asymmetric encryption algorithms used in TLS include:

- **RSA (Rivest-Shamir-Adleman):** RSA is a widely used public-key algorithm in TLS, primarily for key exchange and digital signatures. It is based on the difficulty of factoring large integers. However, due to concerns about security and performance, RSA key exchange has been deprecated in TLS 1.3.
- **Elliptic Curve Cryptography (ECC):** ECC is a more modern and efficient approach to public-key cryptography. It provides similar security to RSA but with smaller key sizes, making it faster and less resource-intensive. The two main ECC algorithms used in TLS are:
  - **ECDSA (Elliptic Curve Digital Signature Algorithm):** Used for signing certificates and authenticating the server in the handshake process.
  - **ECDH (Elliptic Curve Diffie-Hellman):** Used for secure key exchange during the TLS handshake. It is favored over traditional Diffie-Hellman due to its efficiency and security.
- **DSA (Digital Signature Algorithm):** Although supported in some older versions of TLS, DSA is rarely used today due to its lower performance and security compared to RSA and ECC.

Asymmetric encryption in TLS ensures that only authorized parties can participate in the communication, providing authentication and secure key exchange.

Hash Functions

Hash functions play a crucial role in TLS for data integrity and digital signatures. These functions generate a fixed-size hash value from input data, which is used to verify that the data has not been altered during transmission.

Common hash functions supported in TLS include:

- **SHA (Secure Hash Algorithm):** SHA-1, SHA-256, and SHA-384 are the most commonly used hash functions in TLS. The SHA-2 family (SHA-256 and SHA-384) is preferred over SHA-1 due to its stronger security properties. SHA-1 is considered weak against collision attacks and has been phased out in modern TLS versions.
- **MD5 (Message Digest Algorithm 5):** Once widely used, MD5 is now considered insecure due to vulnerabilities in collision resistance. It is deprecated in TLS and should be avoided in favor of more secure hash functions such as SHA-2.

Hash functions in TLS are used for generating message authentication codes (MACs), signing digital certificates, and verifying data integrity.

Key Exchange Algorithms

Key exchange algorithms in TLS are used to securely establish a shared secret between the client and the server. These algorithms play a key role in the TLS handshake process.

Common key exchange algorithms include:

- **Diffie-Hellman (DH):** One of the earliest and most widely known key exchange algorithms. It allows two parties to establish a shared secret over an unsecured communication channel. In TLS, the Ephemeral Diffie-Hellman (DHE) variant is used to provide forward secrecy, ensuring that past communication remains secure even if the server's private key is compromised.
- **Elliptic Curve Diffie-Hellman (ECDH):** An extension of the traditional Diffie-Hellman algorithm that uses elliptic curve mathematics. ECDH provides similar security to DHE with smaller key sizes, making it more efficient and suitable for modern TLS implementations.
- **RSA Key Exchange:** In earlier versions of TLS (up to TLS 1.2), RSA was used for key exchange, where the server's public key encrypted a premaster secret generated by the client. However, the RSA key exchange does not provide forward secrecy and has been deprecated in TLS 1.3.
- **Pre-Shared Key (PSK):** In environments where pre-existing shared keys are used, the PSK key exchange method allows for a simpler and faster handshake process. It is often used in IoT devices and other constrained environments.

Key exchange algorithms determine how securely the encryption keys are generated and shared between the client and server during the handshake.

Cipher Suites

In TLS, a cipher suite is a named combination of cryptographic algorithms used to secure a network connection. A cipher suite specifies the algorithms for:

- Key exchange (for example, ECDH, DHE)
- Authentication (for example, RSA, ECDSA)
- Symmetric encryption (for example, AES, ChaCha20)
- Message authentication (for example, HMAC-SHA256)

Examples of common cipher suites:

- `TLS_ECDHE_RSA_WITH_AES_128_GCM_SHA256`: Uses ECDHE for key exchange, RSA for authentication, AES-128 in GCM mode for symmetric encryption, and HMAC-SHA256 for message authentication.
- `TLS_AES_256_GCM_SHA384 (TLS 1.3)`: Uses AES-256 in GCM mode for encryption, SHA-384 for the hash function, and achieves forward secrecy through Diffie-Hellman key exchange.

The choice of cipher suite determines the security and performance characteristics of a TLS connection, with newer cipher suites offering stronger security and better efficiency. TLS supports a variety of cryptographic algorithms to provide secure communication over the Internet. The use of symmetric and asymmetric encryption, combined with robust hash functions and secure key exchange methods, ensures the confidentiality, integrity, and authenticity of data. The modularity of cipher suites in TLS allows for the use of different algorithms based on the requirements of the application with modern implementations favoring algorithms that offer forward secrecy, efficient performance, and strong security.

Practical Example

To provide a practical example of using TLS, we'll implement a simple client-server communication using Python. In this example, we'll create a basic server that supports TLS to securely communicate with a client over an encrypted channel. We'll use the SSL and socket libraries in Python to demonstrate how TLS works.

Step 1: Generating a Self-Signed Certificate

Before creating a secure server, you need an SSL/TLS certificate. For this example, we'll generate a self-signed certificate using OpenSSL. In a real-world scenario, you would obtain a certificate from a trusted certificate authority (CA).

To generate a self-signed certificate and private key, use the following commands:

This creates two files:

- **server.key**: The server's private key.
- **server.crt**: The self-signed certificate.

Generate Server key and certificate:

```
# Generate private key
openssl genpkey -algorithm RSA -out server.key -pkeyopt rsa_keygen_
bits:2048

# Generate a self-signed certificate
openssl req -new -x509 -key server.key -out server.crt -days 365
```

Step 2: Python Code for the Client

Client-Side Python Code:

```
import socket
import ssl

def create_tls_client():
    # Create a socket
    client_socket = socket.socket(socket.AF_INET, socket.SOCK_STREAM)

    # Wrap the socket with TLS
    context = ssl.create_default_context()
    tls_client_socket = context.wrap_socket(client_socket, server_host-
name='localhost')

    # Connect to the server
    tls_client_socket.connect(('localhost', 8443))
    print("Connected to the TLS server.")

    # Receive data from the server
    message = tls_client_socket.recv(1024)
    print("Received message from server:", message.decode('utf-8'))

    # Close the connection
    tls_client_socket.close()
    print("Connection closed.")

if __name__ == "__main__":
    create_tls_client()
```

The client will connect to the server over TLS, perform the handshake, and then receive the server's message.

Step 3: Python Code for the Server

We'll create a simple server that listens for incoming connections over TLS and sends a message to the connected client.

Server-Side Python Code:

```
import socket
import ssl

def create_tls_server():
    # Create a socket
    server_socket = socket.socket(socket.AF_INET, socket.SOCK_STREAM)
    server_socket.bind(('localhost', 8443))
    server_socket.listen(5)
    print("Server is listening on port 8443...")

    # Wrap the socket with TLS
    context = ssl.create_default_context(ssl.Purpose.CLIENT_AUTH)
    context.load_cert_chain(certfile="server.crt", keyfile="server.key")

    # Accept incoming connections
    while True:
        # Accept a new connection
        client_socket, addr = server_socket.accept()
        print(f"Connection from {addr} accepted.")

        # Wrap the client socket with TLS
        try:
            tls_client_socket = context.wrap_socket(client_socket,
server_side=True)
            print("TLS handshake completed successfully.")

            # Send a message to the client
            tls_client_socket.send(b"Hello, TLS Client! You are
connected securely.\n")
        except ssl.SSLError as e:
            print(f"TLS handshake failed: {e}")
        finally:
            # Close the connection
            tls_client_socket.close()
            print("Connection closed.")

if __name__ == "__main__":
    create_tls_server()
```

Step 4: Running the Server and Client

Start the server first by running the server code in a terminal; the client code can be run in a separate terminal using the commands "**`python tls_server.py`**" and "**`python tls_client.py`**", respectively. You should see the client connecting to the server, performing a TLS handshake, and receiving the message "Hello, TLS Client! You are connected securely."

Explanation:

1. **Generating the Self-Signed Certificate:** In the example, we created a self-signed certificate using OpenSSL. The server use this certificate to establish an encrypted communication channel with the client.
2. **Server Code Explanation:**
    a. A socket is created and bound to port 8443, listening for incoming connections.
    b. The SSL library is used to wrap the server socket with TLS, loading the server's certificate and private key.
    c. The server then accepts incoming connections and performs a TLS handshake with the client. If the handshake is successful, the server sends a message to the client over the encrypted channel.
    d. If there are issues with the handshake (for example, certificate validation problems), an **`ssl.SSLError`** is raised.
3. **Client Code Explanation:**
    a. The client connects to the server using a standard socket wrapped with TLS using the SSL library.
    b. It performs a TLS handshake with the server. Since we used **`ssl.create_default_context()`**, the client will verify the server's certificate.
    c. Once the handshake is complete, the client receives the server's message securely.

Notes:

- ***Self-Signed Certificate:*** *In production, avoid using self-signed certificates. Use certificates issued by a trusted Certificate Authority (CA) to prevent man-in-the-middle attacks.*
- ***Certificate Validation:*** *Ensure that the client verifies the server's certificate to avoid connecting to malicious servers.*

TLS Certificates and Certificate Authority (CAs)

TLS certificates are a critical component of secure communication over the Internet. They are used to establish the authenticity of a server and ensure that the connection between the server and client is encrypted. This section will delve into the purpose and structure of TLS certificates, the role of CAs, and the processes involved in issuing, validating, and managing these certificates.

Purpose of TLS Certificates

TLS certificates serve two main purposes:

- **Authentication:** They verify the identity of the server (or client, in some cases), ensuring that users are communicating with the legitimate entity they intend to reach. This prevents man-in-the-middle attacks, where an attacker could intercept communication between two parties by pretending to be the intended recipient.
- **Encryption:** They enable the secure encryption of data transmitted over the network using the public key contained in the certificate. This ensures that data exchanged between the server and client remains confidential and cannot be easily intercepted or tampered with.

Structure of a TLS Certificate

A TLS certificate contains several key elements, including:

- **Subject Name:** The identity that the certificate is issued for, typically the domain name of the server (for example, www.example.com).
- **Issuer:** The Certificate Authority (CA) that issued the certificate. This helps establish the trustworthiness of the certificate.
- **Public Key:** A public key associated with the certificate's subject. The corresponding private key is kept secret by the server and used to decrypt data encrypted with the public key.
- **Validity Period:** The period during which the certificate is considered valid. This includes the "Not Before" and "Not After" dates.
- **Signature Algorithm:** The algorithm used by the CA to sign the certificate, which ensures its authenticity.
- **Extensions:** Optional information that can specify additional details, such as key usage, subject alternative names (SANs), and certificate policies.

Certificate Authorities (CAs)

CAs are trusted entities that issue TLS certificates to organizations or individuals. They play a central role in the Public Key Infrastructure (PKI) by verifying the identity of certificate requesters and signing the certificates they issue. The process involves the following steps:

- **Certificate Request:** An organization generates a Certificate Signing Request (CSR), which includes the public key and information about the entity requesting the certificate (for example, domain name, organization name).
- **Verification:** The CA verifies the information provided in the CSR. For domain-validated certificates, the CA ensures that the requester controls the domain. For organization-validated certificates, additional checks of the organization's legitimacy are performed.
- **Certificate Issuance:** Once the CA verifies the identity of the requester, it signs the certificate with its private key, thus issuing a certificate that can be trusted by clients who recognize the CA.

Types of TLS Certificates

There are different types of TLS certificates, based on the level of validation performed by the CA and the intended use:

- **Domain-Validated (DV) Certificates:** These are issued after the CA verifies that the requester controls the domain. They provide basic encryption but offer limited information about the entity's identity.
- **Organization-Validated (OV) Certificates:** In addition to domain validation, the CA verifies the organization's details, such as its name and address. OV certificates provide a higher level of trust than DV certificates.
- **Extended Validation (EV) Certificates:** These require the most rigorous verification process, including checking the legal, physical, and operational existence of the organization. EV certificates provide the highest level of trust and are typically used by banks and financial institutions.
- **Wildcard Certificates:** These certificates cover multiple subdomains under a single domain (for example, *.example.com), allowing them to secure mail.example.com, www.example.com, and others.
- **Multi-Domain (SAN) Certificates:** These certificates support multiple domain names and are useful for securing different websites with a single certificate.

Certificate Chain of Trust

The trust model in TLS is based on a "chain of trust." This chain typically consists of:

- **Root Certificate:** The CA's root certificate is a self-signed certificate and is usually pre-installed in the operating system or browser's trusted root store.
- **Intermediate Certificates:** CAs use intermediate certificates to sign server certificates, creating a hierarchical chain. This helps reduce the risk associated with exposing the root certificate.
- **Server Certificate:** The final certificate used by the server to establish secure connections.

When a client connects to a server, the server provides its certificate chain, which includes the server certificate and intermediate certificates. The client verifies the chain against the root certificates in its trusted store, ensuring that the server's certificate is legitimate.

Certificate Revocation

Sometimes certificates need to be revoked before their expiration date due to security concerns, such as private key compromise or changes in domain ownership. The main methods for certificate revocation are:

- **Certificate Revocation Lists (CRLs):** A list of revoked certificates maintained by the CA. Clients download the list to check the status of a certificate.
- **Online Certificate Status Protocol (OCSP):** A more efficient method that allows clients to query the CA's OCSP server in real-time to check if a certificate is revoked.

Challenges with TLS Certificates

Some of the common challenges related to TLS certificates include:

- **Certificate Management:** Keeping track of certificate expiration dates and ensuring timely renewal can be challenging for organizations with many certificates.
- **Revocation Issues:** Not all clients check for revocation status, potentially allowing revoked certificates to be used in some cases.
- **Trust in CAs:** If a CA is compromised, all certificates issued by it may be considered untrustworthy.

Best Practices for Using TLS Certificates

Implementing TLS certificates effectively is critical for ensuring secure and reliable encrypted communications. The following best practices provide actionable steps to maximize the security and performance of TLS deployments.

- **Use Strong Key Lengths:** Choose certificates with adequate key lengths (for example, 2048-bit RSA or higher) to ensure security.
- **Regularly Update Certificates:** Ensure certificates are renewed before expiration to avoid service interruptions.
- **Enable OCSP Stapling:** To improve performance and security, servers can "staple" the OCSP response to the TLS handshake, reducing the need for clients to perform separate OCSP checks.
- **Monitor Certificate Usage:** Keep track of all certificates in use and automate alerts for upcoming expirations or other certificate-related issues.

TLS certificates, issued and verified by trusted Certificate Authorities, form the backbone of secure Internet communication. Understanding their structure, types, and management practices is essential for maintaining a secure communication environment. By ensuring the proper use of TLS certificates, organizations can effectively protect their data and establish trust in digital interactions.

Applications of TLS

TLS (Transport Layer Security) is a vital protocol used to secure communications across the internet. Its primary role is to provide confidentiality, data integrity, and authentication for data transmitted between clients and servers. In this section, we will explore various real-world applications of TLS across different domains, demonstrating how it ensures secure communication and protects data from malicious activities.

Web Security (HTTPS)

One of the most widespread applications of TLS is in securing web traffic through HTTPS (Hypertext Transfer Protocol Secure). When a website uses HTTPS, all data transmitted between the web server and the client (browser) is encrypted, preventing eavesdroppers from accessing sensitive information, such as login credentials, payment details, and personal data.

- **Secure E-commerce Transactions:** Online shopping platforms rely on TLS to secure payment transactions. Without TLS, credit card numbers, bank details, and other financial information could be intercepted during transmission.
- **Protection Against Man-in-the-Middle Attacks:** By encrypting data, TLS prevents attackers from intercepting and modifying communications between the user and the server. This is crucial for avoiding phishing schemes and ensuring the integrity of the data.
- **SEO Benefits:** Web browsers such as Google Chrome and search engines

prioritize secure websites, offering better rankings for websites using HTTPS over insecure HTTP connections.

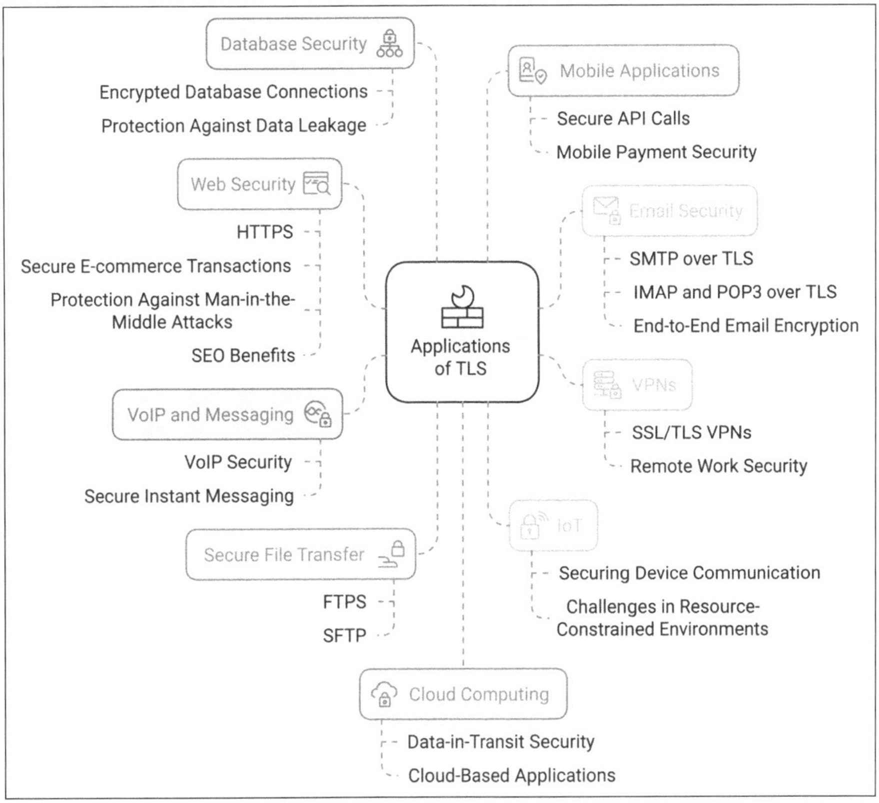

***Figure 9.5**: Applications of TLS*

Email Security

TLS is also widely used to secure email communications, ensuring that email content and attachments are transmitted securely over the Internet.

- **SMTP over TLS:** Email servers use Simple Mail Transfer Protocol (SMTP) over TLS to encrypt email transmissions between servers. This is known as SMTPS or STARTTLS, where STARTTLS is an upgrade command that allows the connection to be secured with TLS without using a separate port.
- **IMAP and POP3 over TLS:** Email clients retrieve emails from mail servers using protocols such as Internet Message Access Protocol (IMAP) and Post Office Protocol (POP3) over TLS, ensuring that email content is not exposed to attackers while being fetched.
- **End-to-End Email Encryption:** While TLS secures email transmissions between servers, it does not protect the content of the email itself. For

complete end-to-end encryption, additional mechanisms such as Pretty Good Privacy (PGP) or Secure/Multipurpose Internet Mail Extensions (S/MIME) are used along with TLS.

Virtual Private Networks (VPNs)

TLS plays a role in securing VPN connections, which are used to create secure tunnels for transmitting data across untrusted networks.

- **SSL/TLS VPNs:** These VPNs use TLS to establish a secure connection between the client and the VPN server, allowing data to be encrypted during transmission. This type of VPN is often used for remote access to internal network resources, especially for corporate employees working from remote locations.
- **Remote Work Security:** With the increasing adoption of remote work, organizations rely on TLS-secured VPNs to provide secure access to company resources, ensuring that sensitive data transmitted between employees and the corporate network remains confidential.

Voice over IP (VoIP) and Messaging Applications

TLS is used to secure real-time communication protocols such as VoIP and messaging services.

- **VoIP Security:** Protocols such as Session Initiation Protocol (SIP) use TLS to secure signaling data, such as call setup and tear-down messages, ensuring that attackers cannot intercept or manipulate call-related information.
- **Secure Instant Messaging:** TLS is used by popular messaging applications, including WhatsApp, Signal, and Telegram, to encrypt messages transmitted between users. This prevents unauthorized access to conversations and protects user privacy.

Secure File Transfer

File transfer protocols that involve the transmission of sensitive data over the internet extensively use TLS for encryption.

- **FTPS (File Transfer Protocol Secure):** An extension of FTP that uses TLS to encrypt data transfers, ensuring that files sent over the network cannot be accessed by unauthorized parties.
- **SFTP (SSH File Transfer Protocol):** Though not directly related to TLS, SFTP offers an alternative means for secure file transfer. However, some file transfer

services integrate TLS to establish a secure connection before using other secure protocols for data transfer.

Internet of Things (IoT)

IoT devices often transmit sensitive data, making them prime targets for attackers. TLS helps secure the communication between IoT devices and cloud services, preventing data breaches and unauthorized access.

- **Securing Device Communication:** By implementing TLS, IoT devices can ensure secure communication with servers and other devices, protecting transmitted data from being intercepted or tampered with.
- **Challenges in Resource-Constrained Environments:** While TLS is effective for securing IoT communications, some IoT devices have limited computational resources, which may necessitate the use of lightweight cryptographic algorithms and optimized TLS implementations.

Database Security

TLS can also be used to secure connections to databases, ensuring that data transmitted between the application server and the database server remains confidential.

- **Encrypted Database Connections:** When accessing cloud-based databases or remote database servers, TLS ensures that sensitive data such as customer information, financial records, and other confidential data remains secure during transmission.
- **Protection Against Data Leakage:** By encrypting the data sent between the database and the application, TLS helps prevent potential data leakage in case of network monitoring or compromise.

Mobile Applications

TLS is an integral part of mobile app security, helping to protect user data, financial transactions, and other sensitive information.

- **Secure API Calls:** Many mobile apps communicate with backend servers via APIs. Using TLS to secure these API calls, developers ensure that the data exchanged between the app and server is encrypted and authenticated.
- **Mobile Payment Security:** Payment apps such as Apple Pay and Google Pay use TLS to secure payment information and transaction details, providing a safe way for users to conduct financial transactions from their mobile devices.

Cloud Computing and Storage

TLS is essential for securing data transmissions between cloud services, clients, and other cloud-based resources.

- **Data-in-Transit Security:** Cloud providers use TLS to secure data as it is transmitted between data centers, clients, and external services, preventing unauthorized access to sensitive data.
- **Cloud-Based Applications:** Web applications hosted on cloud platforms use TLS to secure communication with end-users, protecting login credentials, personal data, and financial transactions.

Blockchain and Cryptocurrencies

Although blockchain technology itself relies on cryptographic algorithms for data security, TLS is still used for securing web-based cryptocurrency wallets and exchange platforms.

- **Securing Web Wallets:** TLS protects the communication between users and web-based cryptocurrency wallets, ensuring that private keys, transaction data, and login credentials are not exposed to attackers.
- **Exchange Platform Security:** Cryptocurrency exchange platforms use TLS to secure user accounts, transaction data, and sensitive financial information, mitigating the risk of data breaches and theft.

The TLS application extends across various domains, providing a foundation for secure communication in web browsing, email, VPNs, VoIP, IoT, and many other areas. By leveraging TLS to encrypt data and authenticate communication endpoints, organizations and users can protect their data from eavesdropping, tampering, and other malicious activities. TLS's versatility and importance in securing digital communication make it one of the most crucial protocols in today's interconnected world.

Future Directions for TLS

TLS continues to evolve to address emerging security challenges, improve performance, and support new use cases. As the internet landscape changes, TLS adapts to protect against more sophisticated threats while maintaining compatibility with existing systems. Here are some key areas where the future of TLS is headed:

Post-Quantum Cryptography

One of the most significant future directions for TLS is the integration of post-quantum cryptographic algorithms. Quantum computers, once powerful enough, could break traditional asymmetric cryptographic algorithms such as RSA and Elliptic Curve Cryptography (ECC), which are widely used in TLS for key exchange and authentication.

- **Quantum-Resistant Algorithms**: Research is underway to standardize post-quantum algorithms, such as lattice-based or hash-based cryptographic schemes, that are resistant to attacks by quantum computers. These algorithms will need to be incorporated into future versions of TLS to maintain long-term security.
- **Hybrid Cryptographic Approaches**: As a transitional solution, hybrid key exchange mechanisms that combine classical and quantum-resistant algorithms may be used. This approach ensures security even if one of the algorithms is broken, providing a gradual path towards full post-quantum cryptography adoption in TLS.

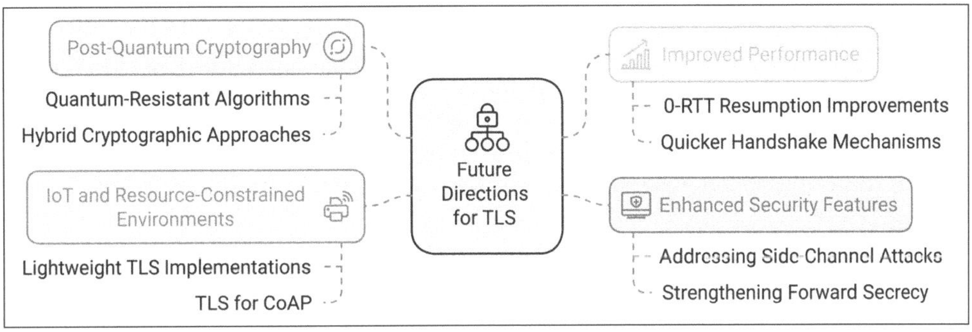

***Figure 9.6**: Possible Future Directions in TLS*

Improved Performance and Latency Reduction

While TLS 1.3 made significant improvements in reducing handshake latency, there is still ongoing work to optimize performance further.

- **0-RTT Resumption Improvements**: TLS 1.3 introduced Zero Round-trip Time (0-RTT) resumption to speed up subsequent connections. However, it comes with security trade-offs such as replay attacks. Future enhancements could focus on making 0-RTT more secure without compromising performance.
- **Quicker Handshake Mechanisms**: Research is being done on optimizing the handshake process to minimize latency, especially for scenarios with high network delays. Techniques such as connection resumption with session tickets and pre-shared keys (PSKs) could see further refinements.

Enhanced Security Features

To keep pace with new threats, future versions of TLS may include enhanced security features to address advanced attack vectors.

- **Addressing Side-Channel Attacks**: Side-channel attacks, like timing attacks, can leak information from encrypted communications. Future developments may include countermeasures to better protect against such attacks in the TLS protocol.
- **Strengthening Forward Secrecy**: Although TLS 1.3 enforces forward secrecy, ensuring that session keys cannot be derived from long-term private keys, future improvements may focus on optimizing algorithms for better forward secrecy in environments with limited computational resources, such as IoT devices.

IoT and Resource-Constrained Environments

As the number of IoT devices continues to grow, securing communication for these devices becomes increasingly important. However, IoT devices often have limited computational and power resources, making the implementation of traditional TLS challenging.

- **Lightweight TLS Implementations**: There is a need for TLS implementations specifically designed for low-power and resource-constrained devices. Future directions may involve optimized cryptographic algorithms and reduced protocol overhead for these scenarios.
- **TLS for Constrained Application Protocol (CoAP)**: CoAP, a protocol designed for constrained devices, can use Datagram Transport Layer Security (DTLS), a variant of TLS. Future enhancements may focus on more efficient integration of TLS/DTLS for lightweight IoT communication.

The future of TLS involves addressing emerging security challenges, optimizing performance, and expanding its applicability to new use cases and protocols. As the internet evolves, so too will TLS, ensuring that secure communication remains a cornerstone of digital interactions. Post-quantum cryptography, privacy enhancements, and IoT-specific optimizations are just some of the areas where ongoing research will shape the next generation of TLS.

Conclusion

In this chapter, we embarked on a comprehensive exploration of TLS Communication, delving into one of the fundamental protocols that underpin secure Internet communication. Our journey began with an Introduction to TLS, where we discussed its evolution from the earlier SSL (Secure Sockets Layer) protocol, the critical reasons behind the transition, and how TLS addresses the shortcomings and vulnerabilities discovered in SSL. We also covered the basic concepts behind TLS, including its role in ensuring confidentiality, data integrity, and authentication in digital communication. Next, we took a deep dive into the TLS Handshake Process, where we outlined the sequence of steps involved in establishing a secure communication channel. We discussed the use of both symmetric and asymmetric cryptography in TLS, explained how certificate-based authentication ensures the identity of communication parties, and explored different key exchange mechanisms, such as RSA, Diffie-Hellman, and Elliptic Curve Diffie-Hellman (ECDH). Our discussion then moved to the Cryptographic Algorithms used in TLS, where we examined the various encryption algorithms, hashing techniques, and cipher suites supported by the protocol. We covered both symmetric and asymmetric algorithms, highlighting their strengths and weaknesses, and explained how these algorithms are employed in different phases of a TLS connection to maintain security. To provide a hands-on understanding, we presented a Practical Example with an End-to-End Use Case, demonstrating how TLS can be implemented in real-world scenarios. The example illustrated the step-by-step process of establishing a secure connection, including using programming libraries and sample code, to give readers a clear view of how TLS functions in practice.

The chapter then transitioned to a discussion on TLS Certificates and Certificate Authorities (CAs), covering the role of digital certificates in authentication and the trust model that underpins secure communications on the Internet. We explored how certificates are issued, validated, and managed, and discussed the importance of CAs in maintaining the integrity of the public key infrastructure (PKI) that TLS relies upon. We also explored Applications of TLS, showcasing how TLS secures a broad range of internet services, from web browsing and email to virtual private networks (VPNs) and secure VoIP communications. We highlighted the widespread use of TLS in protecting sensitive data and ensuring privacy across various industries. Lastly, we touched upon the Future Directions of TLS, where we considered ongoing developments and upcoming enhancements that address emerging threats, optimize performance, and expand TLS applicability to new protocols and use cases. The discussion covered post-quantum cryptography, enhanced privacy techniques, IoT-focused optimizations, and improved automation for certificate management.

In conclusion, this chapter provided a thorough understanding of TLS, covering its evolution, core components, cryptographic underpinnings, and practical implementations. It underscored the significance of TLS in maintaining secure communications and how its continued evolution will shape the future of internet security. In the next chapter, we will dive into "Current Trends in Cryptography," where we will explore cutting-edge developments and emerging technologies in the field. We will examine new algorithms, novel cryptographic techniques, and the impact of advancements such as quantum computing on the future of cryptography. This will provide a forward-looking view of how cryptographic practices are adapting to meet the challenges of an ever-changing digital landscape.

CHAPTER 10
Latest Trends in Cryptography

Introduction

Cryptography, the cornerstone of digital security, continues to evolve in response to new technological advancements and emerging threats. It is not just a static set of techniques, but a dynamic field that must adapt to meet the challenges posed by an increasingly interconnected world. The relentless pace of technological progress brings both opportunities for innovation and new threats that require more sophisticated cryptographic strategies. In this chapter, we will explore the latest trends in cryptography, focusing on cutting-edge research, recent breakthroughs, and emerging technologies that are shaping the future of secure communication.

In the previous chapter, we discussed Transport Layer Security (TLS), an essential protocol for securing communication on the Internet. TLS illustrates the practical application of cryptographic principles, combining techniques, such as key exchange, digital certificates, and encryption algorithms to provide confidentiality, integrity, and authentication for online interactions. Our deep dive into TLS provided insights into how classical cryptographic mechanisms are used to secure real-world systems, setting the stage for understanding more advanced and experimental developments in cryptography that we will explore in this chapter.

As technology advances, traditional cryptographic methods face new challenges. One of the most significant drivers of change is the impending advent of quantum computing. Quantum computers promise to solve complex mathematical problems exponentially faster than classical computers, which could potentially render current cryptographic algorithms, such as RSA and ECC, vulnerable to quantum-based attacks. This impending threat has led to a surge in research into post-quantum cryptography, which aims to develop new algorithms resistant to quantum computing attacks while maintaining performance and efficiency on classical systems.

Another area of active research and increasing practicality is homomorphic encryption. Traditionally, encryption methods ensure data confidentiality but require decryption for data processing. Homomorphic encryption allows computations to be performed directly on encrypted data, enabling data to remain confidential even during processing. This has significant implications for privacy-preserving data analytics, secure cloud computing, and data sharing in regulated industries.

Zero-knowledge proofs (ZKPs), once considered a theoretical concept, are now finding practical applications in various fields, including blockchain, identity verification, and privacy-preserving protocols. These cryptographic techniques allow one party to prove to another that a statement is true without revealing any information beyond the statement's validity. The deployment of ZKPs in real-world scenarios is transforming how privacy and trust are managed in decentralized systems.

The chapter will also explore lightweight cryptography, a field driven by the need to provide strong security guarantees for resource-constrained environments such as the Internet of Things (IoT). As billions of devices become connected to the internet, the need for efficient and secure cryptographic techniques that minimize power consumption and computational resources becomes critical. Lightweight encryption algorithms are designed to strike a balance between security and efficiency, ensuring that even low-power devices can communicate securely.

Privacy-enhancing technologies (PETs) have gained prominence as data privacy regulations, such as the General Data Protection Regulation (GDPR), become stricter. Techniques such as differential privacy, secure multi-party computation, and federated learning integrate cryptographic methods to enable data to be processed securely and privately. The convergence of cryptography and privacy techniques helps organizations comply with regulations while ensuring data confidentiality and integrity.

The increasing complexity of cyber threats necessitates cryptographic agility: systems that can dynamically switch between different algorithms and configurations in response to evolving threats or newly discovered vulnerabilities. This approach provides a future-proof method to address security requirements by allowing seamless transitions to stronger algorithms as needed.

Throughout this chapter, we will delve into these trends and other emerging developments in cryptography, analyzing their potential to shape the future of secure communication and data protection. We will discuss how cryptographic research addresses current security challenges and what lies ahead, providing a glimpse into the innovations that aim to stay ahead of potential adversaries.

As we approach the final section of this book, "Latest Trends in Cryptography" will serve as both a summary and an exploration into the future directions of cryptographic research, touching on recent advancements that push the boundaries of what is possible in securing our digital world. Whether it is quantum-resistant algorithms, privacy-preserving technologies, or new paradigms in encryption, this chapter will provide a comprehensive understanding of the latest and most impactful developments in the field.

Structure

In this chapter, we will cover the following topics:

- Post-Quantum Cryptography
- Homomorphic Encryption
- Zero-Knowledge Proofs (ZKPs)
- Lightweight Cryptography
- Miscellaneous Trends in Cryptography

Post-Quantum Cryptography

Post-Quantum Cryptography (PQC) refers to cryptographic algorithms designed to be secure against the potential capabilities of quantum computers. As quantum computing continues to advance, it poses a significant threat to classical cryptographic systems, particularly those based on mathematical problems that quantum algorithms can solve efficiently. The field of PQC seeks to develop new cryptographic techniques that remain robust even in the face of powerful quantum adversaries, thereby ensuring the continued security of sensitive data in the future.

The necessity for post-quantum cryptography arises from the limitations of classical cryptographic algorithms in the face of quantum attacks. Most of today's widely-used encryption schemes, such as RSA (Rivest-Shamir-Adleman), DSA (Digital Signature Algorithm), and elliptic-curve cryptography (ECC), rely on the computational difficulty of problems such as integer factorization and discrete logarithms. These problems are infeasible for classical computers to solve in a reasonable time frame, which forms the basis of their security. However, with the development of quantum algorithms such as Shor's algorithm, these cryptosystems become vulnerable, as quantum computers can solve these problems exponentially faster than classical computers, potentially breaking the encryption in a matter of seconds.

As a result, there is a pressing need to develop and adopt new cryptographic techniques that can resist the capabilities of quantum computers. Post-quantum cryptography aims to address this by introducing algorithms based on different mathematical problems, such as lattice-based, code-based, multivariate polynomial, hash-based, and isogeny-based cryptography. These approaches are believed to be resistant to quantum attacks and are under active research to be standardized for widespread use.

The urgency of adopting post-quantum cryptography cannot be overstated. Data encrypted today using traditional methods could potentially be decrypted in the future if quantum computers reach a level of maturity where they can break classical encryption. This has implications for long-term data confidentiality, especially for information that needs to remain secure for many years, such as government, financial, or healthcare data. Thus, transitioning to post-quantum cryptographic solutions is not only a matter of future-proofing security but also protecting data that could be at risk from "harvest-now, decrypt-later" attacks.

Post-quantum cryptography serves as a critical step in preparing the world for the age of quantum computing, aiming to maintain the integrity, confidentiality, and authenticity of information in a post-quantum era. The journey toward achieving secure post-quantum solutions involves ongoing research, standardization efforts, and real-world implementations to ensure that future cryptographic systems remain resilient against emerging threats.

Threat of Quantum Computers to Classical Cryptography

Quantum computers represent a significant threat to the security of traditional cryptographic algorithms that have been widely used for decades, such as RSA (Rivest-Shamir-Adleman), ECC (Elliptic-Curve Cryptography), and DSA (Digital Signature Algorithm). These algorithms, which form the backbone of many secure communication systems, rely on the mathematical difficulty of certain problems for their security. The emergence of quantum computing fundamentally challenges these assumptions by enabling powerful quantum algorithms that can solve these problems much more efficiently than classical computers.

Vulnerabilities in RSA

RSA encryption relies on the difficulty of factoring large composite numbers into their prime factors. For classical computers, this problem is considered infeasible to solve in a reasonable time frame as the key size increases, providing strong security for encrypted data. However, using Shor's algorithm quantum computers can factor large numbers exponentially faster than classical algorithms. For instance, while factoring a 2048-bit RSA key would take millions of years on a classical computer, a sufficiently powerful quantum computer could accomplish this task in mere seconds. This capability renders traditional RSA encryption vulnerable, as encrypted data could be rapidly decrypted if the private key is derived through quantum factorization.

Vulnerabilities in Elliptic-Curve Cryptography (ECC)

Elliptic-Curve Cryptography, which offers similar levels of security with smaller key sizes compared to RSA, is also susceptible to quantum attacks. ECC is based on the mathematical problem of finding discrete logarithms over elliptic curves, a problem that is infeasible for classical computers to solve. However, quantum computers can utilize Shor's algorithm to solve the elliptic-curve discrete logarithm problem (ECDLP) in polynomial time. This means that once a sufficiently powerful quantum computer becomes available, it can break ECC-based cryptosystems, compromising the security of systems that rely on elliptic-curve key exchange, digital signatures, and encryption.

Threat of Quantum Computers to Symmetric Cryptography

While quantum computers pose a significant risk to asymmetric cryptographic algorithms such as RSA and ECC, symmetric cryptographic algorithms are also affected, albeit to a lesser extent. Symmetric algorithms such as AES (Advanced Encryption Standard), 3DES (Triple Data Encryption Standard), and various secure hash algorithms (such as SHA-256) are considered more resilient to quantum attacks, but they are not entirely immune.

Grover's Algorithm and Its Impact on Symmetric Cryptography

Grover's algorithm is a quantum search algorithm that provides a quadratic speedup for brute-force attacks against symmetric key algorithms. In classical cryptography, the security of symmetric algorithms is based on the infeasibility of exhaustively searching through all possible keys within a reasonable time. For example, a 128-bit key in AES would require 2^{128} operations to break using a classical computer, which is practically impossible.

However, Grover's algorithm reduces the effective security of symmetric cryptographic algorithms by half. For instance:

- **AES-128**: Instead of requiring 2^{128} operations to brute-force the key, a quantum computer running Grover's algorithm would only need 2^{64} operations, significantly reducing the time needed to break the encryption.
- **AES-256**: Similarly, Grover's algorithm would reduce the effective search space from 2^{256} to 2^{128}, making it theoretically possible to break the encryption, though still challenging due to the very large computational resources required.

Hash Functions and Grover's Algorithm

Grover's algorithm also affects the security of cryptographic hash functions. For example:

- **SHA-256**: With Grover's algorithm, finding a preimage or a collision would take 2^{128} operations instead of 2^{256}, reducing the effective security.
- **SHA-3**: Similarly, hash functions in the SHA-3 family would face a reduction in security levels against quantum attacks.

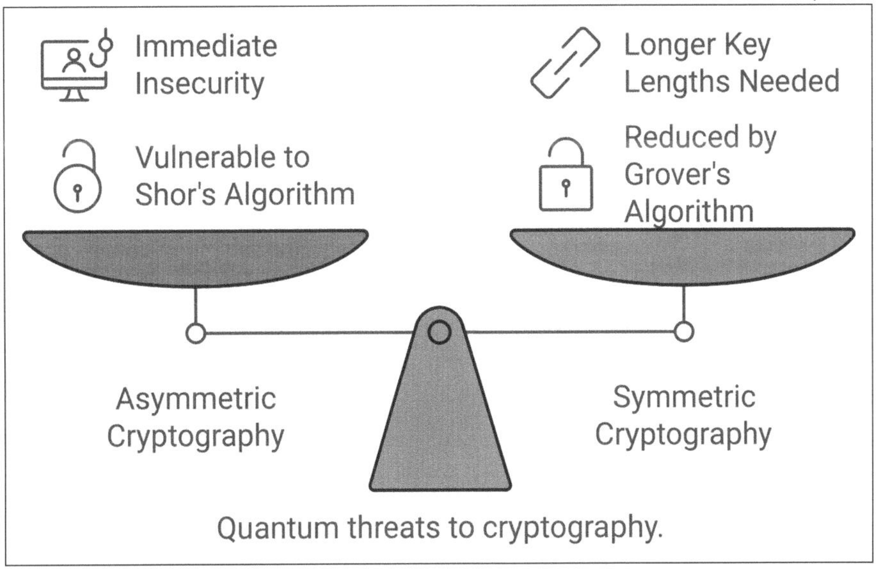

Figure 10.1: *Quantum Threats to Cryptography*

To maintain security levels equivalent to those of classical algorithms, the key lengths and hash sizes for symmetric algorithms would need to be doubled in response to quantum computing threats. For example, using AES-256 instead of AES-128 is recommended to ensure sufficient security in the post-quantum era.

Comparison with Asymmetric Cryptography

The impact of quantum computing on symmetric cryptography is less severe than on asymmetric cryptography. Asymmetric algorithms such as RSA and ECC rely on problems that quantum computers can solve in polynomial time with Shor's algorithm, making them entirely insecure once quantum computers reach a certain size. In contrast, symmetric algorithms "only" lose half their effective security due to Grover's algorithm, meaning they can still be secure with longer key sizes.

Recommendations for Symmetric Cryptography in the Quantum Era

To counter the potential threat posed by quantum computers, several measures can be taken for symmetric algorithms:

- **Doubling Key Sizes**: Using larger key sizes (for example, AES-256) can help maintain strong security against quantum attacks.
- **Strengthening Hash Functions**: Employing larger output sizes for hash functions (for example, SHA-512) helps mitigate the reduced security from Grover's algorithm.
- **Hybrid Cryptographic Approaches**: Combining classical symmetric algorithms with post-quantum cryptographic techniques can enhance overall security.

NIST Post-Quantum Cryptography Standardization Efforts

The National Institute of Standards and Technology (NIST) has been at the forefront of efforts to standardize post-quantum cryptographic algorithms, recognizing the urgent need to secure digital communications against potential future quantum threats. The initiative aims to develop cryptographic standards that will remain secure even when large-scale quantum computers capable of breaking classical cryptography emerge. The NIST Post-Quantum Cryptography Standardization project began in 2016 aiming to select and standardize new algorithms that can resist quantum-based attacks, focusing primarily on public-key encryption, key encapsulation mechanisms (KEMs), and digital signatures.

Phases of the Standardization Process:

The NIST process has been conducted in multiple rounds, progressively narrowing down the pool of candidate algorithms. The main stages of the process are:

1. **Initial Round (2017-2019)**:
    - NIST received 82 algorithm submissions from researchers worldwide, covering various mathematical approaches to post-quantum security. These submissions included encryption schemes, KEMs, and digital signature algorithms.
    - The algorithms underwent an initial review, emphasizing on security, efficiency, and implementation considerations.
2. **Second Round (2019-2020)**:
    - Out of the 82 initial submissions, NIST selected 26 candidates to proceed to the second round: 17 encryption/KEM schemes and 9 digital signature schemes.
    - The second round focused on a more in-depth analysis of the security properties and performance characteristics of the algorithms.
3. **Third Round (2020-2022)**:
    - NIST announced 15 finalists (7 encryption/KEM schemes and 8 digital signature schemes) and 8 alternate candidates, aiming to select the most promising algorithms for standardization.
    - The third round considered attacks, performance optimizations, and a variety of use cases, leading to the selection of a smaller set of algorithms.
4. **Fourth Round and Beyond (2022-present):**

- **NIST selected four algorithms for standardization**: one for public-key encryption/KEM (CRYSTALS-Kyber) and three for digital signatures (CRYSTALS-Dilithium, FALCON, and SPHINCS+).

- Additional algorithms are still under review in a fourth round to identify alternative solutions for specific use cases or to provide additional layers of security.

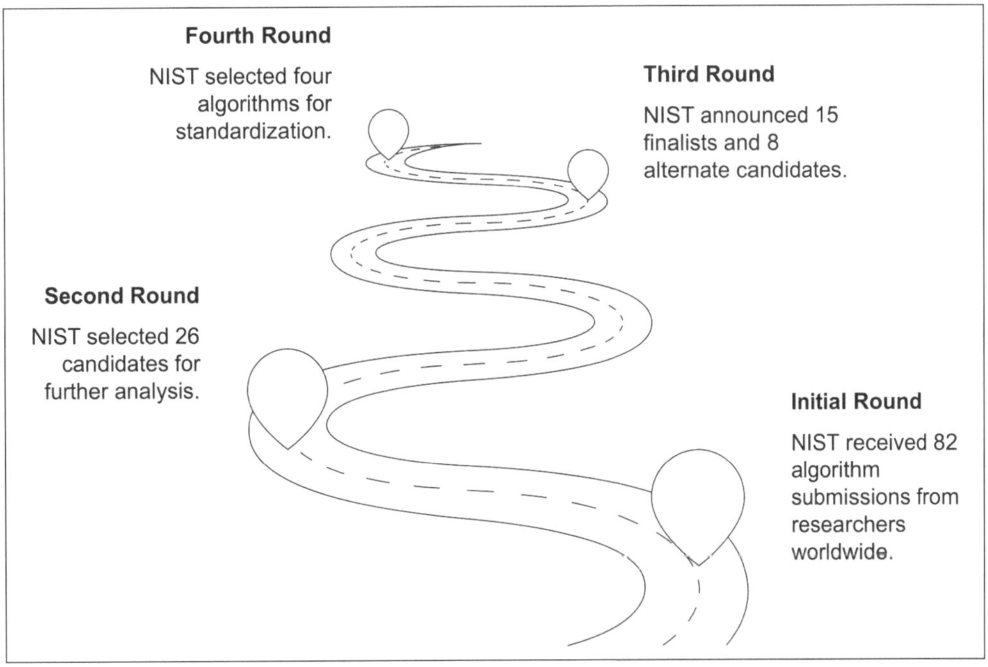

***Figure 10.2**: PQC Standardization Milestones*

Algorithms Selected for Standardization:

The algorithms chosen for standardization represent different mathematical approaches to securing data against quantum threats. Following is an overview of the selected algorithms:

- **CRYSTALS-Kyber (Public-Key Encryption/KEM)**:
  - **Category**: Lattice-based cryptography.
  - **Overview**: CRYSTALS-Kyber is a lattice-based key encapsulation mechanism that relies on the Learning With Errors (LWE) problem. Its security is based on the hardness of lattice problems in high dimensions, making it resistant to quantum attacks.
  - **Strengths**: Kyber offers efficient key generation, encryption, and decryption operations, as well as small ciphertext and key sizes compared to other lattice-based schemes. It is suitable for a variety of applications, including Internet communication protocols such as TLS.

- **CRYSTALS-Dilithium (Digital Signature)**:
    - **Category**: Lattice-based cryptography.
    - **Overview**: CRYSTALS-Dilithium is a digital signature scheme that also relies on lattice problems, specifically the Module Learning With Errors (MLWE) problem. It provides strong security guarantees while maintaining efficient signature generation and verification.
    - **Strengths**: Dilithium features small signature sizes and is well-suited for performance-sensitive environments such as embedded systems.
- **FALCON (Digital Signature)**:
    - **Category**: Lattice-based cryptography.
    - **Overview**: FALCON (Fast Fourier Lattice-based Compact Signatures over NTRU) is a lattice-based signature scheme that uses the NTRU lattice structure. It provides compact signatures with a high level of security.
    - **Strengths**: FALCON is known for its small signature size and efficient verification process, making it a good fit for systems with constrained bandwidth or high verification throughput requirements.
- **SPHINCS+ (Digital Signature)**:
    - **Category**: Hash-based cryptography.
    - **Overview**: SPHINCS+ is a stateless hash-based digital signature scheme that offers security based on the collision resistance of hash functions. It does not rely on any assumptions about mathematical problems that could be broken by quantum algorithms.
    - **Strengths**: As a hash-based scheme, SPHINCS+ provides long-term security even if lattice-based schemes are found to be vulnerable in the future. However, its signature sizes are larger compared to lattice-based alternatives.

Ongoing Efforts and Alternative Algorithms:

Although NIST has selected the primary algorithms for standardization, the need for a diverse portfolio of post-quantum algorithms has led to ongoing evaluations of alternative candidates. These include:

- **SIKE (Supersingular Isogeny Key Encapsulation)**: An isogeny-based encryption algorithm offering small key sizes. However, recent cryptanalytic breakthroughs have shown vulnerabilities in SIKE, leading NIST to reconsider its suitability.
- **Classic McEliece**: A code-based cryptographic algorithm known for its large key sizes but with a long-standing record of resisting cryptanalysis. It remains a viable candidate for specific applications.

Implications of NIST's Standardization Efforts:

The standardization of post-quantum algorithms by NIST will have a profound impact on the future of cryptographic systems. Organizations worldwide will need to transition from classical cryptographic algorithms to post-quantum alternatives, ensuring long-term data security. The selection of lattice-based schemes such as Kyber and Dilithium reflects the current preference for algorithms that balance security, efficiency, and ease of implementation.

NIST's efforts also emphasize the importance of "crypto-agility": the ability to switch cryptographic algorithms quickly in response to emerging threats. As research in quantum computing progresses, it is crucial to stay flexible and prepared to adopt new algorithms or make modifications to existing standards.

Challenges in Implementing Post-Quantum Cryptography

The adoption of post-quantum cryptographic (PQC) algorithms poses several challenges that need to be carefully addressed as the cryptographic community prepares for the quantum era. Despite the promising security offered by PQC algorithms, transitioning from well-established classical algorithms, such as RSA, ECC, and others, comes with significant technical and operational hurdles.

- **Performance Issues**

  One of the most significant challenges with PQC algorithms is performance. Quantum-resistant cryptography, especially lattice-based algorithms, such as CRYSTALS-Kyber and CRYSTALS-Dilithium, requires more computational resources than their classical counterparts. This can manifest in various ways:

  - **Higher Computational Overhead**: The computational requirements for key generation, encryption, and decryption in PQC algorithms are generally more demanding than traditional algorithms. Systems that rely heavily on cryptography, such as web servers and IoT devices, may see increased load and processing time.
  - **Latency Concerns**: In real-time communications, such as TLS handshakes in HTTPS connections, the time required for cryptographic operations can significantly impact latency. For time-sensitive applications, this could lead to performance degradation.
  - **Energy Consumption**: Higher computational complexity leads to increased power consumption, which is particularly concerning for battery-powered devices, such as smartphones, IoT sensors, and other embedded systems.

- **Key Size Considerations**

  Another key issue is the size of the cryptographic keys and signatures used in post-quantum algorithms. Most PQC algorithms, especially those based on lattices and codes, require significantly larger key sizes compared to classical cryptographic algorithms such as RSA and ECC.

  - **Larger Key Sizes**: Algorithms such as Kyber and Dilithium typically use much larger key sizes to achieve the same level of security as RSA or ECC. This increases the storage requirements for cryptographic keys and may impact the bandwidth needed for transmitting encrypted messages or performing handshakes.
  - **Larger Signature Sizes**: Some PQC algorithms, particularly hash-based algorithms such as SPHINCS+, generate very large signatures. This may not be suitable for bandwidth-constrained environments, such as low-power IoT devices or remote connections with limited data transmission capabilities.
  - **Impact on Memory and Storage**: Devices with constrained memory and storage resources, such as smart cards, embedded systems, and IoT devices, may struggle to handle the larger key sizes required by PQC algorithms. Hardware upgrades or optimizations may be necessary to accommodate the increased storage needs.

- **Interoperability with Legacy Systems**

  PQC algorithms are fundamentally different from classical cryptography, and existing systems are primarily built to support traditional algorithms, such as RSA, DSA, or ECDSA. Ensuring backward compatibility and smooth integration with legacy systems is a key challenge in adopting PQC:

  - **Legacy System Compatibility**: Many applications, especially those in critical infrastructure, rely on cryptographic libraries and protocols designed for classical algorithms. Transitioning to PQC would require updating or replacing these libraries, which can be a complex and time-consuming process.
  - **Hybrid Cryptography**: To ensure backward compatibility during the transition, hybrid cryptographic systems that use both classical and quantum-resistant algorithms may be required. However, hybrid systems increase complexity and can introduce additional vulnerabilities.

- **Security Proof and Maturity**

  Although many PQC algorithms have strong theoretical foundations, they are relatively new compared to classical cryptography, which has been rigorously analyzed and tested for decades. Ensuring the security and maturity of PQC algorithms presents several challenges:

- **Lack of Real-World Testing**: PQC algorithms have not been widely deployed, and their real-world security properties have not been extensively tested against advanced attacks, particularly side-channel attacks that exploit hardware or software implementations.
- **Complexity of Cryptanalysis**: While some PQC algorithms are backed by hard mathematical problems (such as Lattice-based or Code-based cryptography), the complexity of cryptanalysis for quantum-resistant algorithms is still an active area of research. The fear remains that future discoveries may reveal weaknesses in these algorithms that we are currently unaware of.

Real-World Applications of Post-Quantum Cryptography

As quantum computing rapidly progresses, organizations, governments, and cryptographic communities are making significant strides toward adopting post-quantum cryptography. While quantum computers capable of breaking current cryptographic standards do not yet exist, early adoption of PQC is seen as a proactive defense against potential future threats. We will now explore the current use cases and real-world applications where PQC is being used or planned for implementation.

- **Government and National Security Agencies**

  Governments and defense agencies are among the early adopters of post-quantum cryptography due to the critical nature of their communications and data security needs. Many government organizations recognize that it may take decades to fully transition to quantum-safe encryption, and any data intercepted today could be decrypted by quantum computers in the future, commonly known as a "harvest now, decrypt later" attack. Some key initiatives include:

  - **NIST and U.S. Federal Agencies**: The National Institute of Standards and Technology (NIST) has spearheaded the Post-Quantum Cryptography Standardization project, working closely with various federal agencies and international organizations to identify and select quantum-safe algorithms. Government agencies such as the National Security Agency (NSA) have also started to issue guidance regarding the transition to quantum-resistant algorithms for securing national security systems.
  - **European Initiatives**: The European Union is investing in quantum communication infrastructure through projects such as the EuroQCI (European Quantum Communication Infrastructure). The goal is to implement post-quantum cryptographic algorithms in critical infrastructures, ensuring long-term security.

- **Financial Institutions**

  The banking and finance industry is particularly sensitive to cryptographic risks, as secure communication, data integrity, and authentication are crucial for protecting sensitive financial data and transactions. Financial institutions are preparing for a future where quantum computers could compromise their cryptographic systems:

  - **Hybrid Approaches in Banks**: Major financial organizations are exploring the use of hybrid cryptographic systems, where both classical and post-quantum algorithms are used in tandem. This ensures backward compatibility with current systems while building quantum-resistant infrastructures for future use.
  - **Blockchain and Cryptocurrencies**: The rise of blockchain and cryptocurrencies has prompted concerns about the security of existing cryptographic protocols, especially in the context of quantum attacks. Some blockchain networks, such as Ethereum and Bitcoin, are actively researching quantum-resistant cryptographic methods to secure their transactions and wallets against future quantum threats.

- **Telecommunications and Internet Infrastructure**

  The telecommunications industry, which forms the backbone of global communication, is actively working on integrating post-quantum cryptographic algorithms into their infrastructure to ensure future-proofing against quantum attacks:

  - **Quantum-Safe TLS**: Companies are working to integrate post-quantum cryptography into existing security protocols such as Transport Layer Security (TLS). The adoption of hybrid TLS, where both quantum-resistant and classical algorithms are used, is gaining traction. Early trials are already taking place with the support of global standards bodies such as the Internet Engineering Task Force (IETF).
  - **5G and IoT Security**: The upcoming 5G networks and the Internet of Things (IoT) revolution will see an unprecedented number of devices connected to the Internet. These networks require scalable and quantum-resistant cryptographic solutions, as IoT devices are often resource-constrained, making traditional cryptography infeasible. Many companies are exploring post-quantum solutions for securing 5G and IoT communications.

- **Cloud Service Providers**

  Cloud computing has become the backbone of modern IT infrastructure, and cloud service providers are now facing the challenge of securing vast amounts of sensitive data in a post-quantum world:

  - **Quantum-Safe Cloud Storage**: Companies such as Google, Amazon Web

Services (AWS), and Microsoft Azure are already investing in research and pilots to secure their cloud environments with post-quantum cryptography. Hybrid cryptographic solutions are being tested to provide cloud customers with forward-looking security that can withstand quantum threats.

- **Key Management and Data Protection**: Quantum-resistant key management systems are being explored to secure the encryption keys used to protect data stored in cloud environments. This is essential for maintaining long-term data privacy in sectors, such as healthcare, legal services, and intellectual property management.

Homomorphic Encryption

Homomorphic encryption is a revolutionary cryptographic technique that enables computations to be performed directly on encrypted data without requiring access to the underlying plaintext. This unique property sets homomorphic encryption apart from traditional encryption schemes, where data must first be decrypted, processed, and then re-encrypted. With homomorphic encryption, sensitive data remains encrypted throughout the computation process, significantly enhancing security and privacy.

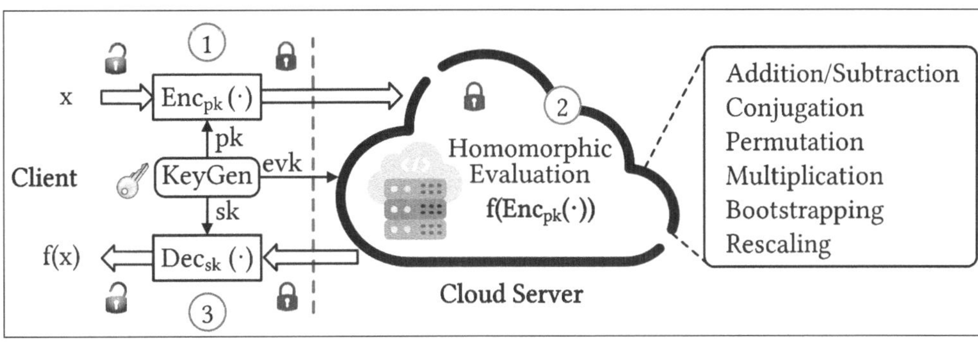

Figure 10.3: *Homomorphic Encryption based crypto system*

At its core, homomorphic encryption ensures privacy-preserving computation: a concept that is particularly valuable in today's data-driven world. As organizations increasingly rely on third-party services for data storage, processing, and analysis, ensuring the confidentiality of sensitive information while still enabling meaningful computation has become a critical challenge. This is where homomorphic encryption shines. Allowing computations on encrypted data minimizes the risk of exposing sensitive information, even in scenarios where data is processed by potentially untrusted parties.

Unique Ability: Computations on Encrypted Data

In traditional encryption, operations on data require access to the original, unencrypted form. For example, in cloud computing environments, if a user wants to perform operations such as searching, sorting, or applying mathematical functions to their data, they typically need to decrypt the data first. This creates a potential vulnerability, as sensitive information is exposed during processing, even if it remains encrypted at rest or in transit.

Homomorphic encryption, however, allows users to delegate computations to third parties–like cloud service providers–without ever exposing the original data. Whether the operation involves simple arithmetic such as addition and multiplication, or more complex functions such as statistical analysis or machine learning model training, the data stays encrypted throughout the entire process. Once the computation is complete, the result, still encrypted, is returned to the user, who can then decrypt it using their private key to view the final result.

This ability has transformative implications across various domains, enabling secure outsourced computation and collaborative data analysis without compromising privacy.

Breakthrough in Privacy-Preserving Computation

The advent of homomorphic encryption represents a major breakthrough in the field of cryptography, particularly as the demand for privacy-preserving computation grows across sectors, such as cloud computing, secure data sharing, and machine learning.

- **Cloud Computing:**

  Cloud platforms are widely used for data storage and processing due to their flexibility, scalability, and cost-effectiveness. However, one of the biggest concerns for users is the security of their data in these environments. Cloud providers may be subject to breaches, insider threats, or government mandates, creating situations where data could be exposed. Homomorphic encryption offers a solution by allowing users to offload data and computation to the cloud without ever needing to reveal the raw data to the service provider. This makes it possible to fully leverage the power of cloud computing while maintaining data privacy and confidentiality.

- **Secure Data Sharing:**

  In scenarios where, multiple parties need to collaborate on sensitive data, such as in healthcare, finance, or research, homomorphic encryption enables secure data sharing and analysis. For example, medical researchers could analyze encrypted patient data from multiple hospitals to generate insights, all without any party gaining access to the actual patient records. This allows for privacy-preserving collaborations and ensures that sensitive data remains protected while still being useful.

- **Machine Learning:**

  Machine learning models often rely on large datasets for training and improvement, but when those datasets contain sensitive information, privacy concerns arise. Homomorphic encryption offers a way to train machine learning models on encrypted data, ensuring that sensitive details remain confidential throughout the process. This can enable privacy-preserving AI solutions in sectors such as healthcare, where patient data must be protected, or in finance, where transaction details are sensitive.

Overall, homomorphic encryption is a key technology that addresses the growing need for secure, privacy-preserving computation in an increasingly connected and data-driven world. It allows organizations and individuals to unlock the full potential of cloud computing, big data analysis, and machine learning without compromising security and privacy. While practical challenges remain, such as the computational overhead associated with homomorphic encryption, its potential to revolutionize how sensitive data is handled makes it one of the most exciting areas in modern cryptography.

Types of Homomorphic Encryption

Homomorphic encryption schemes can be categorized based on the operations they support and the extent to which computations can be carried out on encrypted data. The three primary types of homomorphic encryption–Partial (or Somewhat) Homomorphic Encryption (PHE/SHE), Fully Homomorphic Encryption (FHE), and Leveled Homomorphic Encryption–vary in their ability to handle complex computations, their computational costs, and their practical applications.

Partial/Somewhat Homomorphic Encryption (PHE/SHE)

Partial, or somewhat homomorphic encryption (PHE/SHE), is the simplest form of homomorphic encryption. It allows a limited set of operations to be performed on encrypted data, either addition or multiplication, but not both. Each operation on the encrypted data, or "ciphertext," reflects a corresponding operation on the unencrypted data, or "plaintext," within a restricted scope.

Common examples of somewhat homomorphic schemes include:

- **Paillier Cryptosystem:** Supports additive homomorphism, allowing operations such as the aggregation of encrypted values without decrypting.
- **RSA Cryptosystem (in its multiplicative form):** Allows multiplicative homomorphism, enabling multiplication operations on encrypted values.

Since these schemes restrict the types and numbers of operations that can be performed, they're primarily suitable for use cases where only one type of operation (either addition or multiplication) is needed. For instance:

- **Voting systems:** An additive homomorphic scheme can tally votes in an encrypted format, where each vote is added without decryption.
- **Financial Transactions:** In applications where, aggregating transaction values is required without exposing individual transactions.

While somewhat homomorphic encryption offers practical solutions for specific tasks, its limitation to a single operation type constrains its broader application in complex computations.

Fully Homomorphic Encryption (FHE)

Fully homomorphic encryption (FHE) extends the concept of homomorphic encryption by supporting both addition and multiplication operations on encrypted data, allowing arbitrary computations to be performed securely. This capability enables FHE to execute complex computations on encrypted data without ever decrypting it, making it a cornerstone for privacy-preserving computation.

The concept of FHE was first theoretically proposed in the late 1970s, but it wasn't until 2009 that Craig Gentry proposed a workable scheme using a lattice-based approach. Gentry's construction was groundbreaking but computationally intensive, requiring significant processing power and time for each operation. However, FHE's potential has driven substantial research in recent years, leading to more efficient implementations.

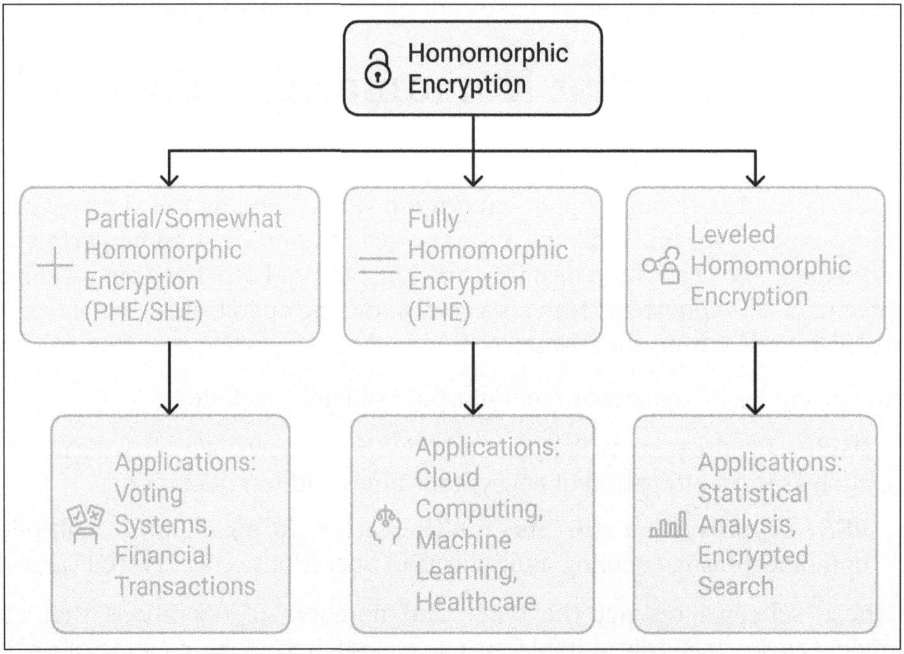

Figure 10.4: *Types of Homomorphic Encryption*

Applications of FHE:

- **Cloud Computing**: Enable cloud providers to perform operations on clients' encrypted data without ever accessing the actual data.
- **Machine Learning on Encrypted Data**: Enables privacy-preserving machine learning where the model can learn from encrypted data without revealing the data itself.
- **Healthcare Data Analysis**: Researchers can analyze patient data stored in an encrypted format, ensuring privacy and compliance with regulations such as HIPAA.

While FHE remains computationally intensive and is not yet widely deployed in production, advancements in FHE libraries, hardware acceleration, and algorithmic optimizations make it more feasible.

Leveled Homomorphic Encryption

Leveled homomorphic encryption, or leveled FHE, is a variation of FHE that supports both addition and multiplication but with a limited depth: the number of operations that can be performed on the ciphertext before decryption is required. This allows leveled FHE to overcome some high computational costs associated with fully homomorphic encryption by trading off unrestricted computational depth.

The leveled FHE approach is especially useful in scenarios where computations can be predefined with a known limit on the number of operations:

- **Statistical Analysis:** Certain types of statistical analyses on encrypted data might involve only a fixed number of additions or multiplications, making leveled FHE a feasible choice.
- **Encrypted Search:** In databases or search engines, where a fixed number of operations are required for search queries, leveled FHE can support efficient, privacy-preserving searches.

Leveled FHE sits at a middle ground between PHE and FHE, offering the flexibility of both addition and multiplication while reducing the computation cost relative to fully homomorphic encryption.

Challenges and Limitations of Homomorphic Encryption

Despite its promise for secure computation and privacy-preserving applications, homomorphic encryption (HE), particularly fully homomorphic encryption (FHE), comes with significant challenges and limitations that hinder its broad adoption. Two of the most critical limitations are performance and scalability.

Performance

The most prominent challenge facing homomorphic encryption is its computational overhead. FHE, in particular, is resource-intensive because of the complex mathematical operations required to ensure that encrypted data can undergo computations without decryption. Here are a few specific performance issues associated with FHE:

- **High Latency:** Each homomorphic operation on encrypted data can take significantly longer than a similar operation on unencrypted data. Simple tasks, such as an addition or multiplication operation, can take seconds or even minutes with FHE, compared to milliseconds or less for standard encryption methods.
- **Increased Processing Power:** HE schemes demand substantial computational power due to the need to maintain privacy during computation. Without specialized hardware, the required computational resources can quickly become prohibitive, making HE unsuitable for real-time or high-throughput applications.
- **Energy Consumption:** With high processing power comes increased energy consumption, which can make HE algorithms impractical for low-power devices or applications requiring efficiency, such as Internet of Things (IoT) devices.

These performance challenges mean that HE, especially FHE, is impractical for many real-world applications today, particularly those requiring rapid or real-time data processing, such as in high-frequency trading, interactive gaming, or emergency healthcare monitoring. Ongoing research focuses on creating optimized algorithms and leveraging hardware acceleration (for example, FPGAs, GPUs, and TPUs) to reduce FHE's computational footprint, but the technology is still maturing.

Scalability

Scalability is another major concern with homomorphic encryption, especially when dealing with large datasets or complex computations that require many sequential operations. Specific scalability issues include:

- **Data Size and Key Management:** HE often requires larger key sizes to maintain security, which, in turn, increases storage demands and complicates key management. For example, FHE keys can be several megabytes or even gigabytes in size, adding complexity and overhead for storage and transfer.
- **Computational Depth:** In FHE, each additional operation (especially multiplications) increases the ciphertext's "noise" or error margin. At a certain depth, the noise becomes too significant, and the ciphertext needs refreshing or "bootstrapping." Bootstrapping is a resource-intensive process, and

although leveled FHE attempts to limit this by capping operations, scalability remains an issue for applications requiring more complex calculations.

- **Data Bandwidth and Communication Overhead:** When dealing with large datasets, the time and bandwidth required to encrypt and send data, perform computations, and decrypt results can increase dramatically. This becomes a bottleneck in applications such as big data analytics and machine learning, where vast volumes of data need constant processing.

Due to these limitations, HE is generally not feasible for handling high-dimensional data or complex models in machine learning, where multiple layers of computation are required. Instead, applications of HE are often confined to simpler operations, smaller datasets, or situations where privacy is a higher priority than efficiency, such as sensitive financial computations or secure medical research.

Current Advancements in Homomorphic Encryption

With homomorphic encryption (HE) offering a revolutionary approach to secure computing, researchers and technologists are actively exploring ways to improve its performance, scalability, and practicality. Despite the challenges HE currently faces, ongoing research and innovative strategies are pushing the boundaries of what homomorphic encryption can achieve, particularly in areas such as performance improvements and hybrid approaches that make it more applicable in real-world scenarios.

Performance Improvements

One of the primary areas of focus in advancing homomorphic encryption is to reduce the computational overhead and increase the efficiency of encryption and decryption processes. Key areas of performance improvements being explored include:

- **Algorithmic Optimization:** Researchers are developing optimized mathematical techniques that streamline the underlying operations in FHE. By refining how addition and multiplication are handled on encrypted data, they aim to reduce the latency of operations while maintaining strong security guarantees. For example, optimized FHE schemes such as the Brakerski-Gentry-Vaikuntanathan (BGV) and Cheon-Kim-Kim-Song (CKKS) have been introduced, each with specific performance benefits in precision or efficiency depending on application needs.
- **Hardware Acceleration:** Another promising approach involves using specialized hardware, such as Graphics Processing Units (GPUs), Field-Programmable Gate Arrays (FPGAs), and Tensor Processing Units (TPUs). These hardware solutions can speed up the mathematical computations required by HE,

reducing latency by orders of magnitude compared to traditional CPU-based processing. Notably, FHE is a focus area in emerging hardware technologies, with companies investing in hardware tailored to support privacy-preserving cryptographic operations.

- **Parallelization:** To improve throughput, researchers are exploring parallel processing techniques where individual operations on encrypted data are distributed across multiple processors or computational nodes. By leveraging parallelism, homomorphic encryption can handle more data and operations simultaneously, making it more feasible for applications such as cloud computing and secure data sharing.

As a result of these advancements, performance gains in homomorphic encryption are expected, which could make FHE suitable for more diverse applications, especially in time-sensitive or high-complexity environments.

Hybrid Approaches

In response to the inherent computational challenges of FHE, researchers are exploring hybrid cryptographic models that combine FHE with other cryptographic techniques to enhance efficiency and functionality. Hybrid approaches aim to leverage the best aspects of each cryptographic method, balancing performance with security, and making homomorphic encryption more feasible for practical use cases.

- **Combination with Symmetric Encryption:** A common strategy involves using symmetric encryption for high-performance bulk data encryption while applying homomorphic encryption to sensitive parts of the data that require computation. For example, in financial applications, a hybrid model could use traditional encryption to protect transaction data, and FHE, only on specific fields where privacy-preserving computation is necessary. This strategy keeps most data processing efficient while ensuring that sensitive computations are securely conducted.
- **Multi-Party Computation (MPC) and FHE:** Some researchers are combining multi-party computation techniques with FHE to create a secure, collaborative environment where data can be processed across different entities without revealing it. In this hybrid setup, MPC handles secure data sharing between parties, while FHE allows computation on the shared data in an encrypted format. This approach has promising applications in sectors requiring secure collaboration, such as healthcare research, collaborative machine learning, and government intelligence.
- **Leveled Homomorphic Encryption (LHE):** Leveled HE schemes provide another layer of practicality by limiting the number of operations that can be performed on encrypted data before re-encryption is required. By restricting operations to a predefined depth, LHE maintains more efficient computations,

making it suitable for scenarios that involve only limited, simpler operations. For instance, LHE could be applied in cloud storage settings where periodic re-encryption is feasible without a major performance impact.

Libraries for Homomorphic Encryption: SEAL and CKKS

Homomorphic encryption is gaining traction as a critical cryptographic tool, and several libraries have emerged to simplify its implementation and foster its adoption. Among these, Microsoft SEAL and the CKKS scheme stand out as prominent tools for implementing homomorphic encryption, offering robust solutions for various use cases.

Microsoft SEAL

Microsoft SEAL (Simple Encrypted Arithmetic Library) is a leading homomorphic encryption library developed by Microsoft Research. It is open-source, written in C++, and designed for both academic research and practical applications. SEAL provides an accessible way to use homomorphic encryption without requiring deep expertise in cryptography.

Key Features:

- **Support for BFV and CKKS Schemes**: SEAL implements two popular homomorphic encryption schemes:
    - **BFV (Brakerski/Fan-Vercauteren)**: Optimized for exact computations, such as addition and multiplication on integers.
    - **CKKS (Cheon-Kim-Kim-Song)**: Designed for approximate computations, such as real-number arithmetic in applications like machine learning and statistical analysis.
- **Highly Optimized**: SEAL is engineered to maximize performance on modern CPUs, leveraging techniques such as polynomial arithmetic and number theory optimizations.
- **Cross-Platform**: It supports various platforms, including Windows, Linux, and macOS, and is compatible with .NET, Python, and other languages through bindings.
- **Flexibility and Security**: The library allows customization of parameters, such as encryption modulus, polynomial degree, and noise budget, enabling users to balance performance, security, and computational depth.

Use Cases:

- **Privacy-Preserving Machine Learning**: SEAL enables secure training and inference on encrypted datasets, making it suitable for privacy-sensitive sectors such as healthcare and finance.
- **Secure Cloud Computing**: The library supports operations on encrypted data in cloud environments without exposing sensitive information.
- **Research and Prototyping**: Academics and developers use SEAL for prototyping and exploring new applications of homomorphic encryption.

SEAL's comprehensive documentation and active community make it a go-to choice for implementing homomorphic encryption in practical scenarios.

CKKS (Cheon-Kim-Kim-Song) Scheme

The CKKS scheme, while supported in SEAL, is also independently implemented in several libraries and frameworks tailored to real-number arithmetic. CKKS is specifically designed for approximate computations, making it uniquely suited for use cases such as privacy-preserving machine learning and encrypted data analysis.

Key Features:

- **Approximate Arithmetic**: CKKS introduces an innovative approach to handling real numbers by encoding them into polynomials and performing approximate computations. This feature is crucial for domains requiring floating-point operations.
- **Efficient Encoding and Scaling**: CKKS balances precision and performance using techniques such as scaling factors and modular arithmetic, ensuring accurate results while managing ciphertext size.
- **Noise Management**: The scheme handles noise growth during operations more efficiently than other homomorphic encryption schemes, enabling deeper computations before re-encryption or bootstrapping is needed.

Use Cases:

- **Machine Learning**: CKKS supports training models on encrypted datasets, allowing for secure collaborative learning without exposing raw data.
- **Statistical Analysis**: Researchers and analysts can perform encrypted statistical computations, ensuring data privacy.
- **Big Data Analytics**: CKKS enables secure computation over large datasets, making it ideal for industries handling sensitive information, such as finance, healthcare, and retail.

Libraries Using CKKS:

- **SEAL**: As noted, SEAL provides comprehensive support for CKKS, allowing developers to leverage its features within a robust framework.
- **HElib**: Developed by IBM, HElib also implements CKKS, alongside other schemes, for advanced cryptographic operations.
- **TenSEAL**: Built on SEAL, TenSEAL extends CKKS support specifically for machine learning applications, offering integration with PyTorch and TensorFlow.

Both Microsoft SEAL and the CKKS scheme play pivotal roles in advancing the practical implementation of homomorphic encryption, offering developers and researchers powerful tools for tackling privacy and security challenges in today's data-driven world.

Real-World Use Cases of Homomorphic Encryption

Homomorphic encryption is finding its way into a range of real-world applications, particularly in sectors where data privacy and security are paramount. By allowing computations on encrypted data, HE provides a groundbreaking approach to protecting sensitive information without sacrificing functionality. The following are some of the key industries leveraging homomorphic encryption, with a focus on healthcare, finance, government, and defense.

Healthcare: Secure Medical Data Analysis

In healthcare, the ability to analyze medical data without compromising patient privacy is critical. Traditional approaches often require healthcare providers to either anonymize data, which may reduce its usability, or process it in a secure environment, which can be costly and complex. Homomorphic encryption offers a solution by enabling secure computations directly on encrypted data. Some of the ways HE is transforming healthcare include:

- **Privacy-Preserving Medical Research:** Medical research often involves processing sensitive patient data across different institutions, from hospitals to research centers. Homomorphic encryption can facilitate privacy-preserving collaborations, allowing researchers to conduct analyses on encrypted patient data without needing to decrypt it. This approach maintains patient confidentiality while promoting data-driven insights in fields such as genetic research and clinical studies.
- **Secure Remote Diagnosis and Monitoring:** With the rise of telemedicine, patient data is increasingly transferred and analyzed over digital platforms. HE allows healthcare providers to securely analyze encrypted data from patients'

devices, such as wearables or home monitoring systems, to offer insights on health trends without exposing sensitive information. This capability is especially useful for chronic disease management and preventative healthcare.

- **Genomic Data Analysis:** Genomic data is highly sensitive but valuable for personalized medicine. By using HE, researchers can analyze encrypted genomic data to identify disease markers or genetic predispositions without compromising privacy. This application enhances data security where patient privacy and data protection are paramount.

Finance: Securely Processing Encrypted Financial Transactions

In the financial industry, security and privacy are both crucial as organizations process millions of sensitive transactions daily. Homomorphic encryption provides a pathway to secure processing in areas, such as fraud detection, risk assessment, and personal data protection:

- **Fraud Detection:** Banks and financial institutions can leverage homomorphic encryption to analyze encrypted transaction data for signs of fraudulent activity without exposing customer information. HE makes it possible to apply machine learning algorithms on encrypted data streams, detecting fraud patterns in real-time and reducing the risk of data breaches.
- **Risk Analysis and Credit Scoring:** Financial institutions use extensive customer data for credit scoring and risk analysis. With homomorphic encryption, they can process customer data securely, performing credit scoring algorithms directly on encrypted data. This helps ensure data privacy while allowing lenders to make informed decisions based on accurate and secure data.
- **Secure Data Sharing Between Financial Entities:** Financial transactions often involve multiple entities, such as banks, credit bureaus, and regulatory bodies. HE enables secure data sharing and computation across entities without compromising customer privacy. For example, different banks could perform joint analyses on shared customer data for loan assessments or market trends without exposing underlying data.

Government and Defense: Secure Communications and Sensitive Data Analysis

In government and defense, data security is critical for maintaining national security and protecting citizen privacy. Homomorphic encryption is an ideal solution for securely handling and analyzing sensitive information in environments where data exposure can have significant consequences.

- **Classified Data Analysis:** Government agencies can use HE to conduct analyses on encrypted classified information, such as intelligence data, to extract actionable insights without exposing the data. This is particularly useful for intelligence agencies where data confidentiality is paramount and information often involves collaborative analysis across different departments.

- **Interagency Data Sharing:** In government operations, secure interagency data sharing is essential for tasks such as criminal investigations and national security initiatives. Homomorphic encryption enables agencies to share encrypted data securely, allowing each party to perform necessary analyses without decrypting the shared data. This mitigates data exposure risks even as government departments work together on shared cases or security operations.
- **Privacy-Preserving Census and Survey Data:** Government agencies frequently collect sensitive information from citizens during censuses or surveys. Homomorphic encryption allows agencies to conduct statistical analyses and extract aggregate insights from encrypted data, ensuring that individual privacy is preserved even as demographic and economic insights are gathered for public policy.

As homomorphic encryption continues to evolve, it is poised to transform more sectors where data privacy and security are critical. Though computational efficiency and scalability remain challenges, ongoing research and advancements in hardware acceleration and hybrid models make homomorphic encryption increasingly viable. By enabling privacy-preserving computations across healthcare, finance, government, and more, HE is setting a new standard for data security in a privacy-conscious world.

Zero-Knowledge Proofs (ZKPs)

Zero-Knowledge Proofs are cryptographic protocols that allow one party, known as the prover, to demonstrate knowledge of a particular piece of information to another party, called the verifier, without actually revealing any details of that information. This seemingly paradoxical concept – proving knowledge without disclosing it – lies at the heart of zero-knowledge proofs. Formally defined in the 1980s by cryptographers Shafi Goldwasser, Silvio Micali, and Charles Rackoff, ZKPs represent a groundbreaking development in cryptography, particularly in privacy-preserving technology and secure communication.

The Foundational Idea Behind Zero-Knowledge Proofs

To understand the fundamental principle of ZKPs, consider that every proof of knowledge can theoretically have two outcomes:

1. The verifier can confirm that the prover indeed possesses the knowledge.
2. The verifier learns nothing else about the actual information beyond its existence and the proof of the prover's knowledge.

This structure ensures that, while the verifier is confident that the prover has the correct information; they gain no advantage in deciphering what that information is. In practice, this ability to confirm validity without exposing content is essential to creating secure, privacy-focused systems.

The Three Core Properties of Zero-Knowledge Proofs

Every ZKP is defined by three essential properties:

- **Completeness:** If the prover is truthful and possesses the required knowledge, an honest verifier will be convinced of this truth by the ZKP.
- **Soundness:** A fraudulent prover cannot deceive the verifier into believing they possess knowledge they do not actually have.
- **Zero-Knowledge:** The proof itself conveys no additional information about the knowledge, apart from the fact that the prover has it.

Proving Knowledge Without Revealing Information

The zero-knowledge aspect is often likened to analogies that simplify complex mathematical processes. One well-known analogy is the "Ali Baba's Cave" thought experiment. In this story, a prover (let's call her Alice) knows the secret phrase to open a hidden door in a circular cave. Alice wants to convince a verifier (let's call him Bob) that she indeed knows this phrase, without actually saying it aloud. Bob watches as Alice enters one side of the cave and returns from the other side without him hearing the phrase. By repeating this process multiple times, Bob becomes convinced that Alice knows the secret, though he never hears it himself. This analogy captures the essence of a zero-knowledge proof – convincing evidence without revelation.

The Importance of Zero-Knowledge Proofs in Cryptography

The ability to prove knowledge without sharing information has significant implications for data privacy and security. In today's interconnected world, there is an increasing need to authenticate information or identities while minimizing exposure to sensitive data. ZKPs address this need by creating ways to verify the validity of information without divulging it, offering a powerful tool for privacy-preserving applications. Examples include verifying identities in secure login processes without storing or transmitting passwords, proving financial solvency without disclosing account balances, and enhancing privacy in blockchain transactions.

Types of Zero-Knowledge Proofs

Zero-Knowledge Proofs (ZKPs) come in various forms, each tailored to specific use cases and designed to meet different practical requirements. Here, we explore the most prominent types of ZKPs: interactive ZKPs, non-interactive ZKPs, SNARKs (Succinct Non-Interactive Arguments of Knowledge), and STARKs (Zero-Knowledge Scalable Transparent Arguments of Knowledge). These categories vary based on interaction requirements, efficiency, scalability, and computational transparency.

- **Interactive Zero-Knowledge Proofs**

  Interactive Zero-Knowledge Proofs (iZKPs) require an interactive, step-by-step process where the prover and verifier exchange information over multiple rounds. During these interactions, the verifier asks a sequence of questions or sends challenges, and the prover responds accordingly. After enough rounds, the verifier gains confidence that the prover possesses the knowledge without learning what it is.

  For example, in a cryptographic scenario involving identity verification, an iZKP might involve a series of back-and-forth challenges that allow the verifier to confirm that the prover knows a particular password without revealing it.

While interactive proofs are secure and relatively simple in design, they have limitations:

- **Real-Time Communication:** Requires both the prover and verifier to be online simultaneously.
- **Multiple Rounds:** The repetitive interactions may increase the verification time, which can be impractical in some real-world applications.

Interactive ZKPs are foundational to the concept of zero-knowledge verification and were among the earliest ZKP implementations. They're particularly useful in settings where real-time verification is possible, and security is paramount, but they can be resource-intensive and challenging to scale.

- **Non-Interactive Zero-Knowledge Proofs**

  Non-Interactive Zero-Knowledge Proofs (NIZKPs) streamline the verification process by removing the need for repeated interactions. In NIZKPs, the prover generates a single, standalone proof that can be verified independently by the verifier.

  This type of ZKP is especially useful in applications where the prover and verifier do not communicate in real-time, such as blockchain transactions or digital signatures. Non-interactive proofs typically rely on a shared reference string (SRS) or trusted setup, which both the prover and verifier can access to ensure accuracy. This SRS, often generated securely in a setup phase, becomes a common anchor for both parties to validate proofs independently.

The main benefits of NIZKPs include:

- **Efficiency:** One-time proof generation and verification eliminate the need for continuous interactions.

- **Practicality:** Suited for distributed environments and batch verification, common in blockchain and authentication systems.

  However, NIZKPs may rely on a trusted setup, where a third party is trusted to create an SRS without any bias or compromise, which can introduce potential vulnerabilities if compromised.

- **Succinct Non-Interactive Arguments of Knowledge (SNARKs)**

  SNARKs (Succinct Non-Interactive Argument of Knowledge) are an advanced form of NIZKPs optimized for efficiency and succinctness. SNARKs generate compact, short proofs that require minimal resources to verify, making them particularly suitable for high-speed applications such as blockchain and complex cryptographic computations. A SNARK proof can convince a verifier of complex computations' correctness without revealing sensitive data or requiring a large proof size.

Key characteristics of SNARKs include:

- **Succinctness:** The proof size remains small, regardless of the computation's complexity.
- **Efficiency:** SNARKs are designed for rapid verification, which is ideal for high-transaction environments.
- **Non-Interactivity:** Verifiers need only a single, compact proof to confirm the computation's validity.

SNARKs have seen widespread use in blockchain platforms such as Zcash, where privacy and efficiency are critical. However, the trusted setup required for many SNARKs introduces potential security concerns since the setup phase must be conducted in a tamper-resistant environment.

- **zk-STARKs (Zero-Knowledge Scalable Transparent Argument of Knowledge)**

  zk-STARKs are an evolution of SNARKs, designed to address some of the scalability and transparency limitations of earlier ZKP implementations. While similar to SNARKs in function, zk-STARKs rely on a transparent setup that doesn't require a trusted third party, significantly enhancing security by removing setup-based vulnerabilities. They also use hash functions instead of more computationally complex elliptic curve pairings, making zk-STARKs more scalable and suitable for larger datasets.

zk-STARKs offer:

- **Scalability:** Efficiently handle large data sets and complex computations without performance degradation.
- **Transparency:** zk-STARKs rely on a "transparent" setup without a need for trusted third parties, reducing vulnerability risks.

- **Longer Proof Sizes:** Although slightly larger than SNARK proofs, STARK proofs are still practical and enable robust data integrity checks.

zk-STARKs are increasingly used in applications requiring both privacy and transparency, such as scalable blockchains. Their transparency and scalability make them ideal for public, decentralized networks. However, zk-STARK proofs are generally larger than SNARKs, which can present minor trade-offs in certain systems.

Applications of Zero-Knowledge Proofs (ZKPs)

Zero-Knowledge Proofs have found significant applications across various fields, particularly where privacy, scalability, and security are crucial. Their ability to verify information without revealing any details about the data makes them ideal for industries, such as finance, identity management, and blockchain technology. Here's an in-depth look at key applications of ZKPs:

- **Privacy in Cryptocurrencies**

  Privacy-Focused Cryptocurrencies: ZKPs play a vital role in privacy-centered cryptocurrencies, such as Zcash, which leverages zk-SNARKs (Zero-Knowledge Succinct Non-Interactive Arguments of Knowledge) to offer confidential transactions. In Zcash, zk-SNARKs allow users to verify that a transaction is valid without disclosing the sender, receiver, or transaction amount. This ensures that financial data remains private while maintaining the network's integrity and compliance with transaction protocols.

Advantages:

- **Confidentiality:** Transaction details remain hidden, protecting user privacy.
- **Security:** zk-SNARKs ensure that transactions follow the correct protocol without needing to reveal details, preserving the blockchain's security.
- **Transparency for Compliance:** Despite the private nature, zk-SNARKs allow selected parties (for example, auditors or regulators) to verify data, balancing privacy with regulatory compliance.
- **Authentication Systems**

  Zero-Knowledge Proofs in Authentication: ZKPs provide a powerful method for identity verification without requiring sensitive information exchange. Traditional authentication systems rely on passwords or biometrics, which can be vulnerable to data breaches. With ZKPs, an individual can prove their identity without exposing credentials, which enhances security and privacy.

  Example Use Case: In authentication for banking services, ZKPs can allow a user to prove that they are an account holder without sending their password or personal information. This way, even if the communication is intercepted, no sensitive data is revealed.

Advantages:

- **Enhanced Security:** Since no sensitive information is exchanged, even if a ZKP-based verification is intercepted, it cannot impersonate the user.
- **Reduced Data Exposure:** Avoiding sensitive data exchange reduces the attack surface for hackers.
- **Privacy Preservation:** Authentication systems using ZKPs are inherently more privacy-preserving, which is advantageous in privacy-critical applications such as healthcare and finance.
- **Blockchain Scalability and Security**
  - **Improving Blockchain Scalability:** ZKPs improve blockchain scalability by reducing the data each participant needs to verify, enabling faster transaction speeds and lowering computational requirements. For example, zk-rollups aggregate many transactions into a single, verified ZKP, which represents the batch as a whole on the blockchain. This allows blockchains to handle larger transaction volumes without sacrificing security.
  - **Security and Verification:** ZKPs also provide a way to verify transactions and blocks without sharing transaction details, enhancing the security of the network. This ensures that the entire network can trust the data integrity without exposing sensitive details, enabling faster consensus.

Advantages:

- **Increased Throughput:** With zk-rollups, thousands of transactions can be verified as a single batch, significantly improving blockchain throughput.
- **Reduced Gas Fees:** Fewer transactions per block reduce gas fees for users, making blockchain applications more affordable.
- **Security and Integrity:** Transaction data remains confidential, preserving privacy while ensuring data accuracy and trust.

Key Advantages of ZKPs in Modern Applications

- **Privacy-Preserving Verification**: ZKPs allow data verification without data exposure, enabling privacy in sensitive transactions.
- **Efficiency in Data Transfer**: Non-Interactive ZKPs reduce the need for multiple back-and-forth communications, lowering data transfer requirements and speeding up processes.
- **Scalability for High-Volume Systems**: In high-volume applications such as blockchain, ZKPs offload computations, enabling better scalability by reducing the amount of data that needs to be processed for verification.

ZKPs are pivotal in achieving privacy, security, and efficiency in modern digital systems, from enabling confidential transactions in cryptocurrencies to optimizing scalability and security on blockchain platforms. As the technology evolves, ZKPs promise to extend their applications, offering transformative potential across industries requiring robust privacy-preserving solutions.

Challenges and Limitations of Zero-Knowledge Proofs (ZKPs)

Despite the powerful applications and security enhancements offered by Zero-Knowledge Proofs (ZKPs), several challenges and limitations remain. These obstacles affect performance, complexity, and scalability, making the deployment of ZKPs challenging in various real-world scenarios. Let's look into some of these issues in more detail:

- **Performance and Computation Costs**

  ZKPs, particularly zk-SNARKs, demand high computational resources for proof generation and verification. This is especially true in environments requiring large-scale or real-time computations, where performance limitations can be critical.

- **Computation Overhead**: Generating and verifying ZKPs typically requires substantial CPU power, which can slow down processes in systems where efficiency is paramount, such as high-frequency trading platforms or large-scale blockchains.
- **Storage Requirements**: Some ZKPs require more memory and storage than traditional systems, especially when dealing with complex proofs. This requirement can add to both infrastructure costs and deployment complexity.
- **Scalability Challenges**: Due to the intensive computation requirements, it can be difficult to scale ZKP-based systems to handle high transaction volumes without impacting speed. Applications that need to handle thousands of transactions per second, such as mainstream payment systems, may struggle with this limitation.
- **Complexity in Design**

  The theoretical foundations of ZKPs are rooted in advanced mathematics and cryptographic concepts. This complexity makes implementing and managing ZKP systems challenging, often requiring expertise that can be difficult to find or costly to maintain.

  - **Mathematical Complexity**: ZKPs rely on complex mathematical constructs, such as elliptic curves, pairings, and polynomial commitments, making design and implementation of ZKPs challenging for even seasoned cryptographic engineers.

  - **Implementation Complexity**: Beyond the theory, building and deploying ZKP systems requires careful consideration of memory, computation efficiency, and security. Any implementation flaws can lead to significant vulnerabilities, which can defeat the purpose of using ZKPs in the first place.
  - **Limited Accessibility**: Due to the high level of complexity, ZKPs are not readily accessible for widespread adoption, especially by smaller organizations or teams lacking deep cryptographic expertise.

- **Trust Assumptions**

  One of the critical limitations of certain ZKP schemes, such as zk-SNARKs, is the need for a "trusted setup." This setup process is crucial to creating parameters that ensure the system's security, but it introduces trust dependencies that can be challenging to manage or verify.

  - **Trusted Setup in zk-SNARKs**: zk-SNARKs require a "trusted setup," where a secure, random key is generated by trusted parties and subsequently destroyed. If this key is compromised, it could theoretically allow malicious actors to forge proofs, breaking the security guarantees of the system.
  - **Transparency in zk-STARKs**: zk-STARKs (Zero-Knowledge Scalable Transparent Argument of Knowledge) have been developed to address the trusted setup issue in zk-SNARKs. zk-STARKs do not require a trusted setup, enhancing transparency and trust in the proof. However, zk-STARKs tend to have longer proof sizes and verification times, affecting the performance.

Zero-Knowledge Proofs hold significant promise but face notable challenges, particularly around performance, complexity, and trust. Efforts are ongoing in the cryptographic community to address these issues by developing more efficient protocols, simplifying implementation, and removing trust dependencies. These advancements are gradually making ZKPs more practical for broader adoption across various industries, from finance and healthcare to government and beyond.

Lightweight Cryptography

Today, technology extends beyond traditional computing environments into devices with limited power, processing capabilities, and memory. From smartwatches to IoT sensors, autonomous drones, and RFID tags, these devices operate under strict constraints that make implementing standard cryptographic solutions challenging. Lightweight cryptography has emerged as a specialized area of cryptography designed to meet the security needs of such constrained devices without overloading their resources. By achieving a careful balance between efficiency and security, lightweight cryptography enables secure data transmission, device authentication, and data integrity across a broad spectrum of low-power, resource-limited environments.

Need for Lightweight Cryptography

In traditional computing environments, security protocols can be built on strong cryptographic algorithms that require significant computational power, memory, and energy. However, many modern devices don't have the resources to support these heavyweight cryptographic algorithms without negatively impacting performance, battery life, or latency.

For instance, in IoT applications, devices often have to run for years on a small battery, making low-power consumption a top priority. Similarly, RFID tags and contactless payment systems require minimal computation time to provide a seamless user experience. Lightweight cryptography addresses these unique needs by offering algorithms that are optimized for:

- **Low computational requirements:** Minimal CPU power to preserve performance.
- **Reduced memory usage:** Efficient use of memory to fit within limited storage.
- **Minimal energy consumption:** Extended battery life for low-power devices.

Applications of Lightweight Cryptography

Lightweight cryptography plays a critical role in securing a range of applications where traditional cryptographic solutions would be impractical. These include:

- **IoT devices:** From home automation to industrial sensors, IoT devices collect and share valuable data, often autonomously. Lightweight cryptography ensures secure communication and data integrity in environments where power and memory resources are highly constrained.
- **Wearable and medical devices:** Wearables such as fitness trackers and medical devices such as glucose monitors require low-power encryption methods to maintain continuous operation without frequent recharging.
- **RFID tags and contactless payment systems:** These systems are commonly used in inventory management, access control, and financial transactions and need fast, low-energy cryptography to provide secure, reliable, and near-instantaneous performance.
- **Automotive security:** Modern vehicles contain numerous embedded systems that communicate with each other and external networks. Lightweight cryptography provides secure in-car and vehicle-to-infrastructure communications without overburdening the vehicle's systems.

Balancing Security and Efficiency

Lightweight cryptography is built on the same fundamental principles as standard cryptography, focusing on confidentiality, integrity, and authentication. However, its design must strike a balance between achieving adequate security levels and respecting the physical and operational limitations of the target devices. For example:

- **Key Size and Computational Complexity:** Lightweight cryptography often uses shorter key lengths and simpler algorithms than traditional cryptography, tailored to constrained environments. While this can potentially reduce security strength, these algorithms are typically designed to ensure adequate protection for the specific applications they support.
- **Trade-offs in Performance and Security:** The primary objective of lightweight cryptography is to create cryptographic solutions that are "light" in terms of resource consumption but still secure enough to deter attacks within the specific risk parameters of constrained devices. Achieving this balance is complex, as it requires designing algorithms that can withstand known attacks (for example, side-channel attacks) without the computational overhead of traditional cryptographic methods.

Lightweight Cryptography vs. Traditional Cryptography

While traditional cryptography, such as AES and RSA, has been highly effective for securing data in high-power environments, these algorithms are not optimized for resource-constrained devices. For example:

- AES encryption, though secure, can be computationally intensive and may consume significant power, making it a less practical choice for very low-power devices.
- Elliptic Curve Cryptography (ECC) provides strong security with shorter key lengths, but it still requires computational resources beyond the capabilities of ultra-constrained devices.

Lightweight cryptography addresses these gaps by creating algorithms specifically tailored to constrained environments. Examples include PRESENT for lightweight symmetric encryption, PHOTON for hashing, and SipHash for message authentication, each offering a streamlined version of traditional cryptographic functions to suit various IoT and embedded systems' limitations.

Standardization Efforts and Global Relevance

Recognizing the need for secure, efficient cryptography in constrained environments, organizations such as the National Institute of Standards and Technology (NIST) have initiated standardization efforts for lightweight cryptographic algorithms. The goal is to develop standardized cryptographic methods that are globally recognized and optimized for use in constrained devices, ensuring interoperability and security across various industries and applications.

As the demand for secure IoT and embedded devices grows, lightweight cryptography is poised to play an increasingly central role in the broader landscape of cybersecurity. In subsequent sections, we'll dive into specific lightweight cryptographic algorithms, their design principles, and use cases to understand how they enable secure and efficient data protection in the most resource-limited environments. This chapter also examines the unique challenges lightweight cryptography faces and how ongoing research aims to expand its capabilities, setting the stage for a more secure future in the age of connected devices.

Design Goals and Challenges in Lightweight Cryptography

Lightweight cryptography is crafted to address the unique demands of resource-constrained environments, which require a delicate balance between security, efficiency, and compatibility. While traditional cryptography provides robust security for high-power computing systems, applying the same algorithms in lightweight devices – where memory, processing, and energy resources are often limited – can significantly hinder performance. Designing lightweight cryptographic algorithms, therefore, involves optimizing security functions to work within these limitations while ensuring sufficient strength against modern attacks.

Efficiency vs. Security: Balancing Low-Power Operations with Robust Protection

One of the primary goals of lightweight cryptography is to create efficient, low-power cryptographic algorithms that can function effectively without compromising security. However, this balance is inherently challenging:

- **Efficiency Needs:** Lightweight devices such as IoT sensors or RFID tags often require extremely low-power consumption to maintain long battery life or even function passively without an internal power source. This requires cryptographic algorithms to be lean, minimizing computational complexity, memory footprint, and energy usage.
- **Security Standards:** Although these devices require lightweight solutions, they still need strong encryption, authentication, and data integrity checks to protect against unauthorized access, tampering, and other attacks. This presents a challenge, as security strength and efficiency are often inversely related: reducing algorithm complexity can inadvertently weaken resistance to attacks.

To address these dual requirements, designers of lightweight cryptographic algorithms often employ strategies such as:

- **Reduced Key Lengths:** Shorter keys reduce the computational load, but the security level must be carefully considered, as it lowers the cryptographic strength.
- **Simplified Mathematical Structures:** Lightweight algorithms may avoid complex operations in favor of faster, lower-cost calculations. However, these structures need rigorous security testing to ensure that they withstand known attacks.
- **Algorithmic Optimizations:** Techniques such as loop unrolling, fixed-point arithmetic, and efficient data encoding can significantly reduce computational effort while preserving essential security properties.

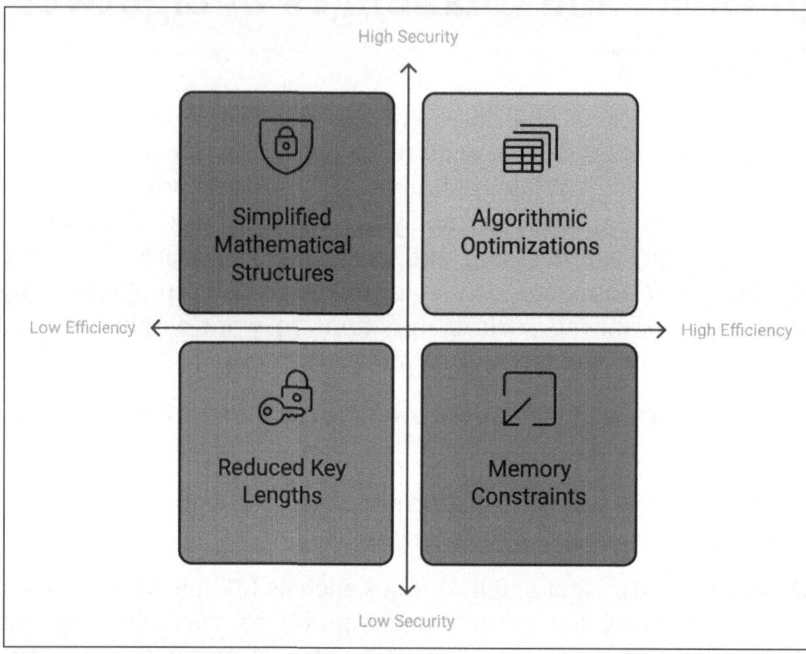

***Figure 10.5**: Security Cost Performance Balance in Lightweight Cryptography*

Achieving this balance is at the core of lightweight cryptographic design and requires innovative approaches to make security both strong and resource-efficient.

Resource Constraints: Overcoming Limited Memory, Processing Power, and Energy Budgets

Resource limitations are a fundamental challenge in the field of lightweight cryptography. Devices designed to operate on minimal resources often face restrictions in memory, processing power, and energy capacity, all of which must be considered in algorithm design.

- **Memory Constraints:** Many embedded devices and sensors have minimal memory, often measured in kilobytes or even bytes. Lightweight cryptographic algorithms must be optimized to operate within these small memory footprints without excessive storage or data overhead.
- **Processing Limitations:** Low-cost devices typically operate with limited processing power, sometimes only a few MHz or less. Cryptographic functions must avoid CPU-intensive operations to allow real-time processing and to avoid interrupting device functionality.
- **Energy Budgets:** In battery-operated devices, energy efficiency is critical, as frequent battery replacements may be impractical. Some devices, such as passive RFID tags, rely on harvesting ambient energy, making low-energy operation essential for continuous functionality. Lightweight cryptographic solutions are, therefore, designed to minimize the number of computational steps, reduce operational power draw, and limit the time required for encryption and decryption processes.

These constraints mean that conventional cryptography, which assumes more ample resources, is generally impractical for lightweight applications. Lightweight cryptographic algorithms must be purposefully designed to fit within these resource limits, ensuring they meet security requirements without draining power or overwhelming memory capacity.

Interoperability and Scalability: Supporting Broad Platform Compatibility and Deployment Scalability

As the ecosystem of connected devices grows, it's increasingly important for cryptographic solutions to support interoperability across diverse hardware platforms and scale effectively within large deployments.

- **Interoperability:** Lightweight cryptographic algorithms must be compatible across a variety of devices and communication protocols. For instance, in an IoT deployment, an algorithm might be required to function on both low-power sensors and more capable edge devices, meaning it must operate seamlessly across varying architectures and hardware capabilities. Designing interoperable algorithms allows more cohesive security measures across device ecosystems, making it easier to integrate lightweight cryptography within existing security frameworks.
- **Scalability:** Many IoT and embedded deployments involve higher volume of devices, often numbering in the thousands or millions. Lightweight cryptography must be scalable to support widespread, simultaneous deployments without introducing significant management overhead. For example, an algorithm should allow for efficient key distribution and periodic updates across a vast array of devices. Additionally, it should support hierarchical or distributed management to accommodate various network topologies.

Meeting these interoperability and scalability needs requires cryptographic solutions that are flexible, adaptive, and easy to deploy across different device types and operational contexts. Standardization efforts, such as those by NIST, help to promote interoperable algorithms, ensuring that lightweight cryptography can be adopted widely and securely across industries.

The Challenge of Future-Proofing

Finally, it's crucial for lightweight cryptographic algorithms to be future-proof where possible, meaning they should be resilient against foreseeable advances in computational power and cryptanalysis. While lightweight cryptography must work within today's resource constraints, it should also consider potential advancements to avoid rapid obsolescence. As more powerful cryptographic analysis techniques emerge, lightweight algorithms must be adaptable, either through flexible key management approaches or algorithmic structures that can evolve.

Balancing these requirements – efficiency, security, resource constraints, and scalability – is essential to advancing the field of lightweight cryptography. As device ecosystems continue to grow, so does the need for cryptographic solutions that ensure robust security across a vast array of low-power, resource-constrained devices.

Types of Lightweight Cryptographic Algorithms

Lightweight cryptographic algorithms are specialized cryptographic protocols that cater to the needs of resource-limited devices, such as IoT devices, RFID tags, and embedded systems. These algorithms are designed to provide essential security features–confidentiality, integrity, and authentication–without imposing a heavy computational burden. We will now explore the four key types of lightweight cryptographic algorithms: symmetric encryption, hash functions, message authentication codes (MACs), and asymmetric algorithms.

Symmetric Encryption

Symmetric encryption is popular in lightweight cryptography because it requires minimal computational resources compared to asymmetric encryption. In symmetric encryption, the same key is used for both encryption and decryption. Here are a few notable lightweight symmetric encryption algorithms optimized for constrained environments:

- **Ascon:**
    - **Overview:** Ascon is a family of lightweight authenticated encryption and hash algorithms that were selected as the winner of the NIST Lightweight Cryptography Standardization project in 2023. Known for its simplicity and efficiency, Ascon provides robust security for both encryption and

integrity with minimal computational and memory overhead. It features a sponge-based construction and operates efficiently in both hardware and software.

  - **Use Cases:** Ascon is ideal for IoT devices, embedded systems, and low-power wireless communication protocols, ensuring secure and efficient data transmission and storage.

- **PRESENT:**
  - **Overview:** PRESENT is a 64-bit block cipher that operates with either an 80-bit or 128-bit key. Known for its simple substitution-permutation network (SPN), PRESENT requires minimal processing power and memory, making it particularly suitable for hardware implementations.
  - **Use Cases:** It is often deployed in applications such as RFID systems, sensor networks, and other devices where memory and processing resources are limited.
- **SIMON and SPECK:**
  - **Overview:** SIMON and SPECK are a pair of lightweight block ciphers developed by the NSA. SIMON is optimized for hardware implementations, while SPECK is tailored for software environments. These algorithms offer a flexible range of key and block sizes, providing users with options to balance between security and efficiency.
  - **Use Cases:** SIMON and SPECK are widely used in IoT security, secure wireless communications, and low-power embedded systems, owing to their efficiency and adaptability to different device architectures.
- **KATAN and KTANTAN:**
  - **Overview:** KATAN and KTANTAN are block ciphers designed for ultra-constrained environments, with block sizes as small as 32 bits. They are optimized to require minimal power and computational resources, making them ideal for passive devices.
  - **Use Cases:** These algorithms are suitable for RFID tags, NFC systems, and other passive devices that need low-cost, efficient encryption.

These symmetric encryption algorithms are foundational to lightweight cryptographic systems, each designed with specific resource constraints in mind to ensure efficient security in constrained environments.

Hash Functions

Hash functions are essential for ensuring data integrity, verifying authenticity, and generating digital signatures. Lightweight hash functions are tailored to deliver these capabilities in environments with limited memory and processing power. Here are some lightweight hash functions widely used today:

- **PHOTON:**
    - **Overview:** PHOTON is a hash function based on the sponge construction, designed specifically for hardware-constrained environments. The low memory footprint makes it ideal for devices with limited resources.
    - **Use Cases:** PHOTON is widely used for data integrity and verification in embedded systems, IoT devices, and RFID applications.
- **SPONGENT:**
    - **Overview:** Similar to PHOTON, SPONGENT is a family of lightweight hash functions also based on the sponge construction, optimized to support different levels of security and resource constraints. Its multiple versions can be adjusted for different block sizes, balancing security and efficiency.
    - **Use Cases:** SPONGENT is commonly used in sensor networks and other IoT systems, where lightweight data integrity verification is essential.
- **Keccak (SHA-3):**
    - **Overview:** While Keccak (SHA-3) is a standard hash function, it is adaptable for lightweight applications by reducing specific parameters. The sponge construction makes it flexible for a range of applications, including constrained environments.
    - **Use Cases:** Keccak is used in secure communications for embedded applications and other lightweight systems that require data integrity and efficient hashing.

These hash functions are integral to lightweight cryptographic protocols, allowing systems to maintain data integrity and authentication without excessive resource demands.

Asymmetric Algorithms

Asymmetric cryptography is typically more computationally intensive than symmetric cryptography, but advancements have led to some lightweight asymmetric algorithms optimized for constrained devices. These are less common in lightweight cryptography but have specific applications where public-key infrastructure is necessary.

- **Elliptic Curve Cryptography (ECC):**
    - **Overview:** ECC is an asymmetric cryptographic approach known for its high security per bit. It offers robust security with smaller key sizes, making it suitable for environments where memory and computational power are limited.
    - **Use Cases:** ECC is used in IoT security, mobile communications, and secure key exchanges in low-power systems where traditional RSA encryption would be too resource-intensive.

- **Ring-Learning with Errors (Ring-LWE):**
    - **Overview:** Ring-LWE is a lattice-based asymmetric cryptographic approach promising for lightweight, post-quantum cryptography. Although not traditionally lightweight, recent optimizations suggest its potential for use in low-resource environments.
    - **Use Cases:** Ring-LWE is primarily in experimental stages for lightweight applications but could be useful in secure messaging and authentication for constrained devices in the future.

These asymmetric algorithms, particularly ECC, are increasingly valuable in applications where public-key cryptography is required but resources are constrained. As IoT and secure, lightweight communication protocols evolve, the role of lightweight asymmetric cryptography will continue to grow.

Each lightweight cryptographic algorithm discussed here has been designed to function efficiently in resource-constrained environments, striking a balance between security and operational feasibility. From efficient symmetric encryption algorithms and specialized hash functions to lightweight MACs and optimized asymmetric algorithms, these techniques collectively enable secure, efficient communication and data integrity in devices where traditional cryptographic approaches would be impractical.

Use Cases of Lightweight Cryptography

IoT and Smart Devices

Lightweight cryptography is crucial in securing Internet of Things (IoT) devices, wearables, and smart devices, which typically operate with limited memory, power, and computational resources. In IoT, data often flows between devices, gateways, and cloud servers, exposing sensitive information to potential risks if left unsecured. Lightweight cryptography offers efficient encryption and authentication for:

- **Data Integrity and Confidentiality:** Lightweight encryption algorithms protect sensitive data collected by IoT devices (such as sensors in industrial or home automation systems) from unauthorized access and tampering.
- **Secure Communications:** Lightweight encryption protocols help ensure secure communication channels between devices and central hubs or servers, protecting against man-in-the-middle and eavesdropping attacks.

RFID and Contactless Payment Systems

RFID tags and contactless payment systems are inherently constrained in terms of power and memory, making traditional cryptographic solutions impractical. Lightweight cryptography enables:

- **Secure Authentication:** Cryptographic algorithms such as PRESENT and SipHash can authenticate RFID tags, ensuring that data exchanged with RFID readers remains secure, even in environments where power and data handling capacity are limited.
- **Data Protection in Payment Systems:** Contactless payment technologies, such as NFC-based payments, use lightweight encryption to protect cardholder data and transaction details, enabling quick, secure payments without excessive power or computational demands.

Healthcare and Medical Devices

In healthcare, devices such as pacemakers, glucose monitors, and wearable health tech generate sensitive medical data that must be protected for both privacy and regulatory compliance. Lightweight cryptography enables:

- **Data Privacy:** Encryption protocols in medical devices ensure that health data remains confidential, and accessible only to authorized personnel, even when transmitted wirelessly.
- **Real-Time Efficiency:** For devices requiring continuous data transmission (such as heart monitors), lightweight cryptography enables secure data exchange without compromising the real-time operation of life-supporting devices.

Automotive Industry

Modern vehicles are equipped with a network of electronic control units (ECUs) and sensors that communicate with each other, often across wireless or remote channels. Lightweight cryptography secures:

- **Vehicle-to-Vehicle (V2V) Communication:** Secure V2V communication prevents attackers from intercepting or tampering with messages, such as those used in collision avoidance systems.
- **In-Vehicle Network Security:** Lightweight cryptography ensures data integrity and authentication across the in-vehicle networks (such as CAN and LIN bus systems), where resource-efficient algorithms protect messages exchanged between various ECUs responsible for critical functions, such as braking and steering.

These use cases highlight how lightweight cryptography is essential in applications that require security without sacrificing performance. By providing tailored solutions for constrained devices, lightweight cryptographic algorithms support secure, efficient data protection across a wide range of modern technology applications.

Challenges and Limitations of Lightweight Cryptography

Performance Limits in Real-Time Applications

One of the primary challenges in lightweight cryptography is balancing security and performance, especially in real-time environments:

- **Real-Time Constraints:** Many IoT devices and embedded systems must process data and respond in real-time. Lightweight cryptographic algorithms must be fast enough to avoid introducing noticeable latency. However, even lightweight algorithms can struggle in extremely resource-constrained settings, like small sensors or medical devices, where delays or interruptions could affect functionality.
- **Processing Overhead:** Despite optimization, even lightweight cryptography adds some degree of computational overhead, which can be problematic in systems with ultra-low processing power. Applications requiring continuous encryption, such as video surveillance or real-time sensor data transmission, can quickly drain limited power resources.

Standardization and Compatibility

The standardization of lightweight cryptography is still an emerging field, and ensuring compatibility with existing cryptographic infrastructure poses additional hurdles:

- **Lack of Universal Standards:** While there has been progress, lightweight cryptography lacks universally accepted standards like those for traditional cryptographic algorithms. The ongoing NIST initiative is working to establish such standards, but until they are fully adopted, there is a risk of fragmentation as developers may adopt different algorithms tailored to specific use cases.
- **Interoperability with Existing Systems:** Lightweight cryptography algorithms must be compatible with existing cryptographic infrastructure to allow seamless data transfer between high-power and low-power devices. Maintaining compatibility while ensuring high security can be challenging, especially in environments where data must travel across different types of networks (for example, between IoT devices and cloud servers).

Risk of Reduced Security

Lightweight cryptography faces an inherent trade-off between efficiency and security, and this can expose devices to potential vulnerabilities:

- **Simplified Algorithms:** Due to the need for minimal resource usage, lightweight algorithms often sacrifice certain security features or adopt simpler designs. While this makes them suitable for low-power environments, it can also make them more vulnerable to attacks, particularly if security parameters are not adequately configured.

- **Emerging Attack Techniques:** Newer attack techniques, such as differential and side-channel attacks, are becoming more sophisticated, and lightweight cryptographic algorithms may be at risk if they're not designed with these threats in mind. This raises the need for continuous innovation to ensure that lightweight algorithms remain resilient against emerging vulnerabilities.

These challenges underscore the complexity of designing lightweight cryptography that is secure and efficient. Balancing performance, compatibility, and security in constrained environments remains a dynamic field of research, with ongoing efforts to standardize and innovate for future-proofed cryptographic solutions.

Miscellaneous Trends in Cryptography

As the field of cryptography continues to evolve, it branches into diverse areas that extend its impact beyond traditional data protection. These emerging trends address pressing challenges in modern security landscapes, enabling innovative applications and improving system resilience. From the foundational role of cryptography in blockchain technology to advancements like decentralized identity, secure multi-party computation, and functional encryption, these trends are reshaping how data is secured, shared, and utilized. Furthermore, the concept of cryptographic agility underscores the importance of adaptability in a rapidly changing digital environment, ensuring that systems can withstand emerging threats and seamlessly integrate cutting-edge cryptographic advancements. Together, these developments highlight the dynamic nature of cryptography and its pivotal role in securing the future of technology.

Blockchain and Cryptographic Innovation

Blockchain technology relies on core cryptographic principles to ensure the integrity, security, and functionality of decentralized systems. Key cryptographic tools used in blockchain include:

- **Hashing:** Each block in a blockchain contains a cryptographic hash of the previous block, forming a secure and immutable chain. Hashing algorithms, such as SHA-256, generate a fixed-size output from input data, allowing quick data integrity checks.
- **Digital Signatures:** Digital signatures use asymmetric cryptography (public and private key pairs) to authenticate transactions. They ensure that only the owner of a private key can authorize transactions, which is essential for secure value transfer and identity verification within the blockchain.
- **Consensus Protocols:** Consensus mechanisms, such as Proof of Work (PoW)

or Proof of Stake (PoS), are cryptographic processes that help decentralized networks agree on a single version of the blockchain. They provide security against malicious actors attempting to alter the chain.

Decentralized Identity (DID) for Data Sovereignty

Decentralized Identity (DID) leverages blockchain's cryptographic properties to give individuals control over their digital identities without relying on a centralized authority. DID systems allow users to store identity credentials on the blockchain, accessible only by their private keys. This approach promotes data sovereignty, enabling individuals to control how, when, and where their identity data is shared.

Secure Multi-Party Computation (SMPC)

Secure Multi-Party Computation (SMPC) is a cryptographic technique that enables multiple parties to collaboratively compute a function over their individual inputs while keeping those inputs private. This allows parties to jointly analyze and derive insights from shared data without revealing any sensitive information to each other. By ensuring that no party learns anything about the others' inputs beyond the final result, SMPC enables secure cooperation in scenarios where privacy is essential.

How SMPC Works

In SMPC, each party's input is split into multiple "shares" and distributed to other parties. Each party then performs computations on their shares without ever seeing the actual data from others. Finally, all parties combine their computed shares to obtain the result of the function, without ever exposing any individual data point. Protocols such as Yao's Garbled Circuits and the GMW (Goldreich-Micali-Wigderson) protocol are commonly used in SMPC to enable secure, privacy-preserving computations.

Use Cases of SMPC

- **Secure Data Sharing in Finance:** In financial services, SMPC enables secure data sharing for fraud detection, risk assessment, and credit scoring without compromising client confidentiality. Multiple institutions can securely collaborate to detect fraud by jointly analyzing transaction patterns without disclosing sensitive client information.
- **Collaborative Analytics in Healthcare:** SMPC is highly valuable in healthcare, where data privacy is paramount. For example, hospitals and research institutions can securely collaborate on analyzing patient data to uncover treatment outcomes or genetic insights without sharing sensitive patient details directly, preserving privacy while facilitating medical advancements.
- **Supply Chain Collaboration:** In supply chains, SMPC can enable collaborative data analysis between suppliers, manufacturers, and distributors to improve efficiency, demand forecasting, and inventory management. This is particularly

useful when parties are competitors or have contractual restrictions on data sharing, allowing them to work together without disclosing proprietary data.

SMPC is a powerful approach in cryptography, offering privacy-preserving data analysis solutions across sectors with strict data privacy requirements.

Functional Encryption

Functional Encryption (FE) is an advanced cryptographic approach where specific functions of encrypted data can be accessed by authorized parties without revealing the underlying data itself. Unlike traditional encryption, which either completely hides or reveals all data upon decryption, functional encryption enables more selective access, where a key can be granted to reveal only a computed function of the encrypted information rather than the raw data. This capability makes FE particularly powerful for cases where data confidentiality and controlled data access are essential.

How Functional Encryption Works

In a functional encryption scheme, the data owner encrypts their data, and the decryption keys are associated with particular functions rather than simply decrypting the data outright. When an entity with the appropriate functional decryption key accesses the encrypted data, it obtains only the result of a specific computation on that data, rather than the data itself. For instance, if a database contains sensitive sales data, an analyst could use a functional encryption key to calculate the total sales without accessing individual transaction records.

Applications of Functional Encryption

- **Privacy-Preserving Analytics:** Functional encryption is valuable in scenarios where analysis of encrypted data is required without exposing the underlying data. For example, in health research, researchers could perform aggregate analyses (such as calculating the average age or health indicators) on patient data while keeping individual patient records confidential, enabling privacy-preserving insights.
- **Access-Controlled Data Sharing:** Functional encryption provides a fine-grained access control method, allowing data owners to share specific functions of their data rather than the raw data. This is particularly useful in finance and government sectors, where sensitive data may need to be shared with third parties, but only for specific purposes. For instance, a tax agency might share encrypted income data with a research body, where only authorized functions (such as income distribution) are accessible, but individual incomes remain hidden.

Functional encryption is a promising direction in cryptography that supports selective data sharing and secure computation, balancing privacy needs with the demand for controlled, useful insights from encrypted data.

Cryptographic Agility

Cryptographic agility is the capacity of a cryptographic system or infrastructure to seamlessly switch between different cryptographic algorithms and protocols with minimal need for extensive re-engineering. This adaptability is increasingly crucial in today's security landscape, where emerging threats and advancements in computing power, such as quantum computing, are constantly challenging traditional cryptographic methods.

Cryptographic agility allows a system to stay resilient by ensuring that outdated or vulnerable algorithms can be swiftly replaced with stronger, more current cryptographic solutions. This quality is especially beneficial in large-scale systems, where rigid cryptographic setups can become costly and time-consuming to upgrade.

Importance of Cryptographic Agility in Modern Security

- **Post-Quantum Readiness:** As quantum computing advances, it threatens to break traditional cryptographic algorithms such as RSA and ECC. Systems with cryptographic agility can transition more easily to post-quantum cryptographic (PQC) algorithms as they are standardized, without requiring an entire system overhaul.
- **Evolving Security Standards:** Security standards evolve as new vulnerabilities are discovcrcd, and cryptographic agility enables compliance with these updates. Agile systems can adapt to meet the latest standards, mitigating risks associated with outdated encryption and enabling interoperability across various platforms. For example, a network with agile encryption capabilities can adopt new cryptographic primitives as soon as they are recommended by bodies such as NIST.
- **Adaptability in Diverse Environments:** Cryptographic agility is essential in ecosystems with heterogeneous devices and systems (such as IoT networks), where different levels of security may be required for different components. By dynamically switching algorithms, cryptographic agility supports compatibility across devices, ensuring they meet appropriate security levels regardless of their computational constraints.

Challenges and Implementation Considerations

Building cryptographic agility into systems can be complex and requires modular design principles to decouple cryptographic algorithms from the core functionalities of applications. This design enables seamless updates and minimizes the risk of incompatibility. Despite the challenges, cryptographic agility is essential for future-proofing systems, ensuring they remain resilient and adaptable in the face of advancing threats and evolving standards.

Conclusion

In this chapter, we explored some of the most transformative trends shaping the future of cryptography, each addressing unique challenges presented by modern security needs. Post-Quantum Cryptography has emerged as an essential area of focus, aimed at safeguarding our digital infrastructure from the imminent capabilities of quantum computers. PQC stands as a foundational move towards resilience in an era where traditional algorithms may no longer suffice. Homomorphic Encryption further pushes the boundaries of secure data handling, enabling computations on encrypted data without compromising confidentiality.

HE is a remarkable advancement for privacy-preserving applications across fields, such as cloud computing, healthcare, and finance, offering robust protection for sensitive information even in outsourced environments. Similarly, Zero-Knowledge Proofs offer unparalleled privacy by enabling one party to prove knowledge of information without revealing the information itself. ZKPs have become pivotal in blockchain and secure authentication systems, making it possible to verify identities and data without unnecessary data exposure.

The Lightweight Cryptography segment demonstrates how cryptographic techniques are evolving to address the resource constraints of IoT, medical devices, and embedded systems, achieving efficiency without sacrificing security. LWC's adaptability is critical for expanding secure technology into new areas that were previously difficult to safeguard. Lastly, the Miscellaneous Trends in Cryptography—from Privacy-Enhancing Technologies and Secure Multi-Party Computation (SMPC) to Cryptographic Agility and Quantum Key Distribution highlight a dynamic landscape where cryptographic innovations are accelerating to meet regulatory demands and adapt to fast-evolving security standards.

Index

D

J

K

L

M

N

P

R